T0342499

Recycling the City

The Use and Reuse of Urban Land

Edited by
Rosalind Greenstein and Yesim Sungu-Eryilmaz

Lincoln Institute of Land Policy
Cambridge, Massachusetts

Library of Congress Cataloging-in-Publication Data

Recycling the city : the use and reuse of urban land / edited by Rosalind
Greenstein and Yesim Sungu-Eryilmaz.
    p. cm.
  Includes bibliographical references and index.
  ISBN 1-55844-159-X (alk. paper)
    1. Urban renewal. 2. Vacant lands. 3. Brownfields. I. Greenstein,
Rosalind, 1955– II. Sungu-Eryilmaz, Yesim.

HT170.R435 2004
307.3'416—dc22
                                      2004017919

Front cover (clockwise from top left): LTV Steel South Side Works, Pittsburgh,
now derelict (Photo by Yesim Sungu-Eryilmaz); Visitors at the Landschaftspark,
Duisburg, Germany (Photo courtesy Tour de Ruhr); Kennedy Community
Garden, Boston (Photo by Martin Bailkey); Armstrong Cork Factory, Pittsburgh,
now abandoned (Photo by Yesim Sungu-Eryilmaz)

Back cover: Landschaftspark at night, Duisburg, Germany (Photo © Christoph
Moseler)

Project management: Julia Gaviria, Lincoln Institute of Land Policy
Design and production: Snow Creative Services
Printing: Webcom Ltd., Toronto, Ontario, Canada

Contents

Part 3: Innovative Uses for Vacant Land

Acknowledgments

This book stems from a collection of research projects funded by the Lincoln Institute of Land Policy. The process of commissioning and collecting these papers gave us the opportunity to learn from a group of scholars with a strong commitment to recycling urban land in a way that is beneficial to the city and its residents. It seemed a good idea, therefore, to make the concepts, hypotheses and empirical evidence presented in these papers available to a larger audience. We asked the authors to revise their working papers for this volume, and invited two others (Alan W. Evans and William Shutkin), whose papers were commissioned specifically for the book, to supply material that would help us round out the collection.

This project has been in the making longer than we care to admit. We are grateful to all the authors for their patience, contributions to the field and enthusiastic cooperation. In addition, we also received much help from our colleagues at the Lincoln Institute. Among those, we would like to give special thanks to Allegra Calder, who provided first-rate project management and research assistance. Laurie Dougherty, out of her deep interest and commitment to sustainable development, provided us with a critical and compassionate eye, as well as fine research assistance. Julia Gaviria brought a gentle hand to the job of copyediting and an impressive professionalism to the management of the production process. We are very grateful for their efforts; they remind us of the social nature of publishing, and we are fortunate to be part of such a work community.

If this volume offers a positive contribution to the field and yields intellectual stimulation and a fresh look at the potential locked into the urban landscape, then this has been made possible by all those mentioned above.

Rosalind Greenstein and
Yesim Sungu-Eryilmaz

Cambridge, Massachusetts
October 2004

Introduction

Recycling Urban Vacant Land

Rosalind Greenstein and Yesim Sungu-Eryilmaz

Vacant land in urban areas can be both an eyesore and an opportunity. In an urban residential neighborhood, vacant land all too often attracts illegal activities such as drug dealing or trash dumping. It also can decrease property values and scare off development for both the actual site and the surrounding neighborhood. But just as vacant land may cause problems, it also provides opportunities. Sometimes scattered parcels, once the site of a corner store or a tenement building, can be magnets for the civically engaged dreamers who, with enormous effort, transform these plots into urban gardens or new housing. Such redevelopment may improve neighborhood livability by bringing jobs, tax dollars, repairexwd infrastructure, and reduced health and environmental risks. Therefore, recycling land is an essential process in the economic, environmental and social sustainability of neighborhoods, cities and regions. The essays in this book address not only the challenges of the redevelopment process, but also the creative uses of vacant land, which are the legacy of industrial and commercial activities, largely from the twentieth century and usually located in urban centers and their close-in suburbs.

The issues presented in this volume, from the causes and extent of the problem of vacant land, to the capacity of government and nongovernmental organizations to deal with it, to the tools utilized, all are affected by how we frame the problem. How, in a period of competing demands for public action and resources, do we understand these abandoned properties and the public and private actions that led to their vacant state? How do we measure the public and private costs that can be traced to these properties? Who is responsible for alleviating the environmental and health hazards and costs associated with these sites? Which sites should be tackled first, and how do we reuse them? And, how do we untangle the issues of environment and economics when so many of these vacant and abandoned properties—those that are contaminated and those perceived to be contaminated—are located in neighborhoods that remain overlooked by private and public investors?

Understanding how and why some parcels are abandoned or substantially underutilized while others are not requires a look at global economic forces. There is great variation in the way such forces affect specific industries, regions, neighborhoods and sites. Because some nations and communities have more resources than others, the social impacts of these economic forces are not random.

Why Is Land Abandoned or Underutilized?

The question of why land is left abandoned or underutilized should be considered through the lens of economic history. The process of deindustrialization in the United States resulted in the shift of manufacturing away from the old industrial areas, of both regions and metropolises, toward the emerging population centers (Bluestone and Harrison 1982). Companies have been moving their production facilities from central cities to the suburbs, from metropolitan to rural areas, and from their home countries to Asia and into developing countries. This capital flight was induced by lower labor costs and growth in new markets. The exodus of the textile and shoe industries is a familiar story to New Englanders (Hekman 1980). Certainly the upper Midwest can point to the decline of the automobile industry as another example of the same phenomenon. The disinvestment of older industries dovetailed with significant investments in military production, from which the South and West benefited (Markusen et al. 1991).

The search for lower-cost production can account for some of these relocations and the subsequent changing fortunes of regions, cities and neighborhoods. However, these industrial changes were accompanied by significant demographic changes, including the move to warmer retirement spots by the first generation of retirees on Social Security. The ascendancy of the new markets increased the demand for a range of goods and services. Some of this new demand, particularly for education, personal and business services, and health care, required the expansion of the service sector in such burgeoning markets.

If sectoral and demographic shifts were largely responsible for the deindustrialization that occurred *between* metropolitan regions, the complex forces that are responsible for the suburbanization that occurred *within* metropolitan areas are more highly contested. For our purposes we do not attempt to sort out the various arguments for suburbanization, but we highlight a few here. The standard neoclassical explanation is that employers moved to the suburbs for cheaper land to build their office buildings, as the role of the service economy increased. Workers continued to minimize their commutes by also moving to the suburbs. Suburbanites imposed zoning regulations that required large lots and low density, sending development even farther out (Mills 2002). Joe Gyourko and Richard Voith (1999) are among the scholars who have argued that federal subsidies, for example, the tax treatment of mortgage interest or the subsidization of infrastructure, have played an important role in this suburbanization. Sectoral changes (the fall of traditional manufacturing and rise of defense and hi-tech), demographic changes (population shifts from the Northeast and Midwest to the South and West), and intra-metropolitan locational changes (suburbanization) have left underinvested neighborhoods and central cities with a legacy of abandoned factories and underutilized land.

What Are the Externalities of Contaminated Land?

The improper disposal of toxic chemicals can result in health and safety problems. Contamination can be found on parcels that were once used for residential, commercial, industrial or military activities; these sites often reflect complex histories of sequential industrial use. Lead paint chips left from demolished or crumbling residential buildings can contaminate soils. Perchloroethylene, an industrial solvent routinely used by dry cleaners, is considered hazardous by the U.S. Environmental Protection Agency (EPA), as well as by many of the states. Thus, its use, removal and disposal are all subject to environmental regulations. Aging storage tanks at gas stations can leak and thereby cause soil contamination. When chemicals or petroleum get into groundwater and streams the contamination spreads beyond the parcel lines and significantly increases remediation and cleanup costs.[1] Many industrial processes, such as metal fabrication and ceramics, create waste as a by-product; earlier waste disposal procedures (legal and illegal) could result in contaminated sludge. According to the World Health Organization, the presence of toxic wastes is among the so-called modern risks that children often face as they play in their neighborhoods.[2]

If the legal entity that once owned the factory is no longer in business, or if the site was used by a number of owners who all contributed to the site's toxicity, then the neighbors are left to wonder, who should pay for the cost of appropriate and safe disposal of industrial waste? In simple economic terms, the answer to the question is straightforward. If the creation of pollution is a by-product of the industrial process, then the safe disposal of this waste is the responsibility of the owners of the production facility. Cutting corners on waste disposal, however, reduces manufacturing costs and, in theory, could end up benefiting owners, workers or consumers. However, those that do not stand to benefit from improper waste disposal are the neighbors of the facility.

Love Canal played an important role in shaping U.S. environmental policy. Located in the city of Niagara Falls, New York, Love Canal was used by the Hooker Chemical Company as an industrial dump for most of the 1940s and 1950s.[3] Prior to that, the Niagara Falls city government and the federal

---

1. The cleanup cost differs depending on many factors. The level, type, amount and extent of contamination are key determinants. For example, the cost of cleanup would likely be much higher if the groundwater beneath the site were contaminated than if only the contaminated soil were. The cost also depends on the use of the property. The cleanup is typically less expensive if a brownfield property is cleaned to commercial use standards rather than residential use standards. Depending on the remediation technologies, unit costs for projects differ from approximately $100 to $300 per ton, or $5 to $350 per cubic yard (EPA Remediation Technology Cost Compendium–Year 2000).

2. World Health Organization, http://www.who.int/world-health-day/2003/infomaterials/Brochure3/en/.

3. For a description of the Love Canal history, see http://www.globalserve.net/~spinc/atomcc/history.htm.

government used the canal to dispose of a variety of toxic and nontoxic wastes. By 1977 the chemicals permeated the neighborhood and even reached inside residences. Citizens raised their concerns, gaining a national audience. Their agitation was likely a driving force behind federal legislation to clean up toxic waste dumps; the Comprehensive Environmental Response, Compensation, and Liability Act (CERCLA)—commonly referred to as Superfund—was passed by Congress in December 1980.

Superfund was to be used in cases where responsible parties could not be found or could not afford cleanup costs. Superfund sites are those that pose the greatest public health hazard. As of 2000, there were 1,210 Superfund sites, which the EPA then estimated would cost $36.3 billion to clean up. RAND studies (1989, 1992) found that it takes an average of three and a half years after a site's listing for inclusion on the National Priorities List (NPL). Furthermore, after a site is included on the NPL it takes on average eight and a half years before remediation work is completed.

While Superfund sites are among the worst in the nation, they do not exhaust the list of all contaminated parcels of land. In many urban neighborhoods abandoned properties, once used for manufacturing, gas stations or dry cleaners, lie dormant. These neglected sites are too small to be on the Superfund list; however, to those living in the neighborhood, their national ranking is unimportant. They may pose public health hazards or be magnets for undesirable activity; they may be unsightly or repel investors to the neighborhood; they may represent an opportunity cost or symbolize the social, political and economic marginality of the neighborhood.

Although many vacant sites are in fact contaminated, other parcels may only be *perceived* as contaminated. In terms of real estate economics, both actual and perceived contamination are a negative externality, since market value is reduced in both cases. Based on economic theory, the drop in market value due to perceived contamination reflects a violation of a foundation of basic economic thought: that buyers and sellers have perfect information. Given the uncertainties of what may have been improperly disposed and over what period of time, and the subsequent environmental damage that may have been caused (e.g., groundwater contamination), combined with the principles of joint and several liability, buyers and lenders have tended to assume that contamination was likely and severe. In practice this assumption is violated. Patchin (1991) and Mundy (1992) add that property value may be reduced due not only to real contamination, but also to perceived risk associated with the effects of stigma.

Why Aren't the Properties Redeveloped?

In many urban markets properties were abandoned, and remain unused, because the old facilities posed problems for efficient industrial use. Some of the problems were technical or physical, as when horizontal facilities were favored over vertical ones. For example, in the beginning of the twentieth century, the industrial architect Albert Kahn designed an auto plant in Highland Park, Michigan, a village only six miles west of Detroit. Just after this four-story factory was built, Henry Ford had Kahn design and build the Ford Rouge plant, a half-mile-long building without interior supports to allow the uninterrupted flow of production.[4] The era of continuous flow production made suburban locations more attractive than urban ones for industrial use.

In some markets, however, old industrial buildings were recycled. Digital Equipment Corporation (DEC), for example, was opened in 1957 in the small industrial town of Maynard, Massachusetts, about 25 miles west of Boston. The old mills dominated this working class town, but were largely unused after the production of carpets and carpet yarn moved out of New England until the arrival of DEC.[5] In a similar process of adaptive reuse, New York City artists found SoHo's industrial lofts, once the home of intermediary businesses serving the textile and apparel trade, could be reused as mixed-use, work-live spaces.

Despite these examples of adaptive reuse, thousands of unused or underutilized industrial sites remain in the cities. The interaction between land values, underinvested neighborhoods and brownfield sites is difficult to unravel. Are neighborhoods with long-abandoned brownfield properties considered relatively unattractive to investors because of the presence of these brownfields? Or have these sites remained unimproved because the neighborhood is unattractive to investors? The Regional Plan Association (RPA 1998) developed a framework to shed some light on the combined question of the redevelopment likelihood of brownfield sites and when it is appropriate for public subsidy of this redevelopment.

The RPA suggested that there are three classes of brownfield sites. Tier one sites are those that are most attractive to the private sector. An example of tier one property might be abandoned or underutilized parcels along waterfronts in thriving metropolises. These are sites for which the likelihood of strong return on investment is high and exceeds the costs of cleanup and redevelopment. Tier two sites are a class of property whose redevelopment is just below the threshold for viability without public-sector incentives. These might be waterfront sites in cities whose economic prospects are uncertain, or in metropolitan areas with strong economies but whose paths of new development bypass the neighborhoods and districts where the parcels are located. These sites, according to the RPA, should be the primary object "of financial incentives, essentially bringing them into 'tier one' category" (RPA 1998, 5).

The final class of sites, tier three, is the greatest challenge to redevelop, less because of environmental conditions and more because of location. Typically, these are the sites with limited access to markets (due to either the poor quality of infrastructure or the distance from inputs, including employees and/or lower-than-average incomes in the surrounding neighborhood, which limit the retail

---

4. http://www.albertkahn.com/cmpny_history.cfm.

5. Maynard's mill closed in 1950, which was relatively late in the decline of the textile industry in New England. This decline was exacerbated in the 1930s by the Depression. New England mills that did not close in the 1930s got a lift from production for World War II, but in the post-war period the trend of early-century decline in the industry resumed (Greenstein and Robertson 2000).

market potential). Tier three sites are orphaned twice. First, when productive users leave them. Second, when the local economy fails to provide a fertile context for development.

Figure 0.1 shows a framework to understand the likelihood of redevelopment for brownfields, vacant, abandoned and other underutilized urban sites, and reformulates the RPA three-tier classification scheme. Here, the likelihood of redevelopment hinges on not only the cost of redevelopment, but on profitability, the behavior of developers, as well as the behavior of public officials. Profitability in Figure 0.1 is represented as a ratio of cost-to-returns on investment. To increase the odds of redevelopment, policy makers must increase the ratio, and there are several mechanisms (or "policy levers") to achieve this. Those that will increase costs or returns are noted with a (+); those that will decrease

Figure 0.1   Likelihood of Redevelopment

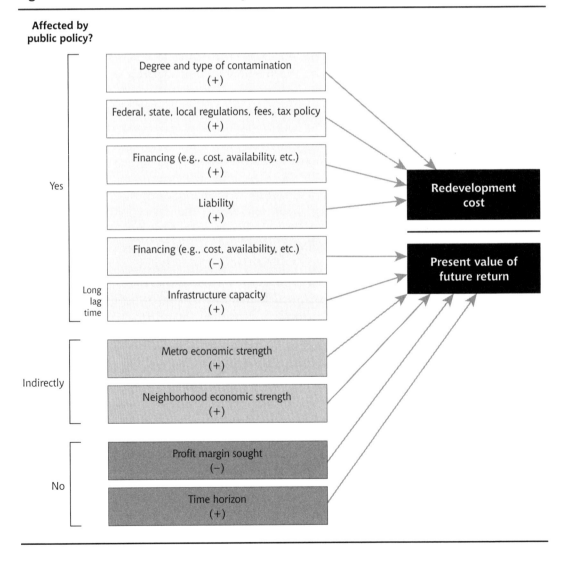

costs or returns are noted with a (–). Whether public policy can actually influence these mechanisms is indicated by "Yes," "No," or "Indirectly," which should be understood as suggestive and useful in policy deliberation, debate and design.

For example, a private developer may not take on a specific brownfield redevelopment project because it costs too much, meaning that the return is "too low" by their determination. Some developers require an 18 percent return, while others desire 12–14 percent; it is the developer, not public policy, that determines the percentage. However, while a public-sector planner or elected official may want the developer to accept a lower profit and consider that as a choice, the developer understands the 18 percent as a real opportunity cost. Public officials might be able to respond with changes in the tax code affecting depreciation, for example, which improve the cost-to-return ratio. The ideas presented in Figure 0.1 could help in constructing development deals and public policy that increase the likelihood of redevelopment.

The answer to the question of redevelopment lies in the strength of the neighborhood and local economies. For example, DEC was able to benefit from the vast Department of Defense expenditures on research and development and new products during World War II and the Cold War. MIT engineers were employed at government labs in New England (Greenstein and Robertson 2000), and the old mill buildings got a new life because Maynard offered cheap land in a resource-rich environment. In this case, the richness was not in hydroelectric power or machine shops, but in the specific human and technological resources needed to launch a new computer industry (i.e., a deep pool of newly trained and experienced engineers and a culture of technological innovation). This provides one example of how context matters.

The literature on brownfield redevelopment focuses primarily on issues surrounding decontamination and cleanup, including risk and liability. However, these can easily be understood as elements that contribute to the cost of redevelopment. The important thing about cost is its relationship to future earnings—if future earnings will be great enough to support redevelopment costs, including the uncertainties about the degree of contamination and liability, redevelopment likelihood will be great. Various public policies have been directed to reducing the redevelopment costs of these brownfields (e.g., providing financial incentives to individual sites or clearly limiting future liability). However, since it is the ratio of cost to future earnings, and not absolute cost, that determines redevelopment likelihood, it is important to focus policy attention on the factors that contribute to future earnings. As shown in Figure 0.1, there are three sets of such factors. The first, local economic competitiveness (i.e., infrastructure capacity, metropolitan economic strength and neighborhood economic strength), is subject to policy intervention only *indirectly*. Profit margins and the time frame for return on investment are assumptions that can vary from developer to developer or from project to project and reflect individual circumstances. Financing affects both the costs of redevelopment and the future earnings of redevelopment, and, unlike the assumptions on profits, can be affected by policy interventions.

While brownfields, vacant, abandoned and otherwise underproductive urban land provide potential opportunity for development, the economic vitality of the local economy may go much further in accounting for the likelihood of redevelopment than would site characteristics alone.

Introduction to the Essays

The vacant land with which we are primarily concerned in the following 11 essays does not represent the most extreme forms of contamination, but, with the exception of the Ruhr Valley, the relatively small-scale and overlooked parcels that are now located in urban neighborhoods and districts that have been disregarded by investors. The essays do not cover all policies comprehensively; rather, they help us understand better the multiple causes of the urban vacant land issue, the extent and depth of the problem, and the responses to it. Most of the chapters refer to the U.S.; however, three authors provide a European viewpoint.

In the first two sections, "The Vacant Land Phenomenon" and "The Vacant Land and Brownfield Redevelopment Process," the authors are concerned with urban land that was once highly productive. Very often the land under consideration is now contaminated or perceived to be contaminated. The authors examine the issue from economic, political and institutional points of view. The first section lays out the context in which urban vacant land and its redevelopment exist. Michael Pagano and Ann Bowman's survey of 70 cities tells us that on average less than one-sixth of a city's land area is vacant. Just as the extent of vacant and underutilized land varies from city to city in the U.S., it also varies between countries. From Wood's studies of four western European countries, we understand that the extent to which land is left vacant depends, in part, on the degree to which property development is guided by the public versus the private sector. Alan Evans's chapter addresses the economic issues relating to land and real estate. While the economic fundamentals are the same in the U.S. and the U.K., from where Evans writes, he does illustrate some points with a British perspective, which helps underscore the notion that while economic fundamentals operate similarly in different settings, the institutional framework has an effect as well. That framework also varies across states and regional markets within the U.S. Evans goes into more detail regarding the connection between vacant urban land and speculation, transitional uses, risk, attachment to a place, and the use of land as a source for future urban development. The realities of real estate investment, including discount rates, also play a role in the use and reuse of urban vacant land.

In the second section the authors grapple with the tools to redevelop these parcels that are available from the state and local levels. Institutional and organizational capacity is needed by state government, local government and the nonprofit sector, which has the potential to play a crucial role in these revitalization efforts. This is so particularly because of the market (and in some cases government) failures that are involved in the abandoned urban sites in under-invested neighborhoods. Nonprofit organizations are in an excellent position to approach the redevelopment of these properties with a different investment calculus. Specifically, if they are willing to adjust their time frame, accept a lower profit margin and/or take some of their return in "community benefit" rather than investor return, these sites have a greater chance of being redeveloped.

Each of the four chapters in the second section focuses on different pieces of the complex puzzle of why some sites are successfully redeveloped and others are not. Because the redevelopment of underutilized urban property usually is addressed site by site, there are important lessons to be learned by examining the actions of local players, such as local government and nonprofit developers (by definition these sites have largely been abandoned by the private sector). However, as Nancey Green Leigh reminds us, there are policies and programs that state governments provide that can facilitate redevelopment of these sites by local actors. Green Leigh presents a survey of U.S. states for an inventory of useful tools.

From Sarah Gardner's work on brownfield redevelopment in four New Jersey cities, we come to understand that local capacity, defined as civic, governmental and private capital resources, accounts for some of the success in redevelopment. As states have delegated responsibility to municipalities for identifying sites, attracting developers, determining cleanup levels, methods of remediation and reuse, local government capacity is stretched. In an era when we have limited political backing of public subsidies for neighborhood redevelopment (as opposed to tax breaks for private investors), we seem unable to muster public support even in cases of classic market failures. Gardner argues that local capacity plays an important role in the implementation of devolutionary programs for brownfields redevelopment, particularly in the near-absolute absence of private and also nonprofit involvement.

Lavea Brachman examines how policies designed and implemented to stimulate brownfield redevelopment have been only partially effective. She provides an examination of the institutional, legal and economic issues with an eye toward understanding the intended and unintended effects of policy remedies in these areas on brownfield redevelopment. Some of the current policy gaps that she addresses include the high costs and delays in the predevelopment stage, the lingering uncertainty associated with legal liability, the obstacles in gaining site control and the disincentives on stakeholder involvement. Brachman emphasizes the need for strong local redevelopment capacity and for this capacity to coexist with existing government programs, private-sector tools and a willingness to use those tools for improving brownfield redevelopment prospects. This local governmental capacity must be fully supplemented by more active nonprofit, community-based efforts and cooperative policy making among agencies at the state level.

Marie Howland's story of a once-thriving industrial district in Baltimore leads us to ask some important questions about the role that economic context plays in successful brownfield redevelopment. In this Baltimore quarter, some small properties were redeveloped, belying the claim that no viable economic activity was possible. However, the events there indicate the need to clarify important land market issues, including cleanup costs that raise expenditures beyond what the market can bear in a weak land economy, outdated and inadequate infrastructure, a mixture of incompatible and adjacent residential and industrial land uses, and obsolete uses that are expensive to demolish (and where sellers are unwilling to lower the cost sufficiently to compensate).

Sabina Deitrick and Margaret Dewar consider brownfield redevelopment success by community-based developers, such as community development corporations (CDCs). Their evidence comes from case studies in Detroit and Pittsburgh. The authors are concerned with whether these organizations can maintain their core mission—to provide benefits to the community—and still meet the financial goals set by lenders that evaluate feasibility on a project-by-project basis and do so within a limited time span. CDCs in both Pittsburgh and Detroit confront the legacy of the U.S.'s industrial past. In both cities the success of nonprofit developers has been a mixed bag, with CDCs having a bit more success in Pittsburgh. The obstacles to brownfield redevelopment are large. The challenges of redevelopment in aging, once-industrial cities are difficult, as are the challenges of real estate development by those with limited experience. And yet, these organizations attempted to beat the odds, gaining some skills on the way and probably increasing their chances for their next try.

In the final section of the book, "Innovative Uses for Vacant Land," we shift our focus a bit to consider some unconventional reuses for vacant, derelict, abandoned and brownfield properties. Martin Bailkey and Jerome Kaufman tell us of the discordant use of abandoned urban land for agriculture. Sometimes these plots are seen as simply transitional. That is, a few plantings are a preferable use to vacant lots rimmed with chain link fence. Or, sometimes the urban agricultural enterprise is just another endeavor in a community group's portfolio of activities. Although there are barriers to entrepreneurial urban agriculture, including local policy makers' negative attitude toward agricultural use of inner-city land and difficult management and marketing issues, the authors argue several benefits accrue to the community. City farms can increase the amount of green space, improve the appearance of blighted neighborhoods, and supply low-income residents with fresher and more nutritious food. Furthermore, they can help economically revitalize poor neighborhoods by creating modest food-based employment, bringing more income into the pockets of residents and building greater neighborhood self-reliance.

In a similar vein, Klaus Kunzmann tells the story of the IBA Emscher Park in Germany's Ruhr region. This is a story known for some time among economic development professionals in the U.S. However, this chapter is one of the few places readers can get it in English. The abandoned industrial landscape has been utilized in a way that was never intended and probably never imagined by the steel workers and other laborers of the last century. The planners did not try to fit the IBA Emscher Park into the existing land uses, but rather reused derelict industrial buildings for cultural purposes, thus creating a new district.

William Shutkin's story of industrial ecology brings us back to the themes of the first two sections of the book. Shutkin considers industrial properties, but he is not simply concerned with production output; he is also interested in the industrial process. If many brownfield sites are contaminated because of choices that were made during manufacturing, then, he reasons, in the reuse of these properties, planners, neighbors, taxpayers and public officials ought to be concerned with new industrial processes and ecologically sound production. From his chapter we are inspired to develop a new model for industry. And to be successful we may have to draw on a number of innovative entrepreneurial experiences.

Industrial ecology attempts to manufacture goods in a way that is ecologically sustainable. It is a mind-set toward production that was absent from earlier times, when the extant production process created the brownfields now part of our urban landscape. Industrial ecology strives to avoid rustbelts in a most fundamental way. However, redeveloping a contaminated site in a city that was formerly dominated by manufacturing for which there is now limited demand, and to do so with a "green" production process, embodies three sets of challenges. The first is environmental cleanup. The second is competing with lower-cost production sites, which may be in other parts of the U.S. or in developing countries. The third is that industrial ecology may add a further cost by internalizing the negative externalities. That is, industrial ecology producers may be increasing their production costs with respect to their competitors, as they alter manufacturing processes to minimize waste. However, it is true that industrial ecology has the potential to contain production costs as new uses for industrial waste are sought and identified.

Conclusion

The forces that created brownfields, abandoned and other underutilized land—such as economic, demographic, social and market forces—are largely the same ones that keep these properties undeveloped. The case studies presented here lend credence to the argument that brownfield redevelopment, particularly of relatively small sites in underinvested urban neighborhoods, must be undertaken as part of a larger community revitalization effort. Under such circumstances, brownfields can provide the organizing focus for the neighborhood. Such an effort should, at a minimum, develop both a neighborhood plan and a neighborhood planning process. The successful redevelopment of a formerly brownfield parcel will then be one element of a larger set of goals. An organized community, working to implement a democratically created plan, will be raising the social value of the neighborhood, which in turn will raise its economic value.

References

Acton, Jan Paul. 1989. *Understanding Superfund: A progress report.* Santa Monica, CA: Rand Institute.

———. 1992. *Superfund and transaction costs: The experience of insurers and very large industrial firms.* Santa Monica, CA: Rand Institute.

Bluestone, Barry, and Bennett Harrison. 1982. *The deindustrialization of America: Plant closings, community abandonment, and the dismantling of basic industry.* New York: Basic Books.

Crane, Randall, and Daniel Chatman. 2003. Traffic and sprawl: Evidence from U.S. commuting, 1985 to 1997. *Planning & Markets* 6(1). http://www-pam.usc.edu/.

Greenstein, Rosalind, and Jemelie Robertson. 2000. The Boston region. In *Global city regions: Their emerging forms,* Roger Simmonds and Gary Hack, eds. London and New York: Spon Press.

Gyourko, Joseph, and Richard Voith. 1999. The tax treatment of housing and its effect on bounded and unbounded communities. Working paper. Cambridge, MA: Lincoln Institute of Land Policy.

Hekman, John S. 1980. The product cycle and New England textiles. *The Quarterly Journal of Economics* 94(4):697–717.

Markusen, Ann, Peter Hall, Scott Campbell, and Sabina Deitrick. 1991. *Rise of the gunbelt: The military remapping of industrial America.* Oxford: Oxford University Press.

Mills, Edwin S. 2002. Why do we have urban density controls? Working paper. Cambridge, MA: Lincoln Institute of Land Policy.

Mundy, Bill. 1992. Stigma and value. *The Appraisal Journal* 60(1):14.

Patchin, Peter. 1991. Contaminated properties: Stigma revisited. *The Appraisal Journal* 59(2): 167.

Regional Plan Association and Lincoln Institute of Land Policy. 1998. Land, capital community: Elements of brownfield and vacant land redevelopment. Briefing book for "Creating the Capacity for Growth," Regional Plan Association's 8th Annual Regional Assembly, New York, NY.

Part 1

The Vacant Land Phenomenon

1 | Vacant Land As Opportunity and Challenge

Michael A. Pagano and Ann O'M. Bowman

The term *vacant land* has a range of meanings, even within a single town. Consider the sprawling city of Phoenix, for example. In its northern reaches, vacant land means virgin desert; in the southwestern part of the city, it refers to farmland. But within the older, built portions of Phoenix, vacant land takes on another meaning: abandoned land or unsafe spaces. Furthermore, there are some vacant industrial properties with real (or perceived) environmental contamination. And the narrow strips of land that run alongside the canal system in Phoenix provide a completely different kind of vacant land. Sharing borders with Phoenix, the cities of Tempe and Peoria have related, but distinct, definitions of vacant land. Tempe, bounded by incorporated jurisdictions on all sides, has precious little vacant land. What it does consider as vacant land is frequently a parcel that, from a development perspective, is deemed underutilized. Peoria, however, similar to Phoenix, has aggressively annexed desert land for future development. Its supply of vacant land is robust and tends to be of the "raw dirt" variety.

The land milieu of cities in the Seattle area is different from that of Phoenix-area jurisdictions. The difference is a result, in part, of the constraining effects of Washington's 1990 Growth Management Act and Arizona's liberal annexation laws. Therefore, a city's supply of vacant land in Washington is more tightly controlled than in Arizona. In Seattle and the neighboring city of Bellevue on the eastern shore of Lake Washington, vacant land, as variously defined, tends to be in short supply. Some land remains vacant by virtue of its physical characteristics and terrain that make it impossible to develop. Other areas that may be considered vacant are those with particular natural resource value such as wetlands or habitat. And, in some instances, the definition of vacant land extends to open space such as dedicated land for parks. Seldom is vacant land in Bellevue identified in terms of dilapidated structures or blight. Surveys of housing conditions in Bellevue typically find about 1 percent of the structures deteriorated. In the late 1990s, virtually any unoccupied residential structure in the downtown area of the city was a redevelopment property awaiting conversion. In Seattle and Bellevue vacant land is only temporarily vacant, as it is primarily a matter of underutilized land. Thus, an important goal in both cities is the redevelopment of existing parcels to intensify use. As one Bellevue planner stated, "the basic question here is how to use the land supply most efficiently."[1] The city of Redmond, Washington, has proportionately more undeveloped land than either Seattle or Bellevue. It tends to have a different definition of vacant land that includes not only redevelopment properties and open space such as dedicated parkland and habitat preserve, but also land reclaimed from mining operations and former farms.

The Philadelphia area offers a quite different perspective on vacant land. In Philadelphia and, across the Delaware River, in Camden, New Jersey, vacant land is in great supply, as it is in nearby Bucks County, Pennsylvania, north of Philadelphia. The abundant vacant land in the two cities, however, is very different from the vacant land in the suburban county. In Philadelphia and Camden, much of the vacant land is composed of abandoned and dilapidated structures or parcels where buildings have been razed. Many of the vacant industrial sites are brownfields, including some toxic properties dangerous enough to be listed as Superfund sites. Given the intensive development patterns in both Philadelphia and Camden, vacant land is defined primarily in terms of abandonment, whether residential, commercial or industrial. In Bucks County, vacant land is mostly acre upon acre of verdant farmland; brownfield sites and blighted parcels are few and far between. Instead, vacant land involves various types of open space—farm sites, wooded terrain and meadows. Bucks County officials are not concerned about the accumulation of more vacant land, but about the rapid consumption of it. The challenge for local policy makers is to moderate the effects of urban sprawl, as bucolic scenes yield to subdivisions and malls.

All of the jurisdictions discussed above contain vacant land. However, the definitions and images of such land vary from one place to another. State governments create at least part of the contextual variation, but even within a single state, vacant land has remarkable depth and range. Here we explore the definitions more systematically and discuss the images of vacant land. We then present data on the amount of vacant land in U.S. cities, explore the reasons for changes in the supply of vacant land, and finally argue that an alternative view of vacant land as opportunity is advisable.

Defining Vacant Land

Table 1.1 categorizes different types of vacant land and assesses their development potential. This categorization is derived from Northam's (1971) classification of vacant land in U.S. cities.

The characteristics of remnant parcels and those with physical limitations, on the one hand, make them unlikely to be developed in the foreseeable future. Among reserve and speculative parcels, on the other hand, vacancy is

---

1. Interview with Bellevue city planner, March 1999.

Table 1.1   Types of Vacant Land

Type of Parcel	Site Characteristics	Probability of Development
Remnant land	Small size, irregular shape	Low: Unsuitable for development
Land with physical limitations	Small or large; unbuildable due to slope, drainage or other physical limitation	Low: Unsuitable for development
Reserve parcels	Held by public and private owners. Located at urban fringe or at the border of existing holdings	High: Eventual development likely
Speculative parcels	May be located in low value or transitional areas; held in anticipation of increased future land values	High: Especially in strong property markets; lower in weaker markets
Derelict land	Damaged parcels; brownfields that are contaminated or perceived to be contaminated	Low: Unless the parcel is restored to an acceptable standard for development

a temporary condition. Even as this land sits idle, development plans may be in place. The last category in the typology, derelict land, refers to land that has been "so damaged by industrial or other development that it cannot be used beneficially without treatment" (Kivell 1993, 51). Brownfields, where real or perceived environmental contamination impedes redevelopment, are examples of derelict land (GAO 1997). Even the perception of contamination can lessen a parcel's redevelopment potential; thus, such sites frequently remain vacant.

City officials conducting land inventories devise their own operational definitions of vacant land. The label is applied to idle or unused land and may be extended to cover underutilized land. For example, a land inventory of a medium-sized southern city classified a parcel as vacant if one of the following characteristics was met: the parcel had a zero-dollar building value in the tax assessor's records; it was a tax parcel that did not have a structure on it; or it was a city-owned property considered vacant and developable, such as a municipal surface parking lot in the downtown area (Jones 1992). This definition is strongly influenced by the city's property tax structure and its development plan, a fairly common characteristic among local jurisdictions.

Another vacant land typology are temporarily obsolete, abandoned or derelict sites (TOADS) (Greenberg, Popper and West 1990; Hampton 1995). TOADS are of three varieties:

- formerly productive and valued sites such as automobile factories, furniture plants, warehouses or textile mills that have since been abandoned by their owners;

- formerly productive but unwanted sites that housed less desirable activities such as slaughterhouses, leather tanneries and paper mills; and

- unused parcels of overgrown land that for various reasons have not been developed.

The third kind of TOADS underscores an important point: vacant land is not necessarily damaged or derelict. It can simply be neglected land that is unused but capable of some beneficial use (Civic Trust 1988). Land that is being held for speculation may take on these characteristics. Or, it might be operational land, an unsightly or underutilized section of a current development. For example, an industrial plant may use a portion of its land for storage; it might lease part of it for pasture. These categorizations are inherently instrumental: the value of land is linked to its economic value.

Images of Vacant Land

Although vacant land is defined differently in various places, it often tends to conjure up negative images: abandoned, unfashionable, empty and dangerous. To describe inner-city decline, former Secretary of Housing and Urban Development Henry Cisneros spoke of "boarded-up buildings and trashed vacant lots" (1996, 118). Alice Coleman offers evocative labels such as *dead space* and *disturbed space* to refer to bare, derelict land, roughly vegetated wasteland, abandoned buildings and an assortment of temporary uses such as materials dumps and construction sites (Coleman 1982). Phrases such as *urban wastelands* and *derelict land* are used in reference to vacant land. Jakle and Wilson describe the condition in this manner:

> [A] place may be considered derelict to the extent that the symbols of disinvestment, vacancy, and degradation dominate. Where disrepair, litter, emptiness, violation, and other signs of diminished habitat prevail, a derelict zone exists in mind if not in reality. It symbolizes failure. (1992, 9)

Similarly, abandoned structures send out powerful signals to passersby:

> Abandoned buildings in our inner-city neighborhoods continue to erode the local social fabric. They signify the ills of neglect, communicating to people the futility of inner-city living.... To invest here is to risk losing money...abandoned buildings are a sign of irreversible deterioration—a process that has attained a critical internal momentum. (1992, 175)

Abandonment of a single building may trigger more abandonment. Store closings tend to reduce retail traffic in an area, thus jeopardizing remaining merchants. If the economic viability of the area weakens, more vacancies occur. Maintenance of the structures may be deferred or stopped, thereby creating potentially unsafe conditions. Some unoccupied structures may be boarded up, their isolation reinforced by chain link fencing. Other buildings may provide "homes" to the homeless.[2] Some may be demolished, leaving gaping holes in the area where the newly vacant lots gradually accumulate litter and trash.

---

2. The occupancy of abandoned structures by the homeless was moved tragically onto the public agenda in 2000, when a fire in an abandoned warehouse in Worcester, Massachusetts, killed six firefighters. The fire had been set accidentally by a homeless couple residing in the building.

Eventually, there may be more vacant lots than occupied buildings. Coleman's label *dead space* might seem especially appropriate to describe the area. Conventional efforts by city government to induce investment are not likely to be sufficient.[3] In fact, unsuccessful attempts by a city government to transform the area add another negative layer to the mix: policy failure.[4]

The public often perceives vacant land as a problem that requires correction. City governments find themselves thrust in the role of fixer—regulating and promoting privately held vacant land. Further, the city may own vacant land itself. After taking ownership, perhaps through condemnation proceedings or direct purchase, the city may improve the vacant parcel and resell it. In this manner, the city is a central participant in the local real estate market. Before exploring the local government's role, however, urban vacant land itself must be better understood.

The Amount of Vacant Land in U.S. Cities

How much vacant land is there in U.S. cities? Are there a few parcels scattered here and there, or is it a widespread phenomenon, dominating the cityscape? The data from our survey of 70 cities with populations of more than 50,000 provide some clarification. (See the appendix for survey methodology.) City officials were asked to estimate the amount of usable vacant land (thus excluding unusable land such as streets, rights of way, submerged land, wetlands and so on) within their corporate boundaries.[5]

Vacant Land

On average, less than one-sixth (15.4 percent) of a city's land area is vacant land (see Table 1.2).[6] This figure includes widely varying types of land ranging from undisturbed open space to abandoned, contaminated brownfields. Twenty-five of the 70 large cities (35.7 percent) that provided vacant land data in the survey reported a higher-than-average percentage of vacant land. The 15.4 percent average reflects a decline in vacant land from national studies conducted in the

---

3. Jakle and Wilson (1992, 107) mention New York City's attempt to do something unconventional. The city once operated a program in which murals were painted on boarded-up buildings. The murals, an effort to project a more positive image of a declining area, depicted family scenes.

4. In the 1980s cities seeking to maintain the central business district's role as a retail center engaged in costly and often unsuccessful interventions, such as prohibiting vehicular traffic and creating pedestrian malls. However, vacant storefronts are vacant storefronts regardless of the mode of transportation.

5. The survey contained this definition: "Vacant land includes not only unused or abandoned land or land that once had structures on it, but also the land that supports structures that have been abandoned, derelict, boarded up, partially destroyed or razed, etc."

6. To make meaningful comparisons across cities with different territorial sizes, total vacant land by acres was converted to a proportion of the city's total land area. This variable, the proportion of usable vacant land to total land area, provides a better indicator of the magnitude of the vacant land situation in a given city than does the absolute "vacant-land acreage" figure.

Table 1.2   The Amount of Vacant Land in U.S. Cities, 1997–1998

Census Region	Number of Cities	Average Population (1995)	Average City Area (acres)	Average Vacant Land (acres)	Average Vacant Land to Total Land (%)	Median Vacant Land to Total Land (%)
Northeast	6	1,345,612	55,122	5,004	9.6	9.7
Midwest	11	240,798	59,433	5,904	12.2	12.4
South	23	326,167	103,869	20,011	19.3	18.0
West	30	274,183	47,232	10,349	14.8	7.8
Total	70	346,639	64,426	12,367	15.4	12.7

1960s. For example, a 1960 estimate using a sample of 48 large cities put the average figure at 20.7 percent.[7]

Previous studies suggested that the amount of vacant land was perilously close to a minimum level that might reduce the potential economic growth rates of cities (Neidercorn and Hearle 1963). Whether the new number showing a decrease in usable vacant land should warrant a general or even faint alarm is unclear. Earlier perspectives about the supply of vacant land were premised on the need for horizontal factory space. Without adequate vacant land, economic growth would have been stifled. But the so-called new economy requires a different kind of land mix. For example, the Seattle metropolitan area, with precious little vacant land supply in the late 1990s, was teeming with job opportunities and growth. The city of Seattle, in fact, estimated its available vacant land at less than 4 percent of its total area. Indeed, as any city's vacant land supply approaches zero, economic repercussions will follow. Whether they are dire for the economic survival of a municipality, however, is another question.

Average population for the large cities reporting vacant land data in the survey is just under 350,000. Eight cities with populations of greater than 250,000—Phoenix, Fort Worth, Mesa, Albuquerque, Nashville, Virginia Beach, Charlotte and San Antonio—reported a higher percentage of vacant land than the survey average. The cities with populations of a quarter million or more, with relatively low levels of vacant land (below 10 percent), include New York, Baton Rouge, San Jose, Atlanta, Kansas City, Louisville, Seattle, Jacksonville, Baltimore and Cincinnati. These two groups of large U.S. cities face very different vacant land situations.

Table 1.2 indicates that the territorial size of the surveyed cities averaged 64,426 acres (roughly 101 square miles). However, land areas of cities varied greatly. On average, cities had 12,367 acres of usable vacant land, although these figures, too, varied considerably. A subset of cities with large amounts of vacant land (e.g., Phoenix) skews the average. Given that, another measure of central

---

7. Neidercorn and Hearle (1963) estimated vacant land in 48 large cities at 20.7 percent of cities' land area. Manvel's study (1968) found that for cities with populations of greater than 250,000, the amount of undeveloped land was 12.5 percent; the median amount of undeveloped, privately held land in those large cities was only 119 acres.

tendency, the median, is perhaps a more useful figure. The median amount of usable vacant land is just under 4,500 acres. The figures in the last column, for example, demonstrate that the median western city contains proportionately less vacant land than cities in the other Census regions.

Cities in the South demonstrated the highest proportionate amount of vacant land (19.3 percent), while western cities reported vacant land proportions similar to the survey average (14.8 percent). Of the 25 cities indicating higher proportionate amounts of vacant land than the survey average, 21 (84 percent) are located either in the South or West. Although cities in the Midwest report less vacant land than these two regions (12.2 percent), it is among northeastern cities that the proportionate amount of vacant land is the lowest: 9.6 percent. No northeastern city showed vacant land figures higher than the survey average.

Southern cities reported a gross vacant land supply that is four times as large as that reported by cities in the Northeast (20,011 acres versus 5,004 acres). As a proportion of total land area, the difference in reported vacant land between southern cities and their northeastern counterparts is a factor of two (19.3 percent versus 9.6 percent). These regional extremes are noteworthy.

Disaggregating the cities by rate of population growth allows a closer look at the regional differences discussed above. Of the 19 cities that increased their populations by at least 50 percent between 1980 and 1995, 18 are located in either the West or South. On average, the 19 fast-growth cities reported 22 percent of their land as vacant, nearly four times the amount reported by cities that lost population during that period (6.0 percent vacant) and 7 percentage points higher than the survey average. Cities that lost population averaged less than half the vacant land within their borders than the survey average (6.0 percent versus 15.4 percent). This appears counterintuitive; one would expect cities with population growth to have less vacant land, as a simple function of demand. After all, one of the primary characteristics of the urban sprawl phenomenon is the comparatively greater consumption of land relative to population increases. The findings reported here suggest that other forces are at work.

Locating more vacant land in fast-growing cities raises questions about vacant land's connection to a city's age. The built environment of cities that grew and matured during the mercantile or industrial epochs of American economic development was designed for horizontal factories or water-related access to transportation routes. As the factories and warehouses are taken out of service, we might expect to find either more vacant land (assuming demolition) or more abandoned structures (assuming less active demolition policies) in these older cities than in new ones. Cities that responded to the survey were classified according to when their population growth rate exceeded the national urban growth rate average.[8] Because our database on vacant land and abandoned structures is not diachronic, it is impossible to compare the rate of change in vacant land and abandoned structures over the past decades to population changes. Consequently, cities were classified into two groups, according to their growth rate exceeding the national average before or after 1970. Based on that

---

8. For a discussion of methodological approaches to measuring city age, see Watkins (1980).

grouping, the average amount of vacant land for older cities was 13.4 percent, and for newer cities whose growth rates exceeded the national average after 1970 it was 18.2 percent. The difference, however, is not statistically significant (T-test of the means is significant at the 0.126 level).

Disaggregating the cities by rate of land area expansion provides another point of comparison. Sixteen cities increased their territorial size by 25 percent or more between 1980 and 1995. Fourteen of them (87.5 percent) are located in either the West or South. Twenty cities reported a negligible land area change (no more than 2 percent) between 1980 and 1995. Cities from all four Census regions are represented among these fixed boundary cities. Expanding cities reported on average 23.3 percent of their land as vacant, almost three times the amount reported by fixed boundary cities (8.8 percent) and 8 percentage points higher than the survey average (23.3 percent versus 15.4 percent). This, too, confounds expectations. It is likely, however, that annexation plays a central role in this outcome. And if so, apparently the territory being annexed adds proportionately more undeveloped land (or raw dirt, as it is often called) to the city's land area.[9]

Abandoned Structures

City ordinances define abandonment of structures differently. For example, some cities contend that a structure is abandoned (and therefore presents an imminent danger to the community or threatens the city's health and safety) if it has been unoccupied for 60 days; others use 120 days or longer as the threshold. Some cities criminalize the abandoning of a structure unless the owner registers it with the city. The survey asked respondents to estimate the number of abandoned structures in the city; it did not request a disaggregation of abandoned structures by use (i.e., single-family residential, multi-family residential, commercial or industrial) nor by the square footage of the abandoned structures.

Sixty cities provided data on abandoned structures within their borders (see Table 1.3). Those cities averaged more than two abandoned structures per 1,000 inhabitants (2.6).[10] The Northeast, the region with the lowest reported percentage of vacant land and the lowest average percent change in city land area, had the highest average number of abandoned structures per 1,000 inhabitants (7.5). Cities in the West, where population growth is high, reported the lowest number of abandoned structures per 1,000 inhabitants (0.6). Northeastern cities averaged more than 10 times the number of abandoned structures per 1,000

9. Only 10 cities reported annexation as a cause for increased vacant land. The empirical data, however, suggest otherwise.

10. Because cities with more people will have more structures, a standardized measure of abandoned structures was created. Of the responding cities, only two-thirds could estimate the number of abandoned structures. Some entered a "0" to denote the very temporary or short-lived nature of the abandonment condition. Much of the difficulty in obtaining an accurate count of abandoned structures resides in the rapid turnover of properties, the definitions imposed by municipalities as to what constitutes an abandoned structure, and the city's administrative capacity to count—and therefore to know about—the number of abandoned structures.

Table 1.3 The Number of Abandoned Structures in U.S. Cities, 1997–1998

Census Region	Number of Cities	Average Change in Population, 1980–1995 (%)	Average Change in Land Area, 1980–1995 (%)	Average Vacant Land to Total Land (%)	Average Number Abandoned Structures per 1,000 Inhabitants	Median Number Abandoned Structures per 1,000 Inhabitants
Northeast	7	–3.1	1.9	8.3	7.5	3.1
Midwest	10	23.7	9.2	11.3	3.1	1.4
South	20	43.7	27.7	17.1	3.0	1.4
West	23	59.1	15.2	15.7	0.6	0.1
Total	60	40.5	16.7	14.8	2.6	0.7

residents than cities in the West, and about two to three times more than cities in the South and Midwest.

However, caution should be exercised in comparing abandoned structure figures across regions. The presence of a city with an exceptionally high number of abandoned structures can skew the regional average. Philadelphia, with a reported 36.5 abandoned structures per 1,000 population, dramatically increases the northeastern average. Baltimore, at 22.2 abandoned structures per 1,000 inhabitants, undoubtedly has a similar impact on the southern regional average. Thus, in these instances, it may be more useful to speak in terms of median numbers than averages. The median statistic for the Northeast is much smaller than the average, or 3.1 abandoned structures per 1,000 inhabitants, although it is still higher than the median figures for the other Census regions.

The cities reporting high proportions of vacant land did not necessarily report disproportionately high stocks of abandoned structures. In fact, comparing the number of abandoned structures between older and newer cities confirms an inverse relationship. The number of abandoned structures per 1,000 people in cities whose population growth exceeded the national urban growth rate prior to 1970 was 5.6, while the comparable figure for newer cities was 0.7, which is statistically significant at the .001 level. Thus, the presence of vacant land and the existence of abandoned structures may be separable situations calling for different policy solutions (Bowman and Pagano 2000).

Describing Vacant Land in U.S. Cities

Although vacant land is present in every city, the phenomenon has not been studied comprehensively. Basic questions about the amount of vacant land and its characteristics have gone unanswered, and more complex questions about the role of city government in regulating and managing vacant land have not been asked. Our survey was designed to probe some of these questions.

The Condition of Vacant Land

Definitions and images of vacant land vary, as the preceding discussion demonstrates. As Figure 1.1 shows, vacant land conditions are also variable.[11] Vacant land in U.S. cities tends to have one or more of the following conditions: parcels are relatively small in size; they are often odd shaped; and, in the view of city officials, they are found in the wrong location. These three characteristics individually, but especially in concert, limit the redevelopment potential of vacant land. Small, odd-shaped parcels in the wrong part of the city complicate the development ambitions of city officials.

Not surprisingly, the supply of vacant land is an issue in most cities. However, in a departure from what might be expected, it is an *under*supply of vacant land, rather than an oversupply, that concerns more cities. Insufficient vacant land may raise questions about a city's ability to accommodate future growth and development. The opposite condition, too much vacant land, distinguishes a different subset of cities.

For most, the temporal condition of vacant land is not an issue. In only about one-quarter of the cities is land considered vacant for too long. This suggests that, as a general rule, vacant land is recycled at an acceptable pace in most places. In 60 cities, "other" conditions are relevant, the most common of which is the holding of vacant land for speculative purposes (in 12). Other notable conditions are the presence of brownfields (in 10) and undevelopable slopes of vacant land (8), the existence of infrastructure problems (6), and classification of vacant land as wetlands (6). The label *vacant land* covers myriad characteristics.

Among larger cities (those with populations of 100,000 or more), vacant land conditions vary by region and growth rate.[12] More than half the cities in the Northeast have land that remains vacant "too long," compared with only 10 percent of cities in the West. More than 80 percent of the midwestern cities have vacant land parcels that are not "large enough" for development purposes, compared with half of cities in the South and 42 percent of cities in the West. Dividing the cities into three equal subsets based on population growth between 1980 and 1995 (slow growth: < 11 percent; average growth: 11–41 percent; high growth: > 41 percent) shows notable variation. Nearly half of the slow-growth cities report the problem of too-small parcels or land that stays vacant too long. Less than one-fifth of cities with average or high growth rates indicate the existence of those conditions.

More than half of all cities cited the problem that vacant land parcels were not large enough for development, and one in four noted that vacant land had been in that state for too long, which are important issues in urban land reuse. Too-small parcels that stay vacant for too long are more likely to characterize cities in the Northeast and Midwest than cities in the West or South. In fact, 45 percent of northeastern cities and 38 percent of midwestern cities list both factors as major impediments to development, compared to fewer than 10 percent

---

11. Survey respondents were asked to indicate which conditions were descriptive of the vacant land in their cities. No limit was imposed on the number selected and no ranking was implied.

12. *Region* refers to the regional designations of the U.S. Bureau of the Census.

Figure 1.1   Vacant Land Conditions

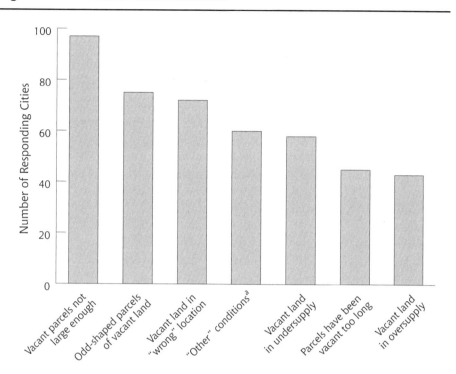

a. "Other" conditions include land that is vacant due to real estate speculation, perceived (or real) contamination, steep slopes, infrastructure problems or wetlands.

of cities in the western and southern Census regions. Slow-growing cities are more likely to exhibit both conditions. One-third (34 percent) of the slow-growth cities identified both vacant land factors, while 13 percent of the average growth group and 7 percent of the high-growth cities selected both factors.

The vacant land conditions displayed in Figure 1.1 present challenges for city governments. How can small parcels, especially when they are not clustered in an area, be assembled into larger ones? What are the development possibilities for odd-shaped vacant lots? How can a "wrong" location be transformed into a "right" one? What can be done to accelerate the movement of long-vacant parcels into productive use? For the analyst, other issues arise, such as a city's successfully bucking regional trends and linking population changes and vacant land conditions.

Changes in the Supply of Vacant Land

An undersupply of vacant land may limit a city's economic potential.[13] An oversupply of vacant land may depress land prices and, more important, be part of a larger downward spiral. It may be useful to think of these supplies as a problem of inventory management, requiring careful assessments of current stocks and anticipated demand (Knaap and Moore 2000). More than half the cities in this

---

13. This was the conclusion of a 1963 study of land use conducted by Niedercorn and Hearle.

study indicated an imbalance in the supply of vacant land: either there was too little (58 cities) or there was too much (43). In each instance, city governments are likely to act to improve the situation. An essential first step in taking remedial action is understanding the causes of the condition. In a separate, but related, question on the survey, officials were asked whether their city had experienced an increase or decrease in its supply of vacant land during the past decade.[14] Further, they were asked to indicate what they considered to be the causes of the increase (or decrease).[15] Table 1.4 presents data for larger cities (populations of 100,000 or more) in which the amount of vacant land had increased.

In cities in which the supply of vacant land had increased, several interrelated causal factors exist. Disinvestment in the city and the flight to the suburbs are the leading causes, according to city officials. If no replacement of the exiting firms and households occurs, the amount of vacant land will increase. Seemingly related to these causes are deindustrialization and out-migration, important factors in a large subset of urban areas. Deindustrialization may have had specific site effects, that is, the closing of old manufacturing facilities may lead to the discovery of contaminated soil at the abandoned sites. Other site-related problems such as limited access to capital (12 cities) or difficulties in assembling land (10) are less important explanations for vacant land increases. In only 10 of the responding large cities annexation said to be responsible for increased vacant land. In very few cities are governmental actions such as land use policies and real estate tax policies linked to growth in the amount of vacant land.

Table 1.5 focuses on cities that experienced a decline in the amount of vacant land in the 1990s. Three causes predominate: a growing local economy; increasing in-migration of population; and the use of private development initiatives. The first two of these items are highly intercorrelated, both substantively and statistically (r = .77). Cities with growing local economies tend to have increased population in-migration. A decline in vacant land availability, especially in cities with limited ability to annex additional territory, is a likely outcome. Private development initiatives also play a significant role. An aggressive private sector, operating in an expanding local economy, may make vacant land scarce. City government, in its land use and reuse policies, is identified as an important factor by more than half the cities with decreased vacant land stocks. Thus, although actions by the city are not among the leading causes of increased vacant land, they are considered important in decreasing the amount of vacant land. This observation, however, is limited to land use and reuse policies; only two cities reported real estate tax policies as causes of decreases in vacant land supply.

The relative lack of importance of real estate tax policies might seem surprising. It is plausible to assume that a city's taxation of land and structures would

---

14. An increase or decrease in the amount of vacant land is not the same as oversupply or undersupply. First, assessments of oversupply and undersupply rely on the perceptions of the city official completing the survey. The increase/decrease question is based on empirical fact. Second, the characteristics are not necessarily parallel. The amount of vacant land in a city may have increased (or decreased) and an under- (or over-) supply could still exist.

15. Survey respondents could select as many causes as were applicable to their city.

Table 1.4. Causes of *Increased* Vacant Land in the 1990s

Causes	Number of Cities
Disinvestment	25
Suburbanization	24
Deindustrialization	18
Contamination of land	15
Out-migration	14
Limited access to capital	12
Annexation	10
Land assembly problems	10
"Other"	7
City land use policies	7
City real estate tax policies	6
Transportation problems	3

Table 1.5 Causes of *Decreased* Vacant Land in the 1990s

Causes	Number of Cities
Growing local economy	55
In-migration	42
Private development initiatives	40
City policy to encourage land reuse (infill)	31
City land use policies	26
"Other"	11
Micro-enterprises	4
Real estate tax policies	2

be directly tied to increases or decreases in the amount of vacant land and, therefore, adjustments to the tax system would have beneficial or detrimental effects on individual decisions to abandon or develop property. However, in our study, we found real estate tax policies were reported to be of little consequence, compared to other explanations.

Urban Vacant Land: Alternative Views

Thus far, this chapter has implicitly examined vacant land as an urban "bad"—a problem for municipal governments. To put it bluntly, "The blight from abandoned property retards economic development severely. It's a threatening appearance to investors" (Moore, quoted in Spinner 2000, 1). But vacant land is not necessarily always a problem. During the nineteenth century the city of Boston aggressively filled wetlands to create more vacant land. Without additional vacant land, the city's development potential would have been limited; it provided opportunity. Barry Wood refers to the French practice of differentiating between industrial vacant land, which reflects past economic use, and urban vacant land, which emphasizes the potential of a site (Wood 1998). Vacant land varies not only by type, but also by its promise and associated perceptions.

Not all images of vacant land are negative. Positive images convey availability, space, opportunity and informality. A survey of vacant land in Great Britain by the Civic Trust noted the more positive view: "(A)n ambivalence to wasteland . . . came through the Trust's survey very strongly. Not all wasteland sites blight their environment, and even those that do sometimes have positive aspects, redeeming features which make them valued by at least some sections of the community" (Civic Trust 1988, 9). For some, vacant land's value rests in its nonproductivity, at least as conventionally measured. That is, its value lies in the indigenous flora and fauna that can be found in these nonmanicured settings. An urban ecology educational effort sponsored by the National Science Foundation in the late 1980s included vacant lots among city parks and rights of way as "nature's classrooms." Similarly, one of the goals of the Portland (Oregon) Metropolitan Greenspaces Program is to shift land use designations from real estate generated labels, such as *vacant* or *undeveloped*, to biologically defined designations, such as *green space* or *greenbelts* (Poracsky and Houck 1994).

Rather than symbols of urban blight, vacant lots along with other open space in a city can be considered fortuitous landscapes (Hough 1994). Thus, instead of seeing a vacant lot as a problem to be managed, city officials are exhorted to consider it instead as an opportunity to be realized. The Philadelphia vacant lot littered with broken glass and discarded mattresses is reborn as a community garden yielding blossoms and vegetables. The parcel may still be in temporary usage, but its value, tangible and otherwise, is quite different.

Still, to most observers the value of vacant land lies not in its ecological characteristics, but in its development potential (Hughes 2000). An example is West Palm Beach, Florida, where the city invested in design-conscious streetscaping and other public improvements in an effort to redevelop a decayed, abandoned downtown area. Vacant land provided the space and the opportunity for the city to encourage infilling and land banking; the commercial and housing markets responded favorably. The result is a lively, café-lined, European-style boulevard, complete with a plaza fountain. The success of the initiative spawned a second effort, this one led by developers, to convert 75 acres of vacant land in the downtown area into a $400 million mixed-use development (Flanagan 1997).

The notion of vacant land as fortuitous landscape is evident in the comments of some city officials. The deputy mayor of Washington, DC, put it this way: "If we're going to create some substantial development, we need to get rid of these abandoned and vacant properties" (Eric Price, quoted in Spinner 2000). In some ways, this is an exercise in visioning, of looking beyond the blight to see what the parcel could become. Abandonment and vacancy, then, are simply stages on the road, perhaps a long road, to renewal. Vacant lots and abandoned properties form the raw material with which a city reinvents itself. Wood quotes an Italian planner on Turin: "The existence of vacant land offers Turin a unique opportunity to refigure the city to meet the needs of the twenty-first century" (Wood 1998, 99).

A less obvious aspect in the reconsideration of vacant land is its ability to offer insights into local culture and society. Archaeologists who conducted fieldwork in 17 vacant lots in Tucson, Arizona, saw the land as a distinct kind of urban space. They argued that vacant lots are not empty in a behavioral sense; that is, they are used for foot travel, refuse disposal, storage, children's play and adult activity (Wilk and Schiffer 1979). A similar theme is voiced by McDonogh who contends that it is through studies of empty spaces rather than the built environment that one learns about a city, its culture and its values. "Whether vacant, reserved, open, or razed, empty spaces thus play crucial roles in the fabric of the city" (McDonogh 1993, 3).

Conclusion

Vacant land is a multifaceted concept, applicable to land that was once developed as well as to land that has never been developed. All cities have vacant land, although the amount, the kind and the conditions vary. In a particular city, vast stocks of abandoned structures line the streets and reflect how far the city has fallen from its glory days of the past. In another city, mile after mile of open space provides the opportunity for expansion and renewal. In its own way, vacant land tells the story of the town and offers a fresh perspective on where it is headed.

Approximately 15 percent of a city's land mass is vacant. Some might ask whether that proportion is too high or too low. Such a question misses the point. The pivotal issue is what city government chooses to do with that 15 percent. As this chapter emphasizes, vacant land and abandoned structures reflect different situations. In growing cities, vacant land represents a resource—a vast supply of potentially developable land that can be harnessed to pursue the city's vision. To depopulating cities, vacant land represents a red flag—an abundance of boarded-up buildings that signals a neighborhood in decline and a city in distress. The successful transformation of both kinds of cities depends on how effectively officials manage vacant land. The circumstances may be different, but the challenge is similar. This revisionist thinking about vacant land appears to be spreading. An article on brownfields in *Governing* in 2000 was subtitled, "You can treat an abandoned industrial site as an environmental problem. Or you can treat it as an opportunity" (Fulton and Shigley 2000, 31). A first step is a reorientation to the concept of vacant land—a new perspective that sees it as an urban resource rather than an urban problem.

References

Bowman, Ann O'M. and Michael A. Pagano. 2000. Transforming America's cities: Policies and conditions of vacant land. *Urban Affairs Review* 35 (March):559–581.

Cisneros, Henry G. 1996. Urban land and the urban prospect. *Cityscape* 3 (December):115–126.

Civic Trust. 1988. *Urban wasteland now*. London: Civic Trust.

Coleman, Alice. 1982. Dead space in the dying inner city. *International Journal of Environmental Studies* 19:103–107.

Flanagan, Barbara. 1997. Good design creates another Palm Beach success story. *New York Times*, June 12, B1, B8.

Fulton, William and Paul Shigley. 2000. The greening of the brown. *Governing* (December): 31.

General Accounting Office (GAO). 1997. *Superfund: Proposals to remove barriers to brownfield redevelopment*. Washington, DC: GAO, GAO/T-RCED-97-87.

Greenberg, Michael R., Frank J. Popper and Bernadette M. West. 1990. The TOADS: A new American urban epidemic. *Urban Affairs Quarterly* 25 (March):435–454.

Hampton, Kumasi R. 1995. *Land use controls and temporarily obsolete, abandoned, and derelict sites (T.O.A.D.S.) in Cincinnati's basin area*. Master's thesis, University of Cincinnati, Ohio.

Hough, Michael. 1994. Design with city nature: An overview of some issues. In *The ecological city*, Rutherford H. Platt, Rowan Rountree and Pamela Muick, eds., 40–48. Amherst: University of Massachusetts Press.

Hughes, Mark Alan. 2000. Dirt into dollars: Converting vacant land into valuable development. *The Brookings Review* (Summer): 34–37.

Jakle, John A. and David Wilson. 1992. *Derelict landscapes: The wasting of America's built environment*. Savage, MD: Rowman and Littlefield.

Jones, David W. 1992. *Vacant land inventory and development assessment for the city of Greenville, S.C.* Master's thesis, Clemson University, Clemson, SC.

Kivell, Philip. 1993. *Land and the city: Patterns and processes of urban change*. London: Routledge.

Knaap, Gerrit and Terry Moore. 2000. Land supply and infrastructure capacity: Monitoring for smart urban growth. Working paper. Cambridge, MA: Lincoln Institute of Land Policy.

Manvel, Allan D. 1968. Land use in 106 large cities. In *Three land research studies*. Research report no. 12. Washington, DC: Prepared for the National Commission on Urban Problems.

McDonogh, Gary. 1993. The geography of emptiness. In *The cultural meaning of urban space*, Robert Rotenberg and Gary McDonogh, eds., 3–15. Westport, CT: Bergin and Garvey.

Moore, Robert. 2000. Quoted in *Decaying buildings targeted*, by Jackie Spinner. *Washington Post*, April 8, E1.

Neidercorn, John H. and Edward F. R. Hearle. 1963. *Recent land-use trends in forty-eight large American cities*. Santa Monica, CA: The RAND Corporation, Memorandum RM-3664-1-FF (September).

Northam, Ray. 1971. Vacant urban land in the American city. *Land Economics* 47:345–355.

Poracsky, Joseph and Michael C. Houck. 1994. The metropolitan Portland urban natural resource program. In *The ecological city*, Rutherford H. Platt, Rowan Rountree and Pamela Muick, eds., 251–267. Amherst: University of Massachusetts Press.

Spinner, Jackie. 2000. Decaying buildings targeted: DC to acquire, repair or demolish 2,000 properties. *Washington Post*, April 8, E1.

Watkins, Alfred J. 1980. *The practice of urban economics*. Beverly Hills: Sage Publications.

Wilk, Richard and Michael B. Schiffer. 1979. The archaeology of vacant lots in Tucson, Arizona. *American Antiquity* 44 (July):530–536.

Wood, Barry. 1998. *Vacant land in Europe*. Working paper. Cambridge, MA: Lincoln Institute of Land Policy.

Appendix

The survey was designed to (1) estimate and assess the amount of vacant land and abandoned structures in U.S. cities; (2) identify and measure the kinds of vacant land–related policies city governments have in place; and (3) analyze the causal factors related to vacant land and city policies. Specifically, the following set of questions was addressed by the survey:

- How much vacant land exists in American cities?

- Is the amount of urban vacant land increasing or decreasing?

- What causes are associated with changes in vacant land supply?

- What are the ownership patterns for vacant land?

- What policies do cities use to regulate or manage their stock of vacant land and abandoned buildings?

- Is vacant land associated with certain characteristics such as region, population change or fiscal stress, or with city policies?

To find answers to these questions, a survey was mailed to city officials (typically, but not always, a planning director) in U.S. cities with populations of 50,000 or more in late 1997 and early 1998. To minimize the likelihood of disparities, a definition of vacant land was printed on the questionnaire:

> Vacant land includes not only publicly-owned and privately-owned unused or abandoned land or land that once had structures on it, but also the land that supports structures that have been abandoned, derelict, boarded up, partially destroyed, or razed.

A four-page questionnaire requested information from city officials about (1) the causes of vacant land and abandoned structures in their cities; (2) policies designed to regulate privately held vacant land and abandoned structures; and (3) policies governing city-owned vacant land and abandoned structures. Although the questions were structured, respondents were provided ample opportunity to explain their answers as well as to offer caveats and clarifications.

Efforts were made to attain an acceptable response rate. A single mailing of the questionnaire, bolstered by reminder postcards and follow-up telephone contacts, produced 186 responses for an overall response rate of 35.0 percent. The response rate for smaller cities (50,000 to 100,000 in population) depressed the overall rate; the response rate for the nation's large cities (the 197 cities with populations greater than 100,000) was 50.3 percent (N=99). An examination of the responses revealed no discernible over- or under-representation of particular regions or government structures.

2 | Western European Vacant Land

An Overview of Its History, Context and Policy in the Twentieth Century

Barry Wood

The experiences of four Western European countries—Great Britain, France, Italy and the Netherlands—represent quite different attitudes toward the role of the city, the legal and institutional frameworks for redevelopment, the roles of the government and the private sector and their relationship with each other, and the tools that are available for redevelopment. The term *economies in transition* generally refers to states in the former Soviet Union that are moving from a planned economy to a market economy. However, the economies of Western Europe are also in a period of transformation, as they are increasingly driven by market decisions. At the same time, the EU is creating regulatory standards across Europe. As a consequence, if one is interested in understanding the differences among Western European countries, with respect to state posture toward the redevelopment and reuse of vacant land and abandoned properties, the situation is more complex than simply saying that the Dutch have more public ownership of land or that the British have a stronger market-oriented development sector.

Context

To get a fuller appreciation requires a look at the historical and cultural context of each country and how that informs state policies toward the use and reuse of vacant land. For example, the Dutch are willing to dedicate public funds for redeveloping and reusing urban sites and will pay a premium for a compact and contiguous metropolitan area. The British, however, have been slow to reinvest in their cities that were hit by the process of deindustrialization through much of the twentieth century. The French did not really identify the issue of vacant land until the mid-1980s. Since then, however, they have been very active in using the already extensive state powers of intervention and traditional planning instruments to deal with the problem. Italy offers what is perhaps the most regulated development process.

Great Britain

England's industrial decline closely mirrored that of the industrial cities of the midwestern–northeastern corridor of the U.S. during the interwar period. In England, though, the destruction of cities during World War II resulted in a substantial process of urban development and redevelopment, which in many ways masked the problem of urban decay that had begun even before the war. By the 1960s, however, it was becoming clear that urban areas, particularly in older cities, were suffering from both economic and social decay, as firms moved to attractive, less-congested, low-density environments in the suburbs and smaller towns, and the "better-off" population moved with them. The land they left behind was not immediately developed, partly because it was often contaminated from industrial processes, but also because there was an overall lack of demand for urban land. In addition, the economy suffered from general deindustrialization, particularly a decline in the manufacturing sector. Even in London, the effects were obvious; the prosperous and growing service sector sat beside a declining industrial base.

While the industrial sector was in decline, between 1945 and 1965, there was a considerable growth in the birth rate until some commentators were estimating a U.K. population of 100 million by the end of the century. This prediction stimulated public building activity and in particular the creation of new towns. After the late 1960s, however, the population pressure relented; it had only reached 58 million by the year 2001, though there remains a steady increase in household formation. Population growth alone now creates no national pressure to use urban vacant land; it is more often the case that local and national authorities are concerned with how they can attract people back to the cities. Although the British do not have a clear conceptualization of the city, the desire to repopulate cities has come, largely, from the wish to protect the countryside as an amenity. More recently support for higher-density urban development on brownfield sites has come as a response to arguments over sustainable development. In particular, there appears to be a consensus that development activity should reduce its greenfield land take.

France

Because France has always had low population density, there was no real need in the early twentieth century to establish systems for the regulation and allocation of land for different purposes. Indeed, during the first half of the 1900s, cities were able to absorb urban growth by extending their urban perimeter. The situation changed with the urbanization that followed post-war reconstruction. The major problem was the lack of appropriate administrative structures to control and organize urban extensions, as only a few cities were developing local policies of land reserves. The government was the first to intervene, and it appeared at the center of the regulatory apparatus created to manage land use problems. This is not surprising, given the very strong role of the state in the French economy: it is the owner of many of the major banks and a substantial shareholder and financier of much of the private sector.

In France the highly structured planning and development process largely restricts development to the already built-up areas of the communes.[1] Yet, even as the state is exerting greater control in some areas of land use planning, the French are in a period that, in general, can be characterized as one of increasing relaxation of land use control. Where the land use plan is the guide to new development, it emphasizes the interest and concern of the French system for intercommunal planning issues, the social and economic contexts of land use planning, and land management. In favoring the recomposition and reconstitution of the city within its own boundaries rather than pushing the limits of the city outward as was the case before World War II—and therefore consuming more green space—more of the city's vacant land is being recycled.

The current French policies that largely encourage the reuse of vacant urban land and the protection of outlying green spaces are grounded in the significant cultural importance of the city, which is considered by the French as the premier place to live and work, quite unlike the somewhat despised suburbs. As such, vacant or abandoned urban parcels become ideal opportunities to increase the use of existing metropolitan amenities and to reknit the urban fabric with new housing, commercial activities and urban green spaces. In contrast to the British, who see the reuse of urban vacant land as primarily an opportunity to create new employment opportunities, the French do not consider employment options to be the driving purpose behind their policy.

Italy

World War II left Italy with heavily damaged buildings and infrastructure. The planning and development of Italian cities went through three phases in the latter half of the twentieth century. On the human side, there was a great deal of movement by the population, including a migration from the southern to the northern regions of the country. In response to both the physical and human needs, the government set about building low-cost neighborhoods in the 1960s. However, while the communes[2] had authority and tools at their disposal, they lacked financing. As a result, large tracts of land remained undeveloped. Much of the development that did occur, however, often resulted in high-rise and other forms of high-density residential buildings with no local public services, development in peripheral areas of the city, and developments with poor access. Today, these developments are often referred to as *quartieri dormitorio* (sleep-only neighborhoods).

---

1. Commune is the lowest tier of the French administrative system. One level of government is generally not subservient to another. As far as municipalities (communes) are concerned, there are about 36,000 of them. One of them is Paris, while there are others that contain only a few hundred citizens. Each commune has the same legal basis and in theory the same powers. Of course, the smaller communes cannot provide all the functions that their citizens require of them, and the regions and departments work to support the smaller communes.

2. Communes (*comuni*) are the lowest tier of the Italian administrative system also. There are three levels of government in Italy: Regions, provinces and communes. In each region, there are several provinces, and in each province, there are several communes.

Since the early 1970s, a key aim for the local authorities was to provide communities with the necessary schools, green space and urban infrastructure. In contrast to the French attitude, the expansion of Italian cities through the development of new monofunctional areas was the prevailing logic behind this approach. There was no relationship among the different parts of the city; each one of them was designed and conceived of in an individual fashion.

The second wave of urban planning and development was ushered in with the 1978 urban restoration law, which was intended to deal with both development and conservation issues. The environment for planning and development now was centralized, complex and highly structured. For example, restoration plans (*piani di recupero*) were required in those communes where the presence of historic heritage was a development issue. These plans typically dealt with the reuse of vacant land and abandoned buildings and became the planning and development framework for reknitting much of the urban fabric in the 1980s. Public intervention became stronger over time, but the general vision was still linked with a monofunctional distribution of space. However, the Italian idea of urban space did not incorporate an understanding of the city that emphasized the relationships among its functional parts. This understanding of urban space was going to have to await the third generation of master plans.

The economic crisis of the late 1970s and early 1980s also had strong repercussions in Italian cities and regions. Italian manufacturers, just like those in other parts of the West, faced decline. Consequently, their suppliers, wholesalers and retailers also faced economic restructuring or more general decline. The city was not only not expanding; large parts of many cities' territory were abandoned, including not only industrial plants, but also huge warehouses, railway stations, storage and military buildings. At the time of their construction, these plants and facilities were usually located in the peripheral areas of the city, but over the years, with constant urban expansion, the sites had become an integral part of the city space. Urban decline as a result of deindustrialization was, therefore, in practice more significant because the vacated sites were strategically located in the city's new configuration. Plant closures resulted in a quick fall in local real estate prices. Inevitably, there was a decline in investment in surrounding areas. Derelict land was thus initially perceived as a problem rather than an opportunity for transformation. Furthermore, the problem of derelict land due to deindustrialization was considered closely tied with the unemployment that accompanied the manufacturing plant closures. As the decade progressed, however, and faced with persistence of the no-growth city, planners eventually saw these vacated land and buildings as an opportunity to give a new sense and character to the whole city.

At the same time as the older parts of the cities were faced with disinvestment and loss of land values, population was moving out from the center, the so-called counter-urbanization process. From an urban planning point of view, this marks the passage from monocentric urban systems to polycentric ones.

The economic crisis of the 1980s was also sharpened by a political crisis, which became clear to the nation's eye at the beginning of the 1990s, with the scandal of *tangentopoli*.[3] The primary issue of this scandal was the longstanding corrupt practice of paying conspicuous amounts of money to the party or person who facilitated the planning license. This graft was often considered a cost of construction, which the *promotore*[4] was happy to pay in exchange for building permission. Indeed, this was often the only way of obtaining permission, because both local and national governments were highly unstable and unable to deliver the new master plans that granted permission. The approval to build could be forthcoming whether or not the development was the best social choice and despite any public opposition. Ultimately, this corruption and the fact that it financed many of the political parties as well as the "pension funds" of some politicians and public officials resulted in the rejection of the political system by a majority of the Italian population. During the 1990s the political process was reformed, but through the decade there was a real reluctance on the part of officials and politicians, fearing accusations of illegal activity, to grant permission to develop.

During the 1990s a new need for regulations pervaded the planning debate as well as the logic behind planning interventions. The challenge, in the political climate after tangentopoli, called for new rules of transparency. This vision was consolidated and reflected in a 1990 law that instituted the plan for the "metropolitan cities." The third generation of master plans came into existence at the same time the problem of derelict lands was acknowledged by the newly elected mayors after tangentopoli, and by the wider political classes in the urban areas. The regeneration of urban derelict land was one of the most important opportunities to implement new and more effective policy instruments.

The Netherlands

In the Netherlands development outcomes are the result of considerable public intervention in the development process, with the government holding spatial planning powers, supplementary powers and landownership powers. Indeed, almost all construction (approximately 80 percent) still takes place on land supplied by municipalities. This illustrates both the Dutch belief in the social role of land development and a pragmatic attitude toward achieving the desired spatial environment.

In contrast to the French, who see the city as a common cultural asset, the Dutch appreciate both the land and the landscape as a common cultural heritage. In service to this land ethic, almost nothing is built without the cooperation of the municipality. However, it may be misleading to describe development as plan-led. Indeed, the initiative often comes from a private developer who wants

---

3. The tangentopoli scandal brought about the collapse of the political parties that had ruled Italy since the late 1940s and scarred the reputations of thousands of politicians, business people and state officials.

4. *Promotore* generally means the person who takes care of the marketing aspects to start the reuse process for abandoned areas (such as brownfields); the Italian word for developer is *costruttore* or *imprenditore*, which refers to the private party who invests money in specific projects to transform the area's land use.

to build contrary to the existing plan. In this context, if the municipality wants to accept the proposal, it first must modify the plan. In most cases, the municipality sets in motion the procedure for changing the land use plan and, most important, it may act in anticipation of the new plan, including supplying serviced land. Both the formal planning and the active land policy of the municipality lead the development process in the Netherlands. Most urban land reclamation today is of former industrial or harbor areas. While much of this is concentrated in the large harbor cities of Amsterdam and Rotterdam, smaller towns all over the Netherlands have reuse schemes for former industrial areas, as well.

By the end of the 1970s, two forces had combined to question the previous form of growth management policy, which concentrated on decanting new development in designated areas away from the donor cities. First, the philosophy of no growth, which arose at the beginning of the 1980s, made the whole idea of growth centers and growth towns seem suspect (even though its manifest aim was to deflect growth from other, more sensitive areas). Second, donor cities increasingly feared that they would be deprived of their most active population and left with people making excessive demands for social provision. Both sentiments coalesced with new "lifestyle living fashions" that emphasized urbanity. After the elections in 1978, the new generation of Social Democrat politicians changed planning policies to strengthen the position of the city (i.e., creating the compact-city policy: concentrating dense development activity in and around existing towns and cities).

The compact-city policy and strategy are obviously very important in regard to vacant land because they support the redevelopment of urban vacant sites rather than building on new sites outside the cities, even though this could be more practical and cheaper. The compact-city policy has been exemplified in a new form of integrated planning, which includes housing, employment opportunities, infrastructure and environmental health. One of the main goals of the compact-city policy has been to bring to the fore the vital importance of big cities for the country as a whole.

The compact-city policy normally ensures that vacant urban sites are allocated for new uses through the existing municipal plan. Where urban changes are perceived to be in the public interest, new plans will be created. Land use policies are connected to both market demands and other public policies. For example, new offices must be located near adequate public transportation, which both reinforces the applicability of the compact-city policy and achieves the environmental objective of reducing car usage. The implementation of this policy could, however, be in conflict with the desire of some businesses to move to new greenfield sites. While the municipalities have strong planning and landownership powers with which to oppose such pressures, they are also able to ensure that suitable sites are made available within the existing urban area. This is achieved partly through public subsidies to remodel land for new uses. In particular, the removal of pollution and old structures by the municipality can guarantee that suitable land is both readily available and competitively priced. In addition, heavy expenditure by the municipality on improving primary and secondary infrastructure ensures that reusable urban sites are well located within the urban area. They are accessible and, therefore, attractive to the private market, which reduces the pressure for greenfield sites.

Tools and Implementation

Each country, because of its planning traditions, physical development processes and industrial history, has approached the problem of vacant land in a different way, resulting in a variety of policy tools.

Great Britain

The connection between vacant land and development is intertwined with Britain's use of development constraints and incentives, on the one hand, and changes in environmental consciousness, on the other hand. During the 1950s greenbelts were created around most major cities as a way to avoid urban sprawl and protect the countryside, which was dominated by agriculture, from development. Development that is compatible with the greenbelt designation is permitted (e.g., golf courses), and on some occasions development has been allowed where the land is already derelict and land improvement forms part of a redevelopment scheme. Where development is proposed, even when it is part of a major national plan, an extensive public enquiry is almost inevitable.

Generally, greenbelts have been highly successful for "growth management" and they remain an important policy instrument. Living close to the greenbelt is desirable, and, as a consequence, land prices in these locations tend to be pushed up. Developers are forced to either concentrate their activity within the city boundaries or move to other locations beyond the greenbelt. The greenbelts, then, are a double-edged sword: they can both concentrate development within city boundaries and encourage new development beyond the reach of greenbelts, which has been a key characteristic of the last two decades, with a few exceptions.

Development constraints alone, however, have been unable to encourage the reuse of all vacant and abandoned sites. It is now widely accepted in Britain that the reuse of vacant land will only occur if development is constrained from locating in more attractive areas, and a "carrot" of subsidy exists in at least some urban locations. Such acceptance is a radical departure from the view of the city as the prime development location. The derelict land grant (DLG), enterprise zones (EZs) and urban development corporations (UDCs) are additional tools meant to provide incentives for the reuse of abandoned and underutilized urban sites.

The derelict land grant provided a subsidy for a redevelopment scheme. At first, bids were made by public agencies; however, by the 1980s, private landowners were permitted to bid for DLGs. The national government contribution varied from 50 percent to 100 percent, with 100 percent contributed to designated "assisted areas." Public contribution to private schemes ranged from 50 percent to 80 percent. The DLG included a claw-back arrangement, under which the grant had to be repaid by the amount the land had increased in value due to the reclamation. Critics saw this as a deterrent to reclamation in some circumstances. However, such an instrument to capture land value increments due to public investment is consistent with the philosophy behind the U.K.'s betterment tax.[5] While the DLG has now been amalgamated into the single regeneration budget (SRB), the procedures and practices can still be used in suitable situations; indeed, the whole logic of the SRB is to integrate existing policies rather than to replace them.

Enterprise zones are also a form of public incentive. They were built, however, on the philosophy that the public sector inhibited private-sector development by imposing taxes and regulations. Within these geographically demarcated areas in cities' distressed zones, businesses received tax exemptions and the easing of some planning and data collection regulations. Each zone would last 10 years. Recently, the government has restricted their designation to "exceptional circumstances," perhaps in response to the widespread criticism that they have been expensive and that they encouraged so-called hedge hopping by local businesses. This form of subsidy must now be approved by the European Commission, and it is unlikely that they will do so except in the most extraordinary cases.

While the zones were conceived primarily as a tool for job generation, they have probably been more successful in bringing disused urban land back into use. In fragile property markets they have tended to concentrate development activity in specific locations; in such markets there is little evidence of positive spillover effects outside of the zones. Certainly, the concentration of development in zones has been important, though the London example is different. In some of the smaller cities, the zone has attracted all the major developments, but the zone has not been large enough to reinvigorate the whole city and generate significant spillover effects. In attempting to create a new entrepreneurial city, the zones clearly failed. The provision of site infrastructure by one main owner/developer is quite common, but often the owners are public bodies, and the EZs, therefore, require additional public funding.

The urban development corporations were entrepreneurial and behaved in ways that look familiar to both private developers and public development agencies. The UDCs were governed by a board of directors that was appointed by the Secretary of State (SoS).[6] They were, however, accountable to existing planning processes. The UDCs were in effect master land developers. For example, they reclaimed and assembled sites using compulsory purchase powers; planned new developments; assisted in the provision of infrastructure; improved the environment; and provided social facilities. In addition, they offered financial assistance to private developers to fund the gap between the costs of development of certain

---

5. The betterment tax existed only from 1976 to 1985. The policy was introduced by a Labour government, and the idea of reclaiming betterment for the public formed a consistent theme in Labour governments from 1945 to 1975. The policies of the present Labour government have departed from this earlier development policy.

6. SoS is the minister in the government responsible for planning. The minister for planning is now the Office of the Deputy Prime Minister.

sites and the value of the finished developments. The goal was to return land to the market and, most important, make locations attractive for private investors and occupiers. UDCs were expected to operate with the maximum amount of private investment, and were time-limited bodies, lasting from five to 15 years. All the UDCs have been wound up since the year 2000, however, and as yet their only replacement is the SRB.

There were 10 UDCs in England and one in Wales. They were an important part of the process of property-led urban regeneration in the 1980s and 1990s. Most of the land that was allocated to them was either derelict or vacant, and, unlike the EZs, the UDCs managed the process of change and represented a proactive response to urban decay. They also signified an explicit recognition of the need for public subsidies for property development, especially in depressed regions.

As with EZs, UDCs were not at their core a policy to address vacant land in a vacuum. Rather, they were understood as a tool for urban regeneration in its physical and social aspects. As such, UDCs have been criticized for concentrating on the provision of high-skilled service jobs, costly housing and leisure activities at the expense of lower-skilled jobs for local workers, labor training and social housing. The largest UDC, the London Docklands Development Corporation (LDDC), has faced particularly strong criticism for using large amounts of public money to subsidize high-quality office developments and executive housing in a locality with serious social problems. LDDC did, however, transform what was by far the largest derelict building site in Europe and invested heavily in land improvement and infrastructure provision.

In other parts of the country, despite some initial local displeasure, the UDCs were more readily accepted because they brought subsidies for land improvement, infrastructure provision and physical development, which are not normally available to local authorities. The creation of new commercial space in some fragile property markets, however, resulted in growing vacancy rates in other parts of the cities. In these markets, the UDCs, like the EZs, largely shifted economic activity from one part of the city to another, rather than create new economic activity.

The experience from all of these programs has pointed to the view that land reclamation is most effective when it is part of a wider strategy of urban regeneration, and is least effective when it is done as an individual project, on an isolated site and without the cooperation of adjacent land users and public authorities.

Before 1980 it was common for developers to buy contaminated land, especially after it had received some treatment, apparently accepting that the land was suitable for development. The situation has now changed, partly because of the rising awareness of environmental issues in Britain, but also because of the evolving contaminated land legislation. The latter is being led by Brussels, with the clear policy objective that the polluter should pay. Developers and investors are increasingly reluctant to buy sites where the level of contamination is not well documented, and even then they fear that additional and more demanding legislation will require new site decontamination in future years. Thus, in a curious way, the effect of environmentalism on land development has been contradictory. The force of new legislation and rules to deal with contaminated properties may lead some developers to skip the older urban centers and seek development opportunities beyond the reach of the greenbelts. In so doing, these new developments may add to urban sprawl and the increased consumption of rural land for urban uses. Perhaps urban land policy in the next decade will work through this conundrum.

France

The French place considerable cultural importance on the city, as well as on its role, function and attractiveness. As a consequence, within a planning and development context, urban vacant land is given an importance that is often far greater than its spatial significance.

In France urban development is understood from the perspective of the recomposition and reconstitution of the city within its own boundaries. Instead of pushing the limits of the city outward—and thereby consuming more green space—the urban policy objective is to use the available vacant land contained within the existing footprint of the city. Underlying this perspective is the view that both industrial and urban vacant land are major development opportunities. At the present time, the French have a particular interest in regenerating and redeveloping such land as a mechanism for enhancing and strengthening the vibrancy of the city. The debates and policies on vacant land are, therefore, part of the strategies for the dynamic management of urban spaces.

The importance of the problems caused by vacant land was highlighted in the engineer general Lacaze's 1986 report, which argued that in order to tackle the issue of vacant land in France, there needed to be a specific policy. Since then, vacant land has become a real consideration in terms of economic development and urban planning. The initial approach saw vacant land as a secondary issue, in comparison with the central policy task of industrial transformation. In the 1990s vacant land policy evolved so that it is now at the heart of the transformation itself. This is mainly explained by the fact that the regeneration and redevelopment of industrial vacant land are very important for the living environment of many regions.

The economic dimension is still cited as major justification for public-sector intervention, as vacant sites are often uneconomical to develop in many highly depressed local markets. The European perspective on vacant land must also be taken into account, which is primarily environmental, as EU legislation dominates the technical specification of cleanup regimes. EU competition policy affects the extent to which local and national governments can subsidize the cleanup, infrastructure provision and property development processes.

In legal terms, France is an extremely codified country in which relationships between public and private initiatives are strictly regulated and ordered. Hence, all forms of policy response require a legislative basis. Planning and development tools are based on the full guarantee of private property rights, but these are guided and regulated as far as their use is concerned. The right of property is expected to perform a social function.

Despite the fact that France is highly codified, there is no legal definition of vacant land in France. The term *friche* is widely used, but there is no consensus on its meaning. For instance, some use it to refer to large, vacant industrial sites located out-of-town, while others apply it only to urban buildings. The central government uses the term to describe built or nonbuilt sites that have previously been used for industrial or similar activity and have been degraded in such a way that any new use is only possible after substantive redevelopment. The concept of a *friche* can refer to a historical use, an environmental problem or a potential opportunity. In one sense, it indicates a point of failure within the urban system. In another sense, it is a recognition that a site has changed from an out-of-town location to an urban location because of the extension of the city. Finally, the *friche* may also be defined as some sort of transitory space awaiting future use. The reason for the variety of definitions is that the term has been used over many years, in a number of contexts, and with differing legal and administrative frameworks. It is only since 1986 that the French have "woken up" to the issue of vacant land as a concept requiring broad policy analysis and response.

Within that legal context, France has experienced a major transformation in political relationships with decentralization since 1983. This decentralization has involved various degrees and types of transfers of power to each of the three levels of subnational authorities (i.e., regions, departments (*départments*), and municipalities or communes). This decentralization has occurred in a variety of public activities including housing, schools, hospitals and land use planning. Since 1983 the local municipalities have been responsible (within limits) for land use plans and building permits; the departments are responsible for rural land reallocation and the protection of the environment; and the regions are merely consulted on land planning matters. Therefore, with decentralization, the management of urban development and local land policy has been transferred to local public bodies, and the power of central government to intervene has been limited, except in the case of large-scale operations. Decentralized land-use planning powers give each of France's 36,000 municipalities a significant role in development; however, the smaller municipalities have a limited ability to find the resources to finance and fulfill these functions.

The provision for private development outside the built-up areas of communes with no approved land use plan (POS) is strictly limited. This has led to strong control over the activities of private development in these communes, because all development is restricted to the built-up area. Although Great Britain has explicit land use regulations to encourage development within designated areas, in France development in existing urbanized areas is encouraged because of the institutional structure. Yet, there is variation across municipalities due to the political strength of the mayor, the particulars of the plan, and the size of the jurisdiction. It is possible for these communes to argue that unsuitable non-residential development should be located outside of the existing built-up area. In the communes with an approved POS, the mayor and the elected members of government determine where new development should go.

While some vacant land issues are clearly in the domain of the local governments, there are conditions that are understood to be national problems. For example, sites previously occupied by old industries, such as coal or shipbuild-ing, are beyond the regeneration capabilities of the local governments. These *très grandes friche*s are usually located out-of-town in relatively undesirable locations for which there is little or no private demand.

The ZAC (Comprehensive Development Area) and the ZAD (Deferred Development Zone) are two positive planning tools that enable public agencies to act as developers and, therefore, complement or counteract market forces. Both were instituted in the 1960s (1969 ZAC and 1962 ZAD). The ZAC pro-vides for contractual arrangements between public and private developers for land assembly, infrastructure investment and development in accordance with an agreed comprehensive plan. The main contribution of the ZAC, however, has been to decentralize the planning and development approval procedures to those communes that have an approved local land use plan. Alternatively, the ZAD defines an area within which a right to acquire land (preemption, with a validity of 14 years) is given to the state or another public body.

The ZAC and the ZAD are the favored tools for the redevelopment of French vacant land because they allow an integrative approach. For example, an intervention strategy for an urban quarter in which the *friche* is located raises the value of the *friche* and makes development more attractive to private inves-tors and developers. These schemes, within the framework of the POS, can range from entirely private to entirely public, or a partnership that allows for the sharing of risk and reward.

Italy

Planning legislation is central to the understanding of the problems associated with vacant land in Italy. The internal debate within the Italian planning system has accompanied the progressive awareness of vacant land as a problem in the 1980s and as a strategic resource for the transformation of cities in the 1990s.

The derelict land issue is linked particularly with the last chapter in the evolution of the Italian planning process, namely with the third generation of master plans. Prior to the 1980s, development projects were linked to the master plan. Italian urban planners, however, had to face a state of no-growth in their cities in the early 1980s. Because no new expansions to the city were foreseen, the principal urban design was to modify the existing situation; the newly vacated land appeared to be an opportunity for the planner to give a new character to the whole city. Within this framework, however, it is possible to distinguish between a first and a second phase, corresponding to the distinctive characteristics of the master plans of the 1980s and those of the 1990s. In fact, the approaches to the role of the master plan were very different.

The first phase was certainly characterized by the debate about the urban project (*progetto urbano*). Projects were developed that had no connection to the master plan strategy, because of a general sense of planning's failure and its inability to cope with new and pressing urban problems. This intermediate level of planning—smaller than citywide master planning, yet larger than an individ-ual site—gave birth to urban planning through projects (*urbanistica per progetti*), of which the urban project represented the main tool. Projects for vacant land areas, when conceived of as an urban project, constituted an opportunity to give a unitary theme to the modification of a large part of the city. The regulatory instrument for this approach was an approved variant (*variante*) to the existing master plan. The three main northern industrial cities, Milan (who appears to have the highest concentration of derelict lands in Italy), Turin and Genoa, were the first to acknowledge the problems due to deindustrialization and its negative externalities, and they were the first to introduce the new approach.

Often, much of the vacant land was already in the public domain or in the property holdings of public (state-owned) companies. This made the process of transformation easier, because in many cases the local government had only to deal with a small number of landowners. The vacant lands were appealing to the developers who were able to obtain variants and to the authorities who, in this deregulatory phase, wanted to free the market and to permit part-by-part development (i.e., urban planning through projects) of their city.

The regulatory framework favored the municipalities in their development activities, vis-à-vis private owners, but because the cost of decontamination of many of the derelict industrial sites was so high, the municipality was forced to enter into negotiations with landowners' associations. Furthermore, with the difficult land expropriation procedures in Italy, it was often easier to work with landowners than try to obtain the landownership via expropriation. The municipality was promoting and controlling the process of change, while the developers were trying to maximize their profits.

The deregulation phase of the 1980s gradually gave way to a more plan-oriented approach in the 1990s, which addressed both the need for comprehensive regulation of development and a more inclusive way of resolving the conflicts between the requirements of individual projects and the needs of the city. During this period—in the aftermath of the tangentopoli scandal—the political climate changed and major reforms of the electoral system took place. One of the main innovations was a directly elected mayor, whose power was crucially strengthened, allowing for a more effective administration of the commune through direct control of local economic initiatives. Along with this change came a stronger role for the executive in promoting the image of the city. Consequently, many local authorities started to promote their city and in particular to promote the redevelopment of the project area as part of the city's transformation.

With the election of new mayors, several local authorities started creating new master plans. In many cases, particular concern was given to the resource generated by vacant land. It is interesting to note that by this time, urban voids, which were traditionally perceived as a problem, were now considered a resource for the city and its development.

The need for new and more interactive tools for planning was envisaged at this time. At the beginning of the 1990s, the complex programs (*programmi complessi*) were instituted by the Ministero dei Lavori Pubblici (ministry of public works) with the help of the Segretariato Generale del Comitato per l'Edilizia Residenziale (secretary general of the housing committee [CER]). The complex programs represent a radical change in dealing with the problem of urban regeneration. The novelty of the approach consists mainly in the way the plan functions; the actors and the resources of the area are an integral part of the plan, which is more collaborative between landowners, developers and the city. In practice, the role played by negotiation in choosing alternatives appears to be even more critical than usual. The last generation of plans not only addresses the problem of collaboration but also that of finance; that is, before the plan is approved, the major sources of finance must be acquired.

The Netherlands

Two of the main causes of vacant land in developed countries are speculation (i.e., landowners holding on to undeveloped land in anticipation of receiving greater profit at a later time) and lack of funds by owners to clean contaminated properties. In the Dutch case, the combination of the compact-city policy and the extensive public ownership of land leaves little room for speculation.[7] Therefore, contamination is the most important cause of vacant urban land.

In the last few years, it has become clear that many urban and recreational uses are located on heavily polluted land. Among the environmental operations of the 1990s, cleaning polluted soil was a major activity. The *Interimwet Bodemsanering* (Ground Cleansing Interim Act) of 1983 constitutes the legislative framework for this operation. The aim of the act is to enable quick action in cases of direct danger to the environment or public health. The provincial governments can oblige the landowners to cooperate in the cleaning program, though the private owners are not compelled to pay for it. The government authorities have the right to expropriate the land and buildings concerned in special cases. Financial responsibility is one of the main stumbling blocks in the redevelopment of this contaminated land. In the most expensive cleanup cases, the municipalities will pay up to 10 percent of the costs, with the national government paying 90 percent. This arrangement between the national and the municipal governments is typical. That is, higher levels of government may require that the municipalities execute the national policies. However, most of the heavy expenditures are financed by the national government. In practice, the dependence on the national government diminished to some degree in the 1990s, with an increasing role played by the private sector, as evidenced by more public-private partnerships.

Another vacant land issue derives from the consequences of sand and gravel extraction. In recent years there has been a shift from passive legislation (approval/rejection) to more active policy making at national and provincial levels. There is now an obligation for provincial and national governments to make operational plans for their jurisdictional areas. The issue of mineral extraction also has to be coordinated with the physical planning of the area. Over the years, and because of inadequate agreements in the past, the aims for the redevelopment of these areas when extraction has finished have changed.

---

7. In the Netherlands the degree of public control over land is extraordinary; approximately 80 percent of all land coming into development goes through the ownership hands of the municipality concerned.

Current practice now highlights the benefit of setting up some kind of public-private enterprise to finance the restoration or redevelopment of the sites. One specific characteristic of the Netherlands is the use of most of these areas for recreation, in part because it is possible to find funding for the redevelopment of vacant land for this purpose. It is much more difficult to finance landscape renewal, and current policy is to try to include a requirement for it within the terms of the extraction concession.

Given the strength of the framework and institutions that support a highly rational land policy, and one for which there is a great deal of public consensus, local governments find little need for additional tools. However, compulsory purchase and preemption rights are available to municipalities under some circumstances. These tools, though, are rarely used. Furthermore, each level of Dutch government supports a very powerful planning process that is able to ensure that some land can be protected from development while development sites in approved locations are made available. When land becomes vacant within the urban area, its owner becomes liable to a range of laws and planning policies. For instance, when a site becomes vacant the owner is responsible for its condition. Local laws normally ensure that the land be returned to some beneficial use, even where substantive development is not immediately possible (it may be, for instance, a parking lot or landscaped area).

Conclusion

The extent to which urban land remains vacant or underused in these four Western European countries is a result of differences in the way industrialization and reindustrialization played out in each area, the requirements of rebuilding in the aftermath of World War II, the social attitudes toward cities and the urban policies that these philosophies generated, as well as differences in social policies and cultural characteristics. In Britain policies toward existing urban vacant land are largely an extension of property-led urban rejuvenation programs, such as enterprise zones, and suffer from the same limitations (e.g., designated revitalization zones simply encourage relocation from one spot to another; developers start to expect subsidies; and development choices become dependent on the subsidy regimes).

In France the vacant land policy is aimed at the reuse of plots in a way that contributes to the city's rejuvenation and enhances the living environment, which is emphasized even when the economic costs of reuse and revitalization are high. Thus, France's practice around the reuse of vacant land reflects the value their citizens place on the city.

In Italy the reuse of vacant land required changes in the planning apparatus and culture. The focus on the project, as opposed to the master-planned city, means that urban changes can occur when large-scale capital investments are limited. And the concentration on negotiations over regulations means that the voices of more affected urban actors are heard.

Outside of the Netherlands, land vacancies were created at a faster pace than reuse and regeneration. There, however, the cleanup of derelict land is not a once-and-for-all issue. Rather, the Dutch have adopted an ongoing public policy approach to the recycling of vacant land. While it is true that the national project of land reclamation and the public ownership of land make the Netherlands quite exceptional, their approach, nonetheless, demonstrates that with the right public and private attitudes, and the willingness to finance the policy, land that becomes vacant can be rapidly recycled into the urban property market. Their emphasis on rapid land recycling is probably a lesson that is worth learning and also one that is actually possible to import into other contexts.

The local and central governments play a significant role in each country studied in this report. The balance between the two is, however, quite variable among countries. Perhaps the critical issue to bear in mind is that in each case, success has depended upon an active interventionist policy; governments have not waited for the market to "solve" the problem. Government intervention, however, may be a necessary but insufficient condition for success. The strongest commitment of government resources, among the four countries studied here, comes from the Netherlands, where land remains vacant for very short periods.

Further Reading

Great Britain

Adams, C. D., A. E. Bau and B. D. MacGregor. 1988. The availability of land for inner city development: A case study of inner Manchester. *Urban Studies* 25:62–76.

Chisholm, M. and P. Kivell. 1987. *Inner city waste land*. London. The Institute of Economic Affairs.

Civic Trust. 1988. *Urban wasteland now*. London: Civic Trust.

Department of the Environment. 1974, 1982, 1988, 1993. *Survey of derelict land*. London: HMSO.

———. 1987. *Greening city sites: Good practice in urban regeneration*. London: HMSO.

———. 1988. *Improving urban areas: Good practice in urban regeneration*. London: HMSO.

———. 1989. *A review of derelict land policy*. London: HMSO.

———. 1996. *Annual report*. London: HMSO.

Elson, M. 1986. *Green belts*. London: Heinemann.

Healey, P., ed. 1994. *Trends in development plan-making in European planning systems: First report of a collaborative project on innovation in development plan-making in Europe*. Working paper no. 56. Newcastle: University of Newcastle upon Tyne.

Healey, P. et al., eds. 1995. *Managing cities: The new urban context*. Hoboken, NJ: John Wiley and Sons.

———. 1992. *Rebuilding the city: Property-led urban regeneration*. London: E&FN Spon.

Kivell, P. 1987. Derelict land in England: Policy responses to a continuing problem. *Regional Studies* 21(3):265–273.

———. 1989. Vacant urban land: Intervention or the market? *The Planner* (August):8–9.

Massey, D. and R. Meegan. 1980. *The anatomy of job losses*. London: Methuen.

Meyer, P., R. Williams and K. Yount. 1995. *Contaminated land*. Chelthenham: Edward Elgar.

Nicholson, D. J. 1984. The public ownership of vacant land. *The Planner* 70(1):18–20.

Thompson, M. J. and D. A. Edmondson. 1984. Whither derelict land grant? *The Planner* 70(1)16–18.

France

Acosta, R. and V. Renard, eds. 1993. *Urban land and property markets in France*. European urban land and property markets, no. 3. London: UCL Press.

Baudouin, T. and M. Collin. 1996. L'Après-friches portuaires. *Urbanisme* (291):24–32.

Bergeron, L. and G. Dorel-Ferre. 1996. *Le Patrimoine industriel, un nouveau territoire*. Paris: Liris.

Biarez, S. and J-Y. Nevers, eds. 1993. *Gouvernement local et politique urbaines*. Actes du colloque international Grenoble, 2–3 February. Paris: CERAT.

Clemenceau, C. 1997. Adieu l'armée. *Urbanisme* (292):14–19.

Comby, J. and V. Renard. 1996. *Les Politiques foncières*. Paris: Presses Universitaires de France.

Duranton, G. and J. F. Thisse. 1996. Land policy in a spatial economy. *Revue Economique* 47(2)227–261.

Enders, M. J. 1986. The problem of land banking: A French solution. *Environment and Planning: Government & Policy* 4(1):1–17.

European Council. 1993. *Requalification urbaine et mutations industrielles*. Commission des Communautés Européennes—Direction générale des politiques régionales.

La Laiterie. 1993. *Friches industrielles. Lieux culturels*. Strasbourg: Laiterie (Centre Européen de la Jeune Création).

Lacaze, J-P. 1986. *Les Grandes Friches industrielles*. Paris: La Documentation Française.

Levy, F. 1995. L'Expropriation des terrains pollués. *Etudes Foncières* (68):27–40.

Malfois, S. 1988. *L'Environnement dans les zones de conversion industrielle. Exemples et propositions*. Paris: DATAR.

Ministère de l'Intérieur et de l'Aménagement du Territoire & Direction Générale des Collectivités Locales. 1994. *Le Guide du maire*. Paris: La Documentation Française.

OCDE. 1992. *Les Marchés fonciers urbains. Quelles politiques pour les années 90?* Paris: Organisation de Coopération et de Développement Economiques.

Renard, V. 1987. Public land banks and private land markets. In *Major urban landowners in Great Britain and in France*. Paris: ADEF.

Renard, V. and J. Comby, eds. 1990. *Land policy in France 1945–1990*. Paris: Association des Etudes Foncières (ADEF).

Savitch, H. V. 1988. *Post-industrial cities: Politics and planning in New York*. Paris, London, and Princeton: Princeton University Press.

Tucny, J. 1996. *Le Traitement des friches industrielles. Logiques d'intervention et procédures de requalification*. Grenoble and Lyon: Institut d'Urbanisme de Grenoble and Institut d'Urbanisme de Lyon.

Wachter, S. 1992. *Redéveloppement des zones industrielles en déclin*. Paris: DATAR/La Documentation Française.

Whitby, M. and J. Ollerenshaw, eds. 1988. *Land-use and the European environment*. London: Belhaven Press.

Williams, R. H., ed. 1984. Planning in Europe. *Urban and Regional Studies* 11. London: George Allen and Unwin.

Wilson, I. B. 1988. French land use planning in the Fifth Republic: Real or imagined decentralisation? *Nijmeegse Planologische Cahiers* 27. Katholieke Universiteit Nijmegen: Geografisch en Planologish Instituut.

Italy

Ave, G. 1996. *Urban land and property markets in Italy.* London: UCL Press.

Bobbio, L. 1990. Archeologia industriale e teziario avanzato a Torino. Il riutilizzo del Lingotto. In *Metropoli per progetti*, B. Dente, L. Bobbio, P. Fareri, and M. Morisi, eds. Bologna: Il Mulino editore.

Forte, F. and Girard L. Fusco. 1997. *Principi teorici e prassi operativa nella pianificazione urbanistica.* Santarcangelo di Romagna, Italy: Maggioli editore.

Russo, M. 1997. *Valutazione e progetto per il recupero della città esistente. La risorsa aree dismesse. Programmi e realizzazioni degli anni 80 e 90.* Ph.D. dissertation, University of Naples "Federico II."

Secchi, B. 1985. Piani della terza generazione. *Casabella* 516.

———. 1986. Progetto di suolo. *Casabella* 520.

———. 1986. Una nuova forma di piano. *Urbanistica* 82.

———. 1989. *Un progetto per l'urbanistica.* Turin, Italy: Piccola Biblioteca Enaudi, Enaudi editore.

The Netherlands

Aitken, P. 1986. Land renewal in South Limburg. *The Planner* 72(9):25–27.

Davies, H. W. E. 1988. The control of development in the Netherlands. *Town Planning Review* 59(2).

Dutt, A. K. and F. J. Costa, eds. 1985. *Public planning in the Netherlands: Perspectives and change since the Second World War.* Oxford: Oxford University Press.

Faludi, A. 1994. Coalition building and planning for Dutch economic development: A new long run data set for the Netherlands 1800–1913. *Netherlands Graphical Studies* 211.

Faludi, A. and P. de Ruijter. 1990. *Dutch growth management: The two faces of success.* Amsterdam: Universiteit van Amsterdam Planologisch en Demografisch Instituut.

Fifty years of Dutch national physical planning. 1991. *Built Environment*, special issue, 17(1).

Jansen, A. J. 1990. Land-development in the balance: The position of environment, nature and landscape in land-development policy. Review of the book by P. P. J. Driessen. *Sociologia Ruralis* 30(3–4):364–365.

Janssen, M. C. W. 1996. The price of land and the process of expropriation: A game of theoretical analysis of the Dutch situation. *Economist* 144(1):63–77.

Koekebakker, P. 1991. Land reclamation. *European Environmental Yearbook 1990*, 287–290. Milan: DOC ter Institute.

Koster, E. 1995. *Eastern Docklands: New architecture on historic ground.* Amsterdam: Architectural and Natura.

Lukkes, P. 1984. Re-use of industrial sites in a rural area: A case study of the province of Friesland. *TESG* 75(3):196–201.

Needham, B. 1985. Urban development in the Netherlands: Who decides and who pays? From the international workshop on urban development control, Institute of Regional Policies, University of Lodz, Poland, 16–21 September.

———. 1988. An approach to land policy: Ideas from the Dutch experience. *Urban Law and Policy* 9(5):439–451.

Pellenbarg, P. H. 1983. Moves of industry to central South Holland in light of regional land-use plans: Results of a study evaluating 25 industrial sites. Book review. *TESG* 74(2):142.

Pistor, R. et al., eds. 1994. *A city in progress: Physical planning in Amsterdam.* Amsterdam: Dienst Ruimtelijke Ordening Amsterdam.

Smit, J. G. 1993. Land-development policy and the chances for local development initiatives in the Netherlands: The Ooijpolder case. *Sociologia Ruralis* 33(2):203–219.

Spit, T. 1993. Strangled in structures: An institutional analysis of innovative policy by Dutch municipalities. *Netherlands Geographical Studies* 5.

van Dinteren, J. H. J., D. A. Hendricks and A. Ruigrok. 1992. City-center management. *TESG* 83(2):138–144.

3 | The Economics of Vacant Land

Alan W. Evans

Before we analyze the economic reasons why land may be vacant, we must consider the question of what is meant by vacant land. There are four possibilities. First, land is vacant if it is owned by someone but not used for anything. The second possibility is that land is used, but for an activity that utilizes it less intensively than might be expected. Sometimes these uses are regarded as temporary, although they may last a long time. The use of sites as parking lots in the central areas of cities is a classic example of such a temporary use. Employing land for agriculture within suburban areas might be regarded as another. Note that while the first definition is absolute, the land is not being used for anything, the second is relative and, when it is applied, involves a subjective evaluation of the possible uses of the site. We shall call both of these *underutilized land*.

The third possibility is that the site is occupied by the buildings or other remains, such as spoil heaps, of activities that were previously held there, and where there is no immediate prospect of change. Sometimes these may be referred to as *derelict sites*. A fourth explanation is that the site has been polluted or otherwise contaminated; extensive and possibly costly work would be necessary to clean it up before it could be used. We shall call both derelict and contaminated sites *brownfield sites*, treating them together because the economic problem is the same for both.

One should be aware, however, that there is possible confusion in the use of the term *brownfield*. In U.S. legal parlance, a site that is contaminated or thought to be contaminated is defined as a brownfield site. In the U.K., however, a brownfield site may be, in planning terms, any site that has previously been developed for a nonrural purpose. The usage in this chapter, which covers a wider range than the U.S. legal terminology, but a narrower one than the U.K.'s, accords with common understanding and usage in both places.

Underutilized Sites

In this section and the next, we explore the reasons a piece of land that could be profitably developed has not been developed to its full potential and perhaps is completely unused. The first reason is because of uncertainty about the future. The economic analysis of this situation was undertaken by Titman (1986). It is interesting that he was not a land economist, and his research focused on finance. Nevertheless, he was motivated to carry out the analysis after observing that there were a number of sites in central Los Angeles that were being used as parking lots but were surrounded by tall office buildings. Why, he wondered, were these sites left vacant in this way?

Titman argued that ownership of a piece of vacant land is like the owner-ship of a stock option. Development of the site is equivalent to exercising the option. Construction and site development are so costly that they are, in practice, irreversible. Acting too soon may result in a development that is less profit-able than it might have been. Therefore, although there is a cost to delay—the revenue forgone from the development that might have been carried out—the owner may still hold on to the site, waiting for the uncertainty to be resolved. The uncertainty may be about the economy of the town or the neighborhood, or about the national or regional economy, but when it has been resolved and the owners feel sure that they know the most profitable use, then the site is developed and the option exercised.

Some uncertainty is inherent in the process of development. It takes time to prepare a site and to erect the buildings; the developer must be sure of the most profitable use, not at the time that development begins, but at that date in the future, which may be in two or three years, when the construction is complete and the buildings can be let or sold. This uncertainty is just as much a problem for the owner of vacant rural land, which may or may not be developed for hous-ing, as it is for the owner of the city-center site, which may be used as a parking lot before an office block is built on it.

Conceptually, uncertainty can be separated from speculation about the future, although in practice the two may be difficult to distinguish. A basic analysis of speculation in land was conducted by Neutze (1987), who pointed out that the owners of a site may choose to delay development because of their expectations regarding the future; they may correctly see that the land they own could be profitably developed for, say, housing at the present time. They may also cor-rectly see that in 10 years, when the surrounding area has become more built up, the site would be even more profitable if it were developed as a shopping center. Clearly, it would not be economical to develop it as housing and then demolish the housing after 10 years and redevelop the site for retail use. The most profitable policy may well be to hold on to the land until the shopping center is financially viable and then develop it. Note that as with the question of uncertainty above it is the costly and long-term nature of development that ensures that land may be left vacant and not developed.

Speculation about the future ensures that some land will be underutilized or left vacant, even when the future can be known with complete certainty. For example, in a planned new town of the kind built in Britain in the 1950s and 1960s, land would be left vacant close to the city center in the early years of the town's life. This was done so the commercial center could be expanded as the town's population grew. Thus, when the town's population was small, the commercial center would also be small, but might be surrounded by a ring of vacant land beyond which were the residential areas. If this had been done through the market, it would have to be called speculation. In fact, of course, it was done through the public sector and called planning. Speculation, therefore, is a kind of planning for the future.

If the future is uncertain, and outside the planned new town it usually is, then it becomes difficult to separate speculation from uncertainty. Owners may be uncertain about the future, then speculate that it may be better to develop the land later. And although speculation has a bad name, the example of the new town given above indicates that speculation is not per se bad, any more than planning is bad.

Land also may be used less intensively and less profitably in the short term than it might have been when it is owned and occupied by the same person or persons (Evans 1983). Because it is their home, residents will have some degree of attachment to the place, which can make them unwilling to move and, therefore, unwilling to sell. For example, the small farmer on the urban fringe may wish to continue farming and so will not sell and move elsewhere. People may be attached to the land that they own through social and economic ties; it may be where their children grew up, and they may consider themselves too old to relocate and start again elsewhere. Moreover, they may feel themselves under no immediate pressure to sell. After all, when land increases in value, it usually does so on a fairly permanent basis. Suppose that the cost of an area of land for farming is $300,000, but that it could be sold for development for $500,000. A 55-year-old farmer may feel that the profit of $200,000 is not enough to compensate for the loss of the family's livelihood if the farm were sold. Since it is likely to be worth this much, if not more, in 10 years time when retirement would be more acceptable, the decision to sell is quite likely to be delayed for a few more years. Thus, the land continues in its previous agricultural use when redevelopment would be profitable.

This would explain, in part, the extent of the urban sprawl around Japan's cities. The farms are very small, and few are for sale for farming at an agricultural use price, because of the pace of urban development. So, the peasant farmers carry on, even when their land is entirely surrounded by urban development, possibly selling a small part of their site when capital is needed, for example, for the wedding of a daughter (Hebbert and Nakai 1988). Often the pieces of land are small so that the peasant farmers work only part-time on their land and work the rest of the time at another job. This makes it easier for them to continue farming, although from our point of view it makes it difficult to distinguish the effects of attachment from the effects of speculation and uncertainty.

There are two further possible explanations for the continued existence of undeveloped sites within urban areas. Both have to do with the nature of land and with the relationship between adjoining pieces of land. The first relates to the availability of land for expansion of a previous development. The owners of factories and offices and other commercial and industrial uses may acquire more land than is necessary for the original development. Thus, a factory may be built and some land left vacant adjacent to it in case the factory has to be extended. It is obvious that it is usually better to be too optimistic rather than too pessimistic; if too much land is acquired, then it can always be sold if it is not needed. If too little land is acquired and the factory needs to expand, but no adjacent sites can be purchased, then the whole operation may have to be moved, which can be costly.

Whether and how much land is held for expansion will depend on its cost. In the early stages of urban expansion when land is cheap, the cost of acquiring surplus land is very low, and many firms will buy more land than they initially need. Later, of course, when what was the urban fringe has moved farther from the center, or when planning controls start to constrain the availability of land for development, the price of these surplus sites rises and their continued ownership becomes more costly. At this point, they may be sold, first, because the cost of holding this "insurance" is now higher, and second, because it is likely by then to have become evident whether it will be needed.

It may be argued that this kind of behavior is speculation or a reaction to uncertainty, but in my view it is clearly distinguishable. In the case analyzed here, the uncertainty relates to the future of the factory and whether it will need to be extended. It does not relate to the future demand for land in the urban area by other firms or households, the relevant factor in the cases discussed above.

In yet another possibility, the city is developed because land is then cheap and activities acquire too much for their immediate use. Nevertheless, there is a significant difference from the previous scenario involving the factory. In this case, an activity such as a suburban rail system acquires adjacent land that is then not worth anything because of its own activities. For example, in building a suburban rail system, the railroad will acquire pieces of land on which to build the line, and in so doing will acquire surplus land beside the track. When the railroad was being built, this land could be bought very cheaply because it was still farmland. After the track was built, however, the land had little or no value because its proximity to the track meant that noise and pollution from the trains lowered the desirability of the sites, and the demand for them was considerably reduced. The land might also be distant from any station and far from the city center. The negative externalities reduce the price any homeowner would be willing to pay to below the original cost of the land and the new construction.

So the sites remain undeveloped until their value rises sufficiently to make their development worthwhile. This will occur either because the city expands so that the sites are no longer at or near the periphery, or because planning constraints such as greenbelts or urban growth boundaries cause the price of land to rise in the urban area generally. Then, although poorly located from an environmental point of view, the sites become economically profitable for housing, industry or commerce. This has been the case in London, where the restrictions on the availability of land outside the existing urban area have substantially raised the price of land within the city. Thus, it was noticeable that land adjacent to suburban commuter lines constructed at the beginning of the twentieth century was bought and developed for housing in the 1970s and 1980s, with occasionally substantial costs incurred to create earth works as barriers to the noise and pollution caused by the trains.

Brownfield Sites

The term *brownfield site* can mean different things in various countries and contexts. Here, I shall employ what I believe to be common usage. First, a brownfield site may be a piece of land that has had a building or buildings erected on it at some point in the past and where these buildings are now derelict. Second, a brownfield site may be a piece of land that has been used for a certain activity in the past that polluted or contaminated it. The common factor is that considerable expenditure on demolition or decontamination is necessary before any new development can be started.

Brownfield site in a narrower sense may cover only contaminated land, as in some U.S. legal terminology, and in a much wider sense to cover any previously developed land, as in British planning terminology. In the latter case, the different meanings of the term create problems, as they conceal differences. The general population understands the term to mean sites that have been contaminated or with derelict buildings and, therefore, favors using such land for housing rather than greenfield sites. Politicians and planners define brownfield land as all previously developed land including gardens and playing fields, which the general public mostly likely would not want to develop.

From an economic point of view, a brownfield site results when the annual revenue that can be derived from the existing use falls below the cost of maintaining and running the building. Since the existing use is unprofitable, that use is closed down or moved elsewhere. To put the site into a state in which it could be used for some other purpose, however, would cost money and resources. The buildings would have to be demolished and the site cleared and/or decontaminated. Then expenditure has to be incurred in developing the site for its new usage. It can be assumed that in most urban areas there is some use that would be profitable. The most profitable alternative use determines the value that could be put on the site if it were cleared and decontaminated. Suppose, however, that the cost of demolition, clearance and decontamination is greater than the value of the site once this work has been done. The clear implication is that it is not worth carrying out the work. From the owner's point of view, the site is best left unimproved.

What we get then is a brownfield site, whether derelict, decontaminated or both. There is no viable alternative use, and the existing building itself would be too costly to operate, given the income that might be obtained. In practice, the position is even messier than this analysis, which indicates that the site's value when the buildings on it are abandoned is effectively negative. But land, or any other asset, is not sold at a negative price. Thus, the owner of the site will put a positive price on the site and then wait until it is offered. A negative price implies that someone else has to be paid to take the "asset" off the owner's hands.

Another factor that makes the position messier is the legal liability of the owner, who is likely to be regarded as responsible for the building. Minimizing the possible damage to the structure and other people involves costs in terms of security and ongoing maintenance. The building may, therefore, stay in use longer since, if costs are to be incurred, it might as well be used. Or, it might be demolished and the site cleared, thus minimizing both the costs of security and the risk of incurring any liability, even though no further development takes place.

Someone could actually be paid to take the site off the owner's hands. According to a chartered accountant in practice in the 1930s (my father), in the depths of the Depression it was not unheard of for the owner of a building in one of the more impoverished parts of Britain to transfer ownership to a "straw man" such as a tramp picked off the street. Having no assets, the new owner was not worth suing, while the previous owner was rid of his or her responsibilities. The new owner received cash and returned some of it as legal consideration; a plain gift would not be legally binding. But this type of transaction is, to say the least, unusual. It goes along with another illegal speciality in that period—paying an arsonist to set fire to the building in order to collect the insurance.

Leaving aside these complicating factors, we turn to the reasons why a site may remain vacant. There are a limited number of possibilities. The income from the existing or any new building must be too low relative to the costs of demolition and clearance of the site and to the construction of any new building. This can, of course, be put the other way around—the cost of construction and of demolition and clearance is too high relative to the income that could be obtained from any new development. Any list of the possible causes of vacancy will inevitably be, in large part, a list of variations on this relationship, the basic economic problem.

The position is most obvious in a rural area, because the best alternative land use is usually agricultural, so land values are low. People are accustomed to seeing derelict buildings in rural areas, such as an abandoned filling station on a former main road that has been bypassed by a highway. In remote areas one can see derelict houses that were once occupied by shepherds or peasants, or former mining "ghost towns." Derelict farm buildings may exist alongside newer ones. In each case, these derelict buildings are not considered abnormal. In effect, people are subconsciously aware of the economic relationship that results when buildings are abandoned rather than demolished and rebuilt. In each case, one is aware that the buildings are left to decay because they themselves yield no return, and the cost of demolition and clearance is high relative to the economic value of the cleared land when the only alternative use is farming.

The economic position is the same within an urban area, but we are not accustomed to it and regard it as counter to the normal order of things. Our perception is different for two reasons. First, there are usually alternative uses for a site within a town that would yield a reasonable income, so buildings are rarely abandoned. They are, in fact, usually rebuilt well before they reach the end of their physical life. Second, an abandoned building in a remote rural area does not affect neighbors with its presence because there are no residents, and the casual visitor may, in some circumstances, regard it as picturesque. But in a city, there are inevitably neighbors of a derelict building who will not regard it as picturesque, but will feel that something should be done.

Economically, however, apart from the negative externalities, there is no greater reason to do something in an urban area than in a rural one. A fence could be put around the site and it could be ignored. Indeed, this might be the best thing to do with sites where the cost of clearance is extremely high because, say, chemicals have been spilled there and the site needs to be decontaminated. The site could be converted into open space, for example, providing recreational area for the local workers and residents, while a greenfield site elsewhere could be developed instead. The urge to redevelop a derelict site sometimes may need to be resisted.

Why Now? The Falling Cost of Transportation

Vacant land and derelict buildings have always been with us. The archaeological excavation of a former Roman town, such as Silchester in southern England, or of the port of Ostia, near Rome itself, can take place only because the sites have been abandoned and then gradually buried. Rome in the Middle Ages, by all accounts, was an abandoned city with people living among the ruins. But, such large-scale abandonment was rare. Most abandonment was on a lesser scale, if only because the population was much smaller and, therefore, the areas developed much smaller.

We may have become more sensitive to the existence of vacant or derelict sites because the population of the world is many times larger, and the urban, developed areas much larger. People, in most developed countries at least, have become aware that there is a limited amount of land and that land should be conserved as a scarce resource. Simply abandoning a developed site no longer seems acceptable.

A general worldwide change in perceptions and specific economic and technical changes explain the existence of vacant land within urban areas. In the past, the cost of transportation within cities was high. Therefore, because it offered significant savings in transportation expense, a piece of land at a central location cost considerably more than a similar site near the city's edge. A steep land value or rent gradient could be identified and measured showing the relationship between land values or economic rents and distance from the center (Clark 1951, 1966). But over the years, transportation technology has changed; motor vehicles have supplanted trains and buses as they had supplanted the horse-drawn carriage and Shank's pony. A location near the city center is no longer so advantageous. Transportation costs have fallen as has the need for centrality, and the slope of the land value gradients has become less steep. Nowadays, in several cities the premium paid for a central-city location may be very small indeed. For many activities, campuslike office parks on fringes of the traditional city provide the fiber optic infrastructure and low-density environment that some industries seek, thus further eroding the premium for a central-city location.

In terms of the analysis set out in the preceding section, one factor, the rent obtainable from the most profitable use of the land, has fallen, while another, the cost of clearing and decontaminating a site, demolishing buildings and tidying up the infrastructure, has not. Thus, the value of an inner-city site is more likely to be low, even negative, than it would have been 50 or 100 years ago. We are more likely to see vacant or derelict sites within urban areas than we ever have been. Because we are conditioned to consider as odd an urban derelict and abandoned site and since there are more people living close to it, the site imposes a greater negative externality than, say, an abandoned mining town in the American West, which few will know about and even fewer will see.

There is a further factor that affects the economic situation of urban sites, which is unlikely to affect rural sites in the same way. In the case of rural sites, it is usually clear that there is no viable alternative use and that the most profitable use of the land is likely to be for agriculture, horticulture or some equivalent. Its value in the past has never been greatly different from this, but the position with respect to urban land is different. An urban site had a significant value in the past and it may have a significant value in the future. Thus, in the minds of the owners there is some uncertainty about its future and, therefore, its present value. As a result of this uncertainty, the landowners may hold on to property in the hope that its value will increase, and, if they put it up for sale, factor this possibility into the asking price.

Suppose, for example, that the current economic value of a derelict site is zero: the value of the site if its buildings were to be cleared would be about equal to the cost of clearing the derelict buildings, etc. Would the owners of the site put it on the market at that price? In most cases, they would not; they would consider the alternatives. The market might improve or it might get worse. If it gets worse, they would lose nothing by continuing to hold on to the site. If economic conditions improve, the value of the site increases, possibly substantially, and they gain. The optimal strategy then is to put the land on the market at a price that is well above zero and wait to see if economic conditions improve so that they get this price. Although it seems at first remarkable that apparently valueless sites are put on the market with appreciable price tags, there is an economic explanation (Evans 2000).

There is one final reason for a discrepancy between asking prices and fundamental values. If a piece of land previously was bought at a substantial price and has since fallen in value, then the owner has sustained a loss. But, although there is a loss on paper, no actual recorded financial loss has been sustained until the property is sold. It has been noted that this reluctance to sell at a loss may be particularly true of public authorities. Once again, land may be put on the market at a price that seems unrelated to the condition and prospects of the property at the time, in the hope that conditions will improve and the earlier paper losses will be recouped. There is a difference, however, between the two cases. In the second case, the public authority has actually sustained a paper loss, while in the first case, the owner is holding out in the hope of making something rather than nothing.

Imperfect Markets

Our discussion thus far has been based on the economists' usual assumption that the way the land and property market works is reasonably efficient. For this there must be many buyers, many sellers, a homogeneous product and full information. In fact, we know that this is not completely true—the product is not homogeneous, people trade infrequently, information is not freely available, so that the land and property market is not completely efficient. Indeed, elsewhere it is characterized as 90 percent efficient (Evans 1995). Such a percentage is good enough, however, for most purposes, and this degree of imperfection would not seem to cause land to be vacant for long periods. It may, of course, slow down the rate at which properties change hands and so cause some land to be vacant for short periods, but this is not a problem with which we are concerned.

There is one kind of market imperfection that can be important, however. The standard economic assumption is that people operating in a market are interested in maximizing their return from it, in this case the buyers, sellers, owners and occupiers of land. But sometimes this may not be correct. Notoriously, in Britain it has been found that much vacant land has been owned by public authorities; indeed, surveys in the mid-1980s suggested that well over half the vacant urban land was owned by public authorities. And because these authorities are not compelled by market forces to maximize their economic returns, they may behave as if the land has no economic value. Sometimes this will interact with the fact that public authorities are putting together large areas of urban land for development in a way in which no private-sector company would contemplate. Land and buildings may be acquired over time for some scheme that is then delayed or canceled. In the 1960s and 1970s local authorities often bought up areas of housing for slum clearance, demolished the housing, and then found that, perhaps after a change in government policy, money was not available to complete the schemes. To cite a more recent example, the U.K. Highways Authority bought up housing along the A40 to Oxford and Birmingham, which it intended to widen and improve, only to find in 1997 that the scheme for which it had planned for 30 years was precipitately canceled. The fact that they had hastened to demolish houses and clear the sites before the scheme was actually approved was criticized by the Public Accounts Committee, since the dwellings were substantial, well-maintained and worth retaining.

In these cases, it is evident that a public authority, which is not subject to competitive pressures, does not necessarily seek to maximize the return from the land it holds, in part because it obtains no direct return from most of its investment; such was the basis of the criticism by the Public Accounts Committee. The U.K. Highways Authority may buy up land on which to build roads, but derives no income from them. Its concern, therefore, primarily is to reduce the cost of acquisition. Sometimes the land holdings of the public authority may be so extensive that no one appears to be responsible. There is a story, which is illustrative though probably apocryphal, that in the 1970s, if a piece of land was seen to be vacant and left for many years, Liverpool Corporation erected a small white hut marked "Property of Liverpool Corporation" on the site and left it there. If no one complained, then the land probably belonged to the authority.

Sometimes problems may occur because of bureaucratic delays. In one case, which is certainly not apocryphal, a community college sought temporary buildings in which to train its motor vehicle engineering students. It found an empty former bus depot, which would have been ideal. It had been built and was owned by the County Council and was in the process of being transferred into the ownership of the town's local authority. The conditions of the transfer were being considered by central government, but had not yet been approved. Because no decision had been made, no one in either local authority was willing to allow the building to be let, even though if it had been controlled outright by either they would have rented it to the college.

Public authorities' actions can be interpreted as not attempting to maximize returns. Alternatively, they can be represented as lacking full information as to the price of their land and its possible uses. The precise interpretation is not really material, however. The point is that their participation in the land market in itself makes that market imperfect, which leads to land being left vacant to an otherwise unwarranted extent.

There are two ways in which market imperfections of this kind can affect the market through the private sector. First, private landowners may hold small parcels vacant because they lack the capital to develop the land themselves, and it may be evident that an area that includes their site should be developed as a whole to achieve economies of scale. Redevelopment of a large site, however, requires a developer to see the possibilities, negotiate with the owners, conclude purchases and, in most countries, obtain planning permission of some kind. But developers who carry out such a scheme may be involved in other schemes; the owners of the different pieces of land that have to be bought may have widely differing views as to the value of their land holdings; and there may be delays in obtaining planning permission. All of these possibilities indicate that the land market is not perfect and that market imperfections may result in land remaining vacant.

These imperfections are the reasons for vacancy that are the most difficult to reduce through government policy. Bringing a perfect market into existence when by its nature it is imperfect is next to impossible.

Conclusions

In this chapter we have set out economic reasons why land may lie vacant or underutilized. With respect to what we have called underutilized sites, we have shown that these may exist for reasons that, from the landowner's point of view, are completely rational. Chiefly, these reasons hinge on the possibility that the landowner will find selling, or utilizing, the land later more profitable than closing his or her options and selling or developing it now.

With respect to what we have called brownfield land, the situation is slightly different. The existence of derelict or contaminated land in urban areas depends on the interrelationships between the cost of clearing the site, the rents available and the cost of construction, as these determine the value of the cleared site. Policies to encourage the redevelopment of such vacant urban sites operate through changing at least one of these factors—the cost of clearance can be reduced, the cost of construction can be reduced or the rents available in the area can be increased. Any of these changes will increase the value of the site. Once it has been moved from near zero or even a negative amount to a figure that is positive, then redevelopment becomes profitable and will take place.

And finally we have pointed out that the land market is an imperfect market characterized by a lack of information. Land, therefore, may be left vacant because the owners fail to realize the value it would have if it were developed, or, in the case of government, fail to respond to the economic incentive.

References

Clark, C. 1951. Urban population densities. *Journal of the Royal Statistical Society, Series A* 114:4.

———. 1966. *Population growth and land use.* London: Macmillan.

Evans, A. W. 1983. The determination of the price of land. *Urban Studies* 20:119–129.

———. 1995. The property market: Ninety percent efficient. *Urban Studies* 32:5–29.

———. 2000. On minimum rents: Part II, a modern interpretation. *Urban Studies* 36:2305–2315.

Hebbert, M. and N. Nakai. 1988. *How Tokyo grows: Land development and planning on the metropolitan fringe.* London: Suntory-Toyota International Centre for Economics and Related Disciplines and London School of Economics.

Neutze, M. 1987. The supply of land for a particular use. *Urban Studies* 24:379–388.

Titman, S. 1986. Urban land price under uncertainty. *American Economic Review* 75:505–514.

Part 2

The Vacant Land and Brownfield Redevelopment Process

4 Turning Brownfields into Community Assets

Barriers to Redevelopment

Lavea Brachman

Over the last decade, brownfield redevelopment has captured the interest of policy makers, government entities, nonprofit organizations and even private-sector developers. For those in the public and nonprofit sectors, brownfield redevelopment represents part of the solution to the twin problems of urban decline and sprawl. For the private sector, under the right circumstances, brownfield properties represent an investment opportunity. However, all these sectors may overrate the potential of brownfields to act as a springboard for economic growth and revenues. The challenge of how to turn brownfields into community assets, particularly in declining and disinvested neighborhoods, continues to elude public policy makers and community leaders.

Policies to stimulate brownfield redevelopment have been only partially effective for several reasons. First, federal and state regulations have had unintended impacts on the operations of the marketplace. Environmental regulations governing brownfields were passed with a single-minded intention: to force the cleanup of contaminated properties. But, as in many arenas where regulations interact with the marketplace, they had an unfortunate effect of generating new problems. For instance, state and federal statutes imposed strict liability on property owners (as a way to compensate for the costs of pollution generated by companies that did not internalize cleanup costs), causing many companies and individuals to abandon their properties or enter into bankruptcy to escape the statutes' reach and consequently discouraging private-sector investors from revitalizing these properties. Second, over the last 40 years, the number of U.S. manufacturing facilities has declined, even while some have shifted location to lower-cost production sites in the U.S. South or overseas. Third, efforts to eradicate brownfield sites are further complicated by the ever-present tension between environmental quality and economic development. These two objectives, traditionally at odds with each other, are often only achievable at the expense of the other, which can prevent brownfield redevelopment projects from going forward. Because environmental problems do not stop at political boundaries, they have been appropriately regulated at the federal level, with implementation delegated to the state level. Yet, regulating for environmental quality at the state and federal levels has interfered with property development in the local marketplace. Since real estate transactions are very location specific, policies regarding property are normally the bailiwick of local government entities closer to the local market.

This chapter analyzes the impacts of these brownfield issues and policy remedies. It sets forth the history and causes of the proliferation of brownfield sites; describes a typical brownfield redevelopment process; breaks down redevelopment issues into three areas, institutional, legal and economic; looks at shortcomings in existing policies and solutions; and finally enumerates some new initiatives for addressing brownfields.

Context: Root Causes of Brownfield Problems

In the last 50 years, the number of brownfield properties has proliferated. Starting in the mid-twentieth century, the steady decline of the industrial sector has resulted in an increasing number of idle factories and manufacturing centers, leaving a legacy of brownfield properties in older industrial cities and districts. As national trends from a manufacturing to a service-driven economy have been compounded by shifts to off-shore production facilities, brownfield properties have multiplied. The adverse impacts of these global economic changes on property use were made worse by statutes enacted to address communities' concerns with the threat to health and safety from environmentally contaminated sites.

In the 1970s and 1980s Congress passed several federal and state hazardous waste cleanup statutes.[1] Superfund in particular held all past, present and future owners strictly liable—that is, without regard to wrongdoing or degree of contribution—for cleaning up pollution found on a property. This specter of liability resulted in many owners abandoning their properties or entering into bankruptcy to avoid financial responsibility for site cleanup. As a consequence, potential investors stayed away from the properties, leaving a landscape of blight in many cities, suburbs and rural areas. Meanwhile, the increased public concern with environmental issues, including preservation of natural settings and cleanup and prevention of pollution, focused a sharper lens on brownfields. The shift in living and work patterns from urban to suburban to exurban made brownfields and future land use inextricably linked to questions of how to combat the phenomenon of sprawl. Finally, early cleanup standards often required all remediation efforts to be completed to background or natural levels. These pristine standards were created without reference to the future use of the property or sometimes without regard to practical concerns about what constitutes true natural conditions.

---

1. Among these statutes are the Comprehensive Environmental Response, Compensation and Liability Act (CERCLA), 42 U.S.C. Secs. 9601 et seq., also know as Superfund, and the Resource Conservation and Recovery Act (RCRA), 42 U.S.C. Secs. 6901 et seq.

Policy makers and economists began to recognize that, left alone, private-sector market forces would push development onto greenfields, or undeveloped properties, mostly outside the urban core; the public benefits of brownfield redevelopment that would bring underutilized land up to its "highest and best use" would go unrealized. Legislative and policy fixes have been introduced to correct some of these unexpected market impacts and related inexorable societal and economic trends, but the question remains, are they the right ones and have they been successful?

On the state level, voluntary cleanup statutes have been passed in more than 40 states that encourage owners to remediate their sites by streamlining the cleanup process and capping the potential for future liability; grants exist to ease the expense of up-front site assessment; and relief from certain corporate and real estate taxes is provided by some states where reuse occurs. In addition, several states have new statutory processes—either existing and adapted for the brownfield context or passed specifically to address these problems—to expedite the elimination of "clouds" on property titles, such as back taxes, mortgages or liens. On the federal level, some progress has been made. The Small Business Liability Relief and Brownfields Revitalization Act (the Act),[2] which Congress passed in 2001, included exemptions from Superfund liability for small businesses and contiguous property owners meeting certain conditions, and for bona fide (as defined in the Act) prospective purchasers; clarification of "all appropriate inquiries"[3] and actions that innocent landowners must take to satisfy their defense; as well as new funding mechanisms. In 1997 the federal tax code was changed to allow companies to deduct "qualified remediation expenditures,"[4] which otherwise would be considered capital expenses, thus deferring the tax benefit over several years. Also, in response to the federal court decision known as Fleet Factors,[5] which stated that a secured lender loses its exemption from Superfund liability under certain circumstances, Congress passed a statute that the lender had to be "actually participating in the management or operational affairs" of facility operations[6] to be held liable. Similarly, the Community Reinvestment Act (CRA),[7] while not targeted specifically at brownfields, requires banks to make a certain percentage of investments—and those in brownfield properties qualify—in low-income neighborhoods.

---

2. P.L. 107-118 (2002).

3. In fact, the U.S. EPA is still developing the federal standards under a negotiated rule-making process to clarify the actions land owners must take to satisfy "all appropriate inquiries."

4. I.R.C. Sec. 198. Qualified remediation expenditures refer to costs paid or incurred in connection with abatement or control of hazardous substances after August 5, 1997.

5. 901 F.2d 1550 (11th Cir. 1990). The Fleet Factors decision held that a secured lender loses its exemption under CERCLA, "by participating in the financial management of a facility to a degree indicating capacity to influence the corporation's treatment of hazardous wastes" (901 F.2d at 1557).

6. 42 U.S.C. Secs. 9601 et. seq.

7. 12 U.S.C. Secs. 2901 et. seq.

Other than these statutes, federal efforts have been limited primarily to administrative initiatives or agency funding programs. In the mid-1990s, the U.S. Environmental Protection Agency (EPA) created a Prospective Purchaser Agreement (PPA), which is utilized primarily for sites remediated under the Superfund program to relieve future owners and users of liability under certain conditions. Current federal funding programs include the Assessment Demonstration Pilots and Grants, which funds brownfield inventories, planning, environmental assessments (EAs) and community outreach; the Brownfields Cleanup Revolving Loan Fund Pilots and Grants, which provides funding to capitalize loans used to clean up brownfields; the Brownfields Job Training Pilots and Grants for environmental training of residents of brownfield communities; and Brownfields Cleanup Grants, which directly support cleanup activities at properties with green space, recreational or other nonprofit uses.

Despite these federal efforts and state statutes, however, according to one report only a small percentage of the total 400,000 to 600,000 estimated brownfield properties in the country have been redeveloped (Northeast-Midwest Institute 2000). Thus, even as brownfield redevelopment has attracted more attention and interest, private investors and market forces have not responded accordingly, because the economics of a brownfield "deal" often do not work. Not surprisingly, the obvious public benefits—such as increased values of surrounding properties, job creation, higher tax revenues, mitigated sprawl, preservation of green space and pollution remediation—are not captured by the developer as a return on investment, thus limiting the private-sector demand for these sites. All too often brownfield sites are located in weak markets, so that even remediated sites may not be particularly marketable. To redevelop many brownfields, multiple solutions are needed from the private and nonprofit sectors, as well as an approach that involves multiple government entities.

A Model Brownfield Property Redevelopment Process

Ideally, brownfield redevelopment begins with an investigation into the ownership status and property conditions of the site. Typically, before a potential buyer can consider purchasing a property and targeting an end use for the site, redevelopment of a brownfield, as differentiated from a regular piece of real estate, requires an extensive due diligence period, during which a potential buyer investigates the property title and conducts an EA. Because brownfields are often abandoned, there are usually liens, mortgages or other burdens from unpaid back taxes that must be extinguished before a buyer can even enter the property legally or take ownership of it. Depending on the state and county, the process for removing these clouds from the title can involve several steps, including a title search, a sheriff's sale, public notices as well as notification of past owners and any other entity with a potential stake in the property. After such a process, a county will typically forgive any back taxes that are owed, and past liens will be extinguished.

At the same time, the buyer will need to undertake a Phase I and perhaps a Phase II EA to determine the extent and location of contamination. A Phase I EA usually does not involve any on-site investigations, but is typically a history of site use and a description of current physical conditions. It indicates whether a Phase II EA is necessary, which involves actual soil borings and testing and additional on-site analysis. The location and type of contamination determined from Phase II will have an important impact on end use (such as industrial, commercial, etc.) and the site development plan. For instance, a contaminated area may need to be "capped" with a parking lot, rather than left as open, green space. Phase II also will lead to a remediation plan that will help determine the redevelopment timeline and the configuration of a site reuse plan.

Local government involvement in brownfield redevelopment varies widely from jurisdiction to jurisdiction; however, in addition to the buyer or developer's investigation process, city or county governments or quasi-public development groups may gather information on the properties, such as ownership and environmental data, to identify prime redevelopment prospects and create a brownfield site inventory. Preliminary title searches or EAs conducted by local entities are helpful to a buyer, as these activities provide information that decrease the risks associated with unknown conditions and thus make the properties more marketable. Local governments are also well-positioned to apply for public brownfield grants and loans, thereby relieving the parties of some financial risk.

Armed with information, a buyer or developer will then negotiate with the seller, reach a contractual agreement that includes terms about the responsibility for remediation of the site, and then take ownership of the property. If it is an orphan property a developer will clear the title by extinguishing all back taxes and liens and then take title to the property. (An interim owner, such as a locality, may take title to clear liens or until the property is remediated.) Simultaneously, the developer will negotiate with financial institutions and potential investors to arrange financing for the project.

A developer may then hold a public meeting to discuss findings and plans for the site. Communities often have a particular interest in these properties because of the site history and concern about a safe reuse, potential adverse health impacts and declining property values of nearby properties. Community input, therefore, is essential to successful redevelopment. In fact, the community may insist on its involvement to ensure that the "right" public benefits derive from redevelopment of the site; citizens may be interested in zoning changes or other local development requirements.

Once preliminary investigations have been completed and a new owner holds title to the property, a developer will obtain financing (possibly including public loans for remediation) and draw up a plan for cleaning up the site's contamination. A developer will get state environmental agency approval for the remediation plan, so that he or she can take advantage of future liability relief the state offers should environmental contamination be discovered after cleanup is completed. Financing and partnerships with other private-sector investors or developers may hinge on these state-authorized liability releases. If the financing comes from conventional sources, then they usually will require submittal of information from a Phase I or Phase II EA.

Current Barriers to Brownfield Redevelopment: Legal, Institutional and Economic

The success of brownfield redevelopment is contingent upon minimizing the barriers to redevelopment so that the process resembles greenfield site redevelopment as closely as possible. It also depends on maximizing inherent brownfield advantages such as existing infrastructure and location. Currently, brownfield redevelopment faces greater challenges than those of a typical greenfield. For discussion purposes here, barriers to redevelopment are grouped into three categories— (1) legal, (2) institutional and political, and (3) economic—to examine their relationship to current policies and assess new remedies.

Legal

Liability
In some senses, liability for the costs of cleanup is the source of all the roadblocks to redevelopment. It certainly has distorted the brownfield market by creating redevelopment disincentives, chilling stakeholder involvement in brownfield projects, increasing costs and interfering with property transfer. Since we as a society have chosen to rely on statutory liability as the method for holding a party or parties responsible for actions that result in property contamination, there remains an ongoing tension between limiting liability to promote redevelopment and continuing to hold parties accountable for their acts.

Legislation imposing liability was intended to address public health and welfare concerns. As part of a group of statutory initiatives, legal liability had the laudable objective of acting as a "hammer" to prevent future disasters such as those at Love Canal[8] and at Times Beach, Missouri,[9] from occurring again and to find a way to force the actors to internalize the costs of activities that posed a danger to public health and the environment. Ideally, imposing liability ensures that only truly responsible parties are held liable, that cleanup results, and that future activities damaging our environment are prevented. Used properly, the legal imposition of liability on responsible parties is a useful tool and must be maintained in the environmental context.

---

8. From the mid-1940s to 1950s, a chemical corporation used Love Canal in upstate New York as a landfill for toxic chemicals from its operations. The land was then covered over with dirt and sold to the local board of education. The next year an elementary school was built near its perimeter and homes were constructed adjacent to it. Two decades later families began to suffer health effects from the leaching chemicals. Love Canal is credited with being a major impetus for passage of the Superfund legislation.

9. Times Beach, Missouri, a small town (population 2,240) 17 miles southwest of St. Louis, was declared a Superfund site and completely evacuated (except for one elderly couple who refused to leave) in 1985 due to dioxin contamination. The site of the town now houses a wild bird sanctuary and a state park.

However, liability has been a damper on development and investment decisions, and also has affected owners' property disposal decisions. It has had a particularly adverse effect on the predevelopment phase of brownfield projects, making it very difficult to get a project started. For example, in the initial phase of EAs, liability has been a disincentive to even investigate whether there is actual or only perceived contamination because of the risks of being tagged with liability and associated financial penalties. Where contamination is unknown, liability cannot be ascertained. In fact, the very potential for contamination, off-site migration or groundwater contamination and the associated liability, which might lead to open-ended cleanup costs, creates a cloud over the property. Experience has shown that the actual contamination of many of the smaller sites throughout the country is often less than speculated, once a site assessment has been completed. Thus, the perception that a property is contaminated stigmatizes it, while information about the type and extent of contamination generally helps alleviate the uncertainty and caps liability.

Property Transfer Decisions

Liability generally affects the decisions of corporate or large property owners differently from small site owners, and it is often a disincentive to transfer or, if ownership is maintained, to redevelop the property. Typically, large corporations assess the best approach for minimizing the liability that these properties represent by weighing the costs and benefits of keeping title, maintaining the property, and fencing it off versus redeveloping or selling it altogether. Where there is no enforcement of cleanup, large Fortune 500 companies often put off decisions about whether or how to dispose of their properties. The advantage of fencing them off is to prevent any future new use of the property that might impose liability on the companies later, while only conducting minimal maintenance and paying the property taxes. Or, if they choose to redevelop, they can control what the use is and ensure that the cleanup is done properly and cost-effectively, to guard against any activities that could increase their liability. Corporations consider this the least risky option. When they are forced to act under law, they prefer to conduct the cleanup themselves. Despite the sustained costs of property maintenance, large corporations will rarely proceed voluntarily. The costs are perceived to outweigh any benefits of sale or redevelopment—and certainly prevail over taking a corporate "good neighbor" approach to help the community by cleaning up a site. Even when a corporation decides to maintain ownership, if its primary business purpose is manufacturing, it generally has neither the expertise nor the inclination to act as a real estate developer.

Despite covenants not to sue available under state statutes, and subsequent agreements between state and federal agencies ensuring these covenants will be federally respected, the uncertainty of enforcement causes many of the large corporate-owned sites to go undeveloped, or be "mothballed."[10] In the early 1990s a corporation chose to do nothing with properties held in Connecticut and Maryland not subject then to regulation. The decision was supported by

---

10. There are no known statistics available on mothballed properties, only anecdotal examples.

a business determination: the costs of maintaining the properties and paying property taxes were relatively small compared with those of remediation and redevelopment. Also, the properties were not easily redeveloped for light industrial use because of the interior location of on-site contamination that would have forced a higher, more expensive cleanup standard and increased complexity of cleanup for a residential or commercial use. In another example, only flexibility in state policies and a great deal of initiative from the property owner resulted in a multinational petroleum refinery corporation deciding not to mothball the site of a former production facility in northern Indiana.[11] To the extent mothballing persists, policies thus far have been inadequate to address this problem. A better understanding of the corporate decisions that lead to mothballing, for instance, could result in important public policies, such as different tax treatment or incentives for owners to convert their properties.[12]

In some locations, corporate decisions to mothball can have a serious detrimental impact on communities. The size and often prominent location of these properties may depress property values and discourage smaller property owners from redeveloping, thus generally restricting economic development throughout the region. For instance, in Gary, Indiana, it is estimated that more than 350 acres of property formerly used by one steel manufacturing company lie fallow. This does not include underutilized property owned by other steel companies or steel-related operators in Gary or in adjacent cities, like East Chicago.

Differential effects of liability on small versus large properties point to the need to craft new policy solutions that encourage redevelopment appropriate to the property's size, owner or scale of on-site operations, and local practices that help businesses reinvest in these sites.

Site Control and Title Problems Affecting Smaller Properties

Liability is a double-edged sword, meant to hold parties accountable but simultaneously resulting in property abandonment and corporate bankruptcy, particularly in the case of smaller properties (20 acres or less) owned by either individuals or small entities. Smaller owners typically lack the resources to maintain ownership of a nonrevenue-producing asset, or, worse, the properties become a financial drain. The fear of liability leads to abandonment in many cases, which has created complications that prevent new parties from taking title. Clear title allows new owners legal access (that is, without trespassing) to conduct site assessments on the property, make site improvements and perform required remediation work. A developer typically cannot develop a property without holding title to it. Financing and public funding are also contingent on ownership.

Clouds on the title from back taxes owed, liens or mortgages complicate and pose a time-consuming hurdle to site control. They prevent an owner from recording the deed with the local recorder's office and getting title insurance. The burdensome process of clearing title through a sheriff's sale and multiple

---

11. Telephone conversation with the current project manager at the facility's corporate owner's office, August 2001.

12. See Hersh and Wernstedt (2003).

notice periods to previous owners common in most states hampers title transfer and prolongs the development timeframe. For instance, a property in a small northern Indiana city containing a former foundry was owned by a bankrupt company. The bankruptcy trustee had no interest in asserting its rights over the property because of the potential for liability claims and because the trust had no money to pay off the liens or back taxes.[13] Left alone, these so-called orphan properties would never be redeveloped and would most definitely remain liabilities to their communities. Some states have expedited the processes by substantially reducing the notice period.[14]

Multiple, small adjacent properties with these problems further impede site control because of the challenge of assembling them into a parcel that is shaped and sized appropriately for redevelopment. This often requires incorporating several contiguous parcels under single ownership. A critical mass of land acreage may not be under single ownership, or the only access to essential roadways or other transportation is through an adjacent, unassembled parcel. It is not unusual for there to be multiple, contiguous vacant or brownfield properties, as a result of the typical local zoning patterns or historical growth of an industrial area of a community, thus providing ample opportunity for property assembly.

Unwilling sellers who fear uncapped liability, such as large property owners or those who are holding out to negotiate a better price if improvements are being made in the area, also promote mothballed properties. Sometimes no entity is willing to take title to these "pariah" properties, especially prior to remediation. Then a buyer may only be interested if the property is clean and the purchase-and-sale agreement includes indemnification terms that protect him or her from liability for any contamination from past sources. An indemnity, however, is only as effective as the party making it. These challenges argue for remedies not targeted at individual sites, but those where local intervention results in comprehensive plans or neighborhood-wide redevelopment and local government assistance with property title.

Institutional and Political

Reluctant Stakeholders and Bureaucratic Delays

Current policies have skewed the decisions of essential stakeholders, causing them to be reluctant to get involved in brownfield deals. The potential for legal and financial liability has deterred investors, financial institutions and new property owners alike, so the time, cost and delay in corralling their involvement discourages demand for these properties. New state statutes—including the voluntary cleanup programs passed in the last five to 10 years—offering legal

---

13. This property and other Indiana properties referenced were part of work done by Northern Indiana Center for Land Reuse (NICLR), at the time a 501(c)3 subsidiary of the Delta Institute.

14. A custodial trust was an innovative solution to orphan property in one case in the late 1980s. Created in 1989 pursuant to a judicial consent decree, the trust took title to a 120-acre orphan property located adjacent to corporate-owned property, part of a Superfund site located in Woburn, Massachusetts, to manage remediation and redevelopment. See Wernstedt and Probst (1997).

promises not to pursue new owners for additional cleanup under certain conditions have improved reuse prospects. As more brownfield deals are done and the technology behind engineering protections improves, financial institutions become increasingly comfortable with the liability protections.

Although these legal covenants have allayed the concerns of some parties, property owners are still wary of ultimate liability. And statutory reform efforts have their own pitfalls, including bureaucratic hassles, delays in approving the site cleanups and issuing the covenants, as well as some inconsistencies in cleanup levels on the part of the state environmental agencies and ineligibility of certain sites for the state programs. These problems lead to property owners' lack of confidence in the long-term enforceability of the covenants, fear of future litigation expenses and suspicion of the agency bureaucracy administering these programs. The need for timeliness to fill a market niche and desire for certainty can still force developers and end users to look elsewhere other than brownfields.

Because brownfields involve both economic development and environmental protection issues, in most states two agencies that commonly are not aligned need to coordinate their programs. This has been a challenge, but not surprisingly, state brownfield regulatory efforts with financing programs specifically targeting brownfield situations, such as in Pennsylvania and Wisconsin,[15] have achieved more success than those without targeting funding. (These states' positive results may be attributed to a range of factors, but available and accessible grant and funding programs are definitely significant.) For instance, in Ohio, until passage of the Clean Ohio Revitalization Fund (CORF) in 2001,[16] there was a gap between state environmental laws and economic development incentives, both institutionally and effectively. Typically run out of different state departments—the Environmental Protection Agency and the Department of Development—these programs had very different, and sometimes opposing, missions. Despite passage of Ohio's statutory Voluntary Action Program (VAP) in 1994, no economic incentives tailored for brownfields were in place to reduce the high costs of redevelopment; therefore, relatively few brownfields were redeveloped.[17] Since the passage of CORF, 35 projects have been funded in two years at up to $3 million per project. However, the true impact of the fund on brownfield redevelopment and its ancillary impact on property values and on the marketplace is still to be judged and may be limited by other institutional or economic factors.

Lack of Local Political Will and Leadership

Strong local leadership is an absolute prerequisite to the success of brownfield redevelopment, whether in single or multiple projects. Leadership can mean an active community leader or an elected official, such as a mayor or a city

---

15. See Hersh and Wernstedt (2003) for discussion about the evolution of Wisconsin's brownfield policies and programs.

16. Ohio Rev. Code Ann. Secs. 122.651-659.

17. Green Environmental Coalition (2001). This study found that only 11 sites had entered the Ohio VAP after seven years of operation.

council member, who will champion the cause of redevelopment, apply for funding sources, and galvanize support from disparate sectors, including the business community, residents and others. Lack of leadership is devastating to redevelopment efforts. In one northern Indiana town, the mayor that was the chief redevelopment proponent was voted out of office at a crucial juncture, creating a leadership vacuum. The city council then failed to support a bond that would fund infrastructure improvements related to redevelopment of several downtown sites, and redevelopment was permanently stalled. All potential local government roles require community support, without which local government leaders are unlikely to risk their political capital by carrying out the roles.

A number of barriers to building local brownfield programs and local support and leadership exists, including a lack of understanding and sophistication about what is needed to accomplish brownfield redevelopment and to address deep-seated economic development challenges. Conflicts over redevelopment goals can arise from pre-existing community divisions, particularly in weak markets. Coalescing support around the success of a project with potential benefits for everyone can mollify these rifts, which often have their roots in economics, ethnicity or race. In disinvested areas, particularly those most in need of revitalization—where there are multiple vacant and brownfield properties—communities suffer generally from lack of organization, inexperience with complicated projects like brownfield redevelopment and mistrust of outside parties. Nevertheless, local support is pivotal to the success of redevelopment on a procedural level to approve permits and zoning changes and on a policy level to spearhead redevelopment efforts.

Location and property condition make a difference in community support. A property's situation, past use, impact on public health or proposed future use can fuel community opposition to redevelopment, even in communities that have some knowledge about how to carry out brownfield redevelopment. These sites tend to be located within or adjacent to residential or retail areas and not in clearly industrial zones, or are slated for a new use that is "messy" or unattractive (e.g., an incinerator) or may bring surplus traffic. Community resistance may be justified, and finding the right beneficial reuse for the community results in community "buy-in." Communities affected by these factors could benefit from leadership by local nongovernmental organizations, such as universities or hospitals that have a stake in neighborhood improvement.

Sites that are either relatively isolated or squarely in industrially zoned areas are less controversial and tend to be obvious candidates for industrial or commercial use redevelopment; the community is accustomed to such a use in that part of town. For instance, a 70-acre former chemical production facility, nestled between the Ohio River and the Appalachian mountains outside a medium-sized West Virginia city, is relatively isolated and has always been a source of industrial jobs. The community, the local government entities (county and city), and the regional economic development organization supported redevelopment. In the case of the former foundry in northern Indiana, the property is separated from the residential and retail parts of town and located in an industrially zoned area. In that city, local economic development efforts are under way, in large part because the local economic development organization and the city are redevelopment proponents.[18]

Similarly, in those communities with a high rate (30 percent or more in most places) of vacant and blighted land,[19] including brownfield properties, the problems extend beyond the brownfields, so that working on a site-by-site basis is ineffective. These communities are usually inexperienced, overwhelmed and lack political will to make changes. Often, new users are deterred from buying or leasing property in these areas for all kinds of reasons, including the high property taxes (because there are fewer entities to absorb the tax burden), high incidence of crime and a general stigma associated with the parcels. For example, a master plan study done for an area in Gary, Indiana, found negative perceptions about the city as a whole were a major barrier to redevelopment of individual sites. The notion of a crime-ridden city with a reputation for lacking the capacity or leadership to provide assistance and support to a developer deters economic development and brownfield redevelopment. In places like Gary and the southern suburbs of Chicago, such as Robins, Chicago Heights, Dalton and Riverdale, the perception often matches the reality. To varying degrees, these cities are not set up to provide technical assistance to developers or to partner with the private sector on public projects, funding applications, or providing permits that developers and construction companies need on a timely basis. These are areas most in need of special local intervention or comprehensive planning.

Areas suffering from this degree of urban disinvestment commonly lack the political will or power to press for targeted legislative remedies of the type that could assist these neighborhoods and redevelop properties. Such a lack of local institutional capacity makes it even less likely that there will be a community-wide plan for redevelopment and, therefore, unlikely that redevelopment of a single property will increase nearby property values and stimulate additional redevelopment. There are some isolated incidents where wholesale programmatic changes are being implemented, such as in Flint, Michigan, where the poverty rate hovers at 40 percent. The county in which Flint is located has adopted a proactive approach to vacant property redevelopment through aggressively taking ownership of property, rezoning, and working with private and non-profit redevelopment partners. However, it is too early to measure the ultimate success of such a program in redeveloping properties, eradicating urban blight and remedying disinvestment.

Economic

Despite lingering institutional barriers, at the same time that new statutes have begun to address certain legal problems, financial assistance programs have started to break down economic barriers and to level the playing field somewhat

---

18. Other challenges to this property's redevelopment, including clouds on the title, lengthened the predevelopment period, but were eventually resolved.

19. For more informaton on the degree of vacant property in cities nationally, see Pagano and Bowan (2000).

between brownfields and greenfields. However, real economic blocks to striking a brownfield deal remain, and these obstacles may exist either as an unexpected result of existing policies or in spite of them.

The legacy of brownfields is due to both macroeconomic trends and the behavior of economic actors. On the macroeconomic front, deindustrialization and technological change led industrial plants to be abandoned. At the same time, factory owners sometimes failed to dispose of industrial waste properly, leaving these sites contaminated. As a society we still bear the cost of these past actions. The conditions are now being remedied both retroactively and prospectively through regulation that attempts to shift the costs back to the private sector. The question then remains, who should be paying for these externalized costs? The expense and the resulting economic barriers manifest themselves at each crucial phase of the brownfield redevelopment process: before development is even contemplated, at the predevelopment stage, and during development and remediation phases. The poor economics of these properties are exacerbated where widespread urban disinvestment exists or where voluntary cleanup statutes and/or deal-by-deal financial incentives are insufficient. These programs have only partially addressed the expensive and time-consuming predevelopment period that chills brownfield development.

Lengthy Predevelopment Due Diligence Period

A lengthy due diligence period increases costs. An up-front investment in information gathering to determine the extent and nature of the contamination is the primary way to break this cycle. Besides the Phase I and II EAs, further investigations are needed to satisfy regulatory requirements, which dramatically increase the costs of brownfield predevelopment and prolong the development timeframe. Although an EA as well as other due diligence activities during the predevelopment stage are not particularly costly compared with remediation, they are viewed as risky, since the potential for return on the investment is extremely low. Besides "characterizing" the contamination (understanding its type, degree and location) with the EAs, development is prolonged by the need to address all the title problems discussed earlier. Other costly predevelopment activities include site preparation (grading, demolishing existing buildings and removing waste); dealing with unknown or unanticipated levels of on-site or groundwater contamination; formulating a remediation plan for agency approval; and holding community meetings. Early local intervention and information gathering provides strategic assistance.

Remediation Expense and Inadequate Public Funds

On average, remediation—including the assessment and demolition—accounts for at least 50 percent of the total project costs.[20] These expenses can be at least partially met now with public funds, but lack of flexibility on the part of state

---

20. This estimate is based on information from the Ohio Department of Development, which oversees the state's brownfields redevelopment program. The percentage of which remediation costs constitute total project costs may differ in projects involving a lower proportion of public funds.

agencies administering the cleanup programs can also add to redevelopment costs. For instance, where there is a choice among different remedial action plans with cost differentials, state agencies can approve a less expensive plan that is equally protective of human health; this helps the private sector improve the economics of the project, making it more likely to occur. Transaction costs associated with negotiating with regulators over the remediation plan and the appropriate cleanup levels—the approval of which is necessary to obtain the all-important liability releases that make a property marketable—mount up. However, the economics of a particular deal may be improved by the negligible purchase price of the property itself, and by using multiple federal and state programs, where possible. The accumulated effect of the above additional costs and delays can significantly increase the expense of doing a brownfield deal and the cost of capital, since it may be tied up for a longer period of time. The incentive programs are meant to reduce costs by matching cleanup standards to the future use, streamlining regulatory action, and reducing bureaucratic oversight.

Conditions such as urban disinvestment cannot be helped with public brownfield funds alone but must be addressed with an entirely different set of programs and policies. This chapter suggests that the availability of public funds for individual sites is a necessary but not sufficient remedy for the economic challenges of brownfield redevelopment.

Evolving Solutions: Filling the Current Policy Gaps

The remaining gaps created by current policies—risky costs and delays in the predevelopment stage, lingering uncertainty over legal liability, problems gaining site control, disincentives on stakeholder involvement, and the general challenge of developing blighted properties—need to be addressed with more targeted regulations. In addition, new private-sector tools and institutional adjustments, such as local programs and capacity building, more active nonprofit-sector efforts and cooperative policy making among state agencies with different or conflicting missions, are needed to supplement these public policies.

States have realized the need to revamp statutes, such as their property disposition laws, to align them with this contemporary vacant property problem. Acknowledging that brownfields are not just an environmental issue is crucial to breaking down barriers to redevelopment and addressing it in a more holistic fashion. However, the most likely sources for improving brownfield redevelopment prospects are local programs and nonprofit organization intervention—in conjunction with existing government programs and private-sector tools. Where local entities take a leading role in eradicating brownfields, there has been a much greater potential for success. These roles include identifying sites, conducting an inventory, brokering a deal and owning or developing property, among others. Some examples of local intervention, such as taking site control, have already proven effective.

Private-Sector Mechanisms: Reducing Costs and Limiting Liability

Up-front costs are viewed as highly risky. Public funds are available, but the gap between public funds and what private developers or property owners are willing to invest underscores the need for a private-sector funding mechanism. Fortunately, this and other brownfield financing gaps have been recognized, and new mechanisms are being forged in a few regions around the country. One fund, called the Great Lakes Redevelopment Initiative Fund I, will offer technical assistance, loans and equity investments to brownfield projects in Illinois, Indiana and Wisconsin for all project stages—acquisition, demolition, soft costs, environmental testing, and remediation and construction. It will leverage New Markets Tax Credit investor equity with loans from financial institutions and government grants for qualified projects.[21] In addition to its wide range of project lending areas, another innovative aspect of this fund is the involvement of the financial institutions that traditionally have been reluctant to invest in or lend on contaminated property because of their concerns about liability and using brownfield properties as collateral.

Although the rules surrounding these financing intiatives differ from region to region, they are used primarily in the predevelopment and remediation phases. They tend to provide debt financing for redevelopment projects with "sweeteners," or outright equity in early phases of actual development. Besides a return on their investment, the banks may be eligible to receive credit under the federal Community Reinvestment Act where the properties financed under the fund are located in low- to moderate-income areas. These types of funds are structured specifically to address the liability concerns of the financial institutions by diffusing both the legal and financial liabilities. The shared risk resulting from the number of parties involved, the arm's-length relationship of the institutions to the projects, environmental insurance, and the use of limited liability corporations together minimize the overall risks. The pooled funds, then, both limit liability and manage costs, and also address the ubiquitous gap in brownfield investment.

Public and private solutions to brownfield redevelopment are interrelated; for instance, understanding the extent and type of on-site contamination not only limits liability, removes the stigma attached to a brownfield property, and provides key information needed to form a remediation plan, it also offers important information to the surrounding community. The community can then put in place mechanisms to protect the public health.

State programs should be used in conjunction with other mechanisms that limit liability. Relief from statutory liability to the government does not protect owners, for instance, from third-party suits, adjacent property owners, future owners or any other party that may claim injury. Insurance can also reduce a property owner's risk of liability that arises from contamination discovered after the sale of the property.

---

21. For more information, see www.chicagoredi.org.

In the last 10 years, environmental insurance mechanisms have become increasingly sophisticated and popular for managing third-party liability. For example, Secured Creditor Insurance protects lenders against the loss of collateral value, inability of a borrower to repay a loan because of cleanup costs incurred, and liability for environmental conditions at properties foreclosed on by the lender. The Cleanup Cost Cap Insurance covers cleanup expenses that far exceed the estimates, thus also managing the costs. Environmental Impairment Insurance handles claims from third parties for personal injury or property damage and pays costs for cleanup of contamination unknown at the time the policy was issued.[22]

Another legal tool for controlling the liability of future owners is the limited liability corporation (LLC), a state statutory construct that is a hybrid of a legal corporation and a partnership. The LLC acts as a vehicle for property ownership and investment, with the tax advantages of a partnership and the liability protection of a corporation, meaning there is no individual liability. LLCs are used in many different contexts besides brownfields. In Michigan City, Indiana, a nonprofit organization took title to a property and transferred it to an LLC that maintained ownership and facilitated the transaction and redevelopment. This permitted the parties forming the LLC to cap their liability: only the assets of the LLC could be used to satisfy any unexpected cost or liabilities.

Finally, remediation plans that are developed pursuant to EAs may include institutional and engineering controls that supplement other liability protections. Institutional controls can be implemented through government controls (e.g., local zoning regulations, state statutes), contractual controls ("deed restrictions"), or using property law mechanisms, such as easements, restrictive covenants and deed notices. Engineering controls are usually on-site physical barriers or restrictions.

Institutionalizing Local Intervention

The structures are in place. However, for the most part, the regulatory and policy framework has not encouraged a strong local role. Some state grant or loan programs do require localities to be the applicants, and cities are involved through the normal zoning or development review process that must occur with any project. But localities as well as community-based organizations (CBOs) can play a much bigger role. By reducing predevelopment and development timeframes, targeting uses and leveraging other properties, local involvement can enhance the brownfields as assets and, thus, draw the market to these properties. Local governments' roles vary. They can (1) conduct and maintain a brownfield property inventory; (2) land bank brownfield and other vacant properties; (3) create neighborhood master plans; (4) target tax incentives for redevelopment; or (5) use eminent domain or a statutory mechanism to relieve back taxes and/or improve site conditions before turning the properties over for redevelopment. From large cities, such as Chicago, to small cities, such as Springfield, Ohio, targeted programs make a documented difference in the brownfield development

---

22. See Meyer, Yount and Wernstedt (2002).

rate. Chicago was the first city in the country to set up a brownfield task force.[23] Springfield, population 60,000, located between Dayton and Columbus, where 30 percent of its developable properties are brownfields, has a property inventory and a regular community input process as well as an active assessment process.[24] These predevelopment efforts have contributed to Springfield's success in obtaining several federal grants as well as state money for brownfield work.

Different solutions are appropriate depending on the nature of the community in which the property is located. For highly disinvested neighborhoods, towns or cities also containing a high percentage of brownfield properties, the antidote is far different than for those areas with a few scattered brownfields that are merely inexperienced with redevelopment and/or lack the resources to identify the missing components and go after financial resources. Besides local government intervention, supplementary community-based initiatives are needed. Forums that allow the community to participate in the decision-making processes about the reuse plan and sessions that disclose any information about the site's history or contamination help demystify the process, remove the property's local stigma, increase trust in the parties involved in the redevelopment, and ultimately bolster community support. An educated community is likely to be in a better position to engage the private sector in the public-private partnership so crucial to ultimate redevelopment, especially in managing the costs and obtaining site control.

Educational efforts are often led initially by nonlocal entities or organizations. In smaller communities with only a few brownfields, they can provide an important catalytic role to encourage communities to leverage change in a blighted area through cleanup and redevelopment and ultimately to enhance the local quality of life. In one small town in Georgia dominated by a single brownfield property, the redevelopment that did occur was accomplished by a local leader, but stimulated by intervention from an outside group. Ironically the insularity characteristic of those communities most in need of assistance—the least sophisticated and most disinvested—often breeds mistrust of outside sources bringing the valuable information. CBOs can play several roles that either supplement or augment local government actions to turn brownfields into community assets: as deal broker or mediator among the different stakeholders; as property owner; as neighborhood-wide planner for multiple brownfields and vacant properties; as community advocate to ensure reuse benefits the community; and even as developer (Brachman 2003).

---

23. In 1993 representatives from Chicago's departments of Environment, Planning and Development, Buildings, Law, and the Mayor's Office came together to develop a strategy for promoting cleanup and redevelopment of the city's brownfield properties. The Brownfield Forum—a broad-based public/private policy group composed of real estate developers, industrialists, bankers, lawyers, representatives from local, state and federal government agencies, environmental advocates and community groups—grew out of the city's strategy. Between December 1994 and June 1995, Forum participants attended working meetings and developed and implemented recommendations for promoting brownfield redevelopment. As a result, hundreds of acres of brownfields have been developed over the last 10 years.

24. See www.ohiobrownfields.com, Appendix C, and www.ci.springfield.oh.us.

For those communities with a high percentage of vacant and abandoned property, where brownfields constitute only part of the problem, working on a site-by-site basis is not going to be effective. Only a wholesale economic development plan has a chance of leading to new users and to redevelopment. Generally, in these communities, organization and capacity building for broad-scale economic development planning and implementation—not just limited to brownfield redevelopment—is the only approach that will lead to new users and to redevelopment. Training local nonprofit CBOs to do brownfield work, or alternatively creating new "cross-jurisdictional" CBOs or local economic development organizations to do work in blighted areas that cross village, city or town boundaries, could support formulation and implementation of these broad-scale plans.

One nonprofit intermediary organization working in Chicago has implemented a range of approaches with some success.[25] Working closely with low-income villages in the south Chicago suburbs, the intermediary has helped bring in resources and relationships; set up a local CBO by outlining a business plan and writing job descriptions; encouraged them to take ownership of the properties they want to develop; and recommended certain economic development tools (like tax increment financing [TIF]) to implement their redevelopment plans. Usually, CBOs have not addressed brownfields, focusing instead on affordable housing, crime and job creation. They view brownfields as overly complicated, expensive, risky and uncertain. In addition, these types of large-scale economic development and planning efforts have a very long lead time (at least five years). It is extremely difficult to locate funding sources to support the planning stages of these efforts.

Even communities without large blighted areas benefit from master plans. One town in central Wisconsin hitched a brownfield redevelopment plan to a transportation improvement program. The program had full-scale community support because of deep frustrations with longstanding traffic backups. Once the city made the connection that redevelopment of brownfield and other vacant sites would improve traffic circulation and create an integrated plan with both components, it leveraged community support for the brownfield redevelopment as well.[26]

Expediting Site Control

A redevelopment scenario may play out in several ways depending on the property and its history. Utilizing the public sector or a nonprofit organization as a transitional owner is becoming more common while a property is being remediated and otherwise prepared for redevelopment. Other times, a city has no choice but to take control of a property that either poses a threat to public health or has extensive back taxes owed. Through a tax benefit available to an owner who donates a brownfield property to a nonprofit organization, the federal tax law

---

25. This refers to the work of the ChicagoLand Redevelopment Institute (REDI), a 501(c)(3) affiliate of the Delta Institute.

26. See Brachman (2003).

also provides an incentive for a reluctant owner to transfer property.[27] Where an owner is holding out because his or her parcel is particularly valuable to the project (e.g., one that provides essential roadway access), then the local government may elect to take a more proactive stance. A locality can resort to the power of eminent domain, if it provides just compensation to the property owners.[28] However, many communities are reluctant to resort to a property taking, given the near-sacred place accorded private property rights in this country.

In many jurisdictions, where there might be an unwilling seller, existing statutory authority—giving localities the power to obtain title without resorting to a taking—is now being applied in the brownfield context. For example, the state of Indiana gives its localities statutory authority to declare an area blighted or economically depressed and take ownership of specific parcels, as long as the locality has a redevelopment plan under the state's Blighted Areas Act.[29] In one project in northern Indiana, in which no back taxes were owed, a recalcitrant property owner with the largest parcel that linked the rest of the four brownfields continually refused to sell his property, even though it was underutilized and had a 100,000-square-foot dilapidated building on it. The city's Redevelopment Board considered but rejected utilizing this authority to take ownership of the parcel. In Ohio a statutory tool for tackling site control that can be applied in the brownfield context is one that authorizes localities to take title through the receivership process (although the statute's constitutionality has been challenged in court).[30] Nevertheless, it can be expensive for a government entity to act under these statutory processes or carry out a taking. Also, the processes required pursuant to the statutes may be long and attenuated, which is undesirable; deliberate speed is necessary, or development opportunities may be lost.

Nonprofit organizations are also important players in the chain of title to transform the property back into active use. Public or nonprofit ownership can come about through several channels, and it may be permanent or transitional. In the case of the former foundry in Indiana, the property was saddled with three liens and back taxes. Before the title could be transferred, release of the liens had to be negotiated. Also, the county forgave the back taxes, took title to the property under a statutory process that included several public notices and a public sale, and transferred the title to a nonprofit organization, as required by the statute (to ensure that no private entity was unduly enriched by the transfer).[31] The nonprofit held the property until it was transferred to an LLC, whose members were two nonprofit organizations, created specifically for the purpose of redeveloping the property. Other states have similar processes for

---

27. The benefits of donation vary from site to site and depend on the appraised value of the property both "as is" and after remediation. Those who are considering this form of property transfer should investigate the options and determine what is most cost-effective.

28. Fifth Amendment, U.S. Constitution. In the 1990s a series of Supreme Court cases slowly enhanced property rights protection by giving greater meaning to "just compensation."

29. Ind. Code Secs. 36-7-14-1 et seq.

30. Ohio Rev. Code Ann. Secs. 323.49-51.

31. Ind. Code Secs. 6-1.1-24-1.5.

taking ownership of property where substantial and longstanding back taxes are owed.[32]

Public- or nonprofit-sector entities are willing owners and effective partners at this stage because their ownership can often expedite the process. In locales where there are several, adjacent vacant properties with multiple owners—in Gary, Indiana, for instance—it makes sense for redevelopment to begin with government-owned property or parcels that have fallen into the hands of public or nonprofit entities (i.e., through a tax redemption process); title and access issues are not barriers, redevelopment for the public interest is more likely, and the deal economics are less risky. Moreover, in many places a public- or non-profit-sector owner may transfer the property to a private entity or partner with a private developer for redevelopment. Then, redevelopment of these proper-ties may stimulate redevelopment of privately owned adjacent lots, as property values potentially increase, despite initial liability concerns.

Conclusion

Current solutions to transform brownfields into community assets are often inadequate, and additional research is necessary to identify factors that improve the prospects for redevelopment, and under what conditions, and to suggest new policies that correlate with these findings. In the end, not all brownfield properties can or will be redeveloped. Nevertheless, the funding programs and liability protection mechanisms are in place so that with strong local involvement and special attention to weak markets, redevelopment is more likely. The focus and content of these programs vary depending on factors such as size, location and history of the city. Local initiatives are critical to spur marketplace change. Therefore, future policies should be crafted to help build local capacity to craft brownfield programs that address local conditions. The nonprofit sector—which encompasses both CBOs and other nongovernmental organizations, such as hospitals and universities—can play a significant role.

Second, policies need to be tailored to address the property transfer challenges faced by large property owners and the site control challenges more common in smaller transactions. In many cases abandonment has already occurred, so future remedies might best be focused on the resulting title problems. Recently enacted legislation in New Jersey, for example, takes into account some of the development challenges specific to abandoned properties.[33] Also, localities need to be active in crafting remedies that allow for these different property qualities, particularly property size and type of owner, and formulate different incentives accordingly.

Third, funding programs that are integrated with brownfield cleanup stat-utes are most successful, and funds that target the predevelopment phase of brownfield properties most dramatically improve redevelopment prospects. Any

---

32. See Ohio Rev. Code Ann. Secs. 1728.01-13.

33. New Jersey Abandoned Properties Rehabilitation Act, P.L.2003, c. 210.

financial solutions, however, should focus on addressing the larger urban disinvestment problems discussed and not just individual brownfield transactions. Also, any programs that increase the legal and financial comfort level of private-sector investors will improve the leveraging capacity of public programs.

Fourth, certain conditions more readily give rise to the synergies of public-private partnerships. As better public laws have passed that address the private sector's chief concerns, such as liability, the private sector crafts innovative market and legal mechanisms that facilitate completion of these projects. For redevelopment of the commonplace, smaller and non-complex brownfield properties to occur, this combination of conditions—public law, private-sector mechanisms and local support—must exist, or multiple barriers to redevelopment may persist.

Finally, tension remains between environmental quality and community and economic development, but it may be addressed partially with active dialogue between state institutions to find an overlap of interests, more attention paid to sustainability issues by the planners of development projects, and a greater appreciation of the public benefits these projects generate.

In the end, a brownfield "glass ceiling" may exist, whereby some sites may never be redeveloped, regardless of the policies, market mechanisms or other suggested remedies. Ultimately, an underlying demand and viability for any real estate development project must exist, and in today's global economy, demand may be insufficient to meet the supply. Brownfield properties for which the hurdles are too high or too numerous to warrant the effort and expense of investment may need to be appropriately remediated and fenced off with engineered and institutional controls until new policies create demand for them.

Acknowledgments

I gratefully acknowledge the staff and affiliates of The Delta Institute, where I had the opportunity to work on many of the projects discussed in this chapter. I also thank the staff of the Ohio Department of Development for its comments and input. Finally, I am grateful to the Lincoln Institute of Land Policy for its financial support and to Rosalind Greenstein who gave me valuable feedback on previous drafts. I alone am responsible for any remaining errors.

References

Bartsch, Charles and Elizabeth Collaton. 1996. *Coming clean for economic development*. Washington, DC: Northeast-Midwest Institute.

Brachman, Lavea. 2003. Three case studies on the roles of community-based organizations in brownfield and other vacant property redevelopment: Barriers, strategies and key success factors. Working paper. Cambridge, MA: Lincoln Institute of Land Policy.

Breggin, Linda. 1999. *A guidebook for brownfield property owners*. Washington, DC: Environmental Law Institute.

City of Gary Route 912 industrial park: Conceptual master plan. 2001. Prepared for Gary Urban Enterprise Association by Northern Indiana Center for Land Reuse, The Lakota Group, and V3 Consultants. May. Unpublished.

Gerrard, Michael B., ed. 2001. *Brownfields law and practice: The cleanup and redevelopment of contaminated land,* vol. 1. New York: Matthew Bender and Co., Inc.

Green Environmental Coalition. 2001. *The State of Ohio's voluntary action program: Findings and recommendations*. http://www.greenlink.org/brownfields/findings/VAP_findings.html.

Hersh, Robert and Kris Wernstedt. 2003. *The brownfield bargain: Negotiating site cleanup policies in Wisconsin*. Discussion paper 03-52. Washington, DC: Resources for the Future. December.

Howland, Marie. 2003. Private initiative and public responsibility for the redevelopment of industrial brownfields: Three Baltimore case studies. *Economic Development Quarterly* 17(4).

Meyer, Peter B., Kristen R. Yount, and Kris Wernstedt. 2002. Brownfield redevelopers' perceptions of environmental insurance: An appraisal and review of public policy options. Working paper. Cambridge, MA: Lincoln Institute of Land Policy.

Northeast-Midwest Institute. 2000. Brownfields: A state by state analysis. Washington, DC: Northeast-Midwest Institute.

Pagano, Michael A. and Ann O'M. Bowman. 2000. *Vacant land in cities: An urban resource*. Washington, DC: Brookings Institution Center on Urban & Metropolitan Policy.

Wernstedt, Kris and Katherine M. Probst. 1997. *Land use and remedy selection: Experience from the field—The Industri-Plex site*. Discussion paper 97-27. Washington, DC: Resources for the Future. July.

5 | Is Contamination the Barrier to Inner-City Industrial Revitalization?

Marie Howland

As smart growth and its promise of more livable cities catches the imagination of planners, academics, developers and citizens, the redevelopment of inner-city brownfield sites becomes an even higher priority. To justify limiting the development of greenfield sites, city governments must find buildable land within existing city limits. Contamination—the legacy of nonexistent environmental laws[1] and our industrial past—is widely perceived to be a deterrent to central-city revitalization.

Are the costs of cleanup so high relative to land values that government has to step in to provide subsidies? Is there a market failure in central-city industrial land markets, due to the refusal of banks to finance such transactions or the lack of information about the risks and costs of dealing with contamination? To what extent is contamination deterring central-city revitalization, and to what degree are other factors impediments to central-city redevelopment? This chapter attempts to answer these questions by tracking all sales, the selling price, existence of contamination and length of time on the market of more than 5,500 acres in one industrial area in southwest Baltimore. The data-intensive methodology and interviews allow us to document the degree to which contamination inhibits market demand and the extent to which other roadblocks are to blame for what is perceived as a relatively sluggish central-city industrial land market. The quantitative analysis sheds light on the impact of contamination on land sales and price discounts, while the interviews provide nuanced insights into how contamination and other factors affect sales and prices. For example, without a district-wide analysis of all sales, we could not know that contaminated parcels were selling without government assistance and that the failure to sell was often the result of asking prices that were too high. The interviews reveal the nonmeasured factors that influence sales and prices.

---

1. The federal government passed the Comprehensive Environmental Response, Liability, and Compensation Act in 1981.

The results of the quantitative analysis indicate that since the mid-1990s, contaminated parcels are selling and the market has adjusted to contamination by lowering sales prices. In fact, contamination does not appear to be a barrier at all when the intended land use is also industrial. The interviews suggest that to seriously implement smart growth and central-city revitalization, advocates will have to tackle the often ignored problems of older industrial areas, such as outdated parcel sizes, inadequate roads for modern truck access, aging infrastructure, incompatible land uses and unrealistic assumptions about the land's possibilities. The sole focus on contamination obscures other equally important barriers to the redevelopment of industrial central-city districts.

Literature Review

Although polluted sites exist in rural and suburban jurisdictions, contamination is often seen as a central-city problem (Staley 1996; De Sousa 2001). Of the 925 sites on the National Priorities List, 17 percent are in inner cities and 57 percent are in metropolitan areas (Wernstedt and Hersh 1998, 460). More pertinent, however, than central cities' overall share is the fact that they are more likely to radiate negative externalities than sites in less dense settings and more likely to create barriers to the implementation of smart growth objectives.[2]

Contamination is viewed as the most significant barrier to the redevelopment of urban industrial parcels. There are two reasons the literature has come to this conclusion. One is by definition: the Environment Protection Agency defines a brownfield as an "abandoned, idled, or under-used industrial and commercial facility where expansion or redevelopment is complicated by real or perceived environmental contamination" (U.S. EPA 1997). This definition excludes all the other contaminated sites on which development did occur, thereby exaggerating the overall role that contamination plays in discouraging development. Second, both the literature and public policy overemphasize contamination as a redevelopment impediment, because the data have not been available to indicate otherwise. Case studies, which comprise the most common methodology in the brownfield literature, usually highlight either best practices (ICMA 1998; Wernstedt and Hersh 1998) or the barriers to redevelopment. Literature of the latter focuses on cleanup costs, fears over future liability, the difficulty of obtaining private financing (Bartsch 1996; Swartz 1994; Yount and Meyer 1994; Staley 1996; Yount 1997; De Sousa 2000; and De Sousa 2001), and the legal and litigation costs associated with any purchase agreements and collection of damages from other legally liable parties (Duff 1994). Most often these cases focus on sites that have reached public attention because of a lack of private-sector interest, giving the impression that contamination is the major roadblock to central-city industrial redevelopment. Additionally, case studies examine individual sites in isolation, and, therefore, public officials and policy makers can miss the fact

---

2. We refer here specifically to smart growth strategies that direct new growth to areas with existing infrastructure.

that the land is sitting idle because the seller has overpriced the land in light of its contamination and market demand.

In spite of extensive literature that documents cases where the price cannot be dropped low enough to compensate for the costs, risks and liability of owning a contaminated site (Bartsch 1996; Bartsch and Collaton 1996; Green Leigh 1994; Greenberg et al. 2000; Page and Rabinowitz 1993; Schriner 1998), several decades of successful cleanups and redevelopment projects reflect the existence of situations where developers find it profitable to absorb the risks of purchasing, cleaning and reusing contaminated parcels (Pepper 1997). Meyers and Lyons (2000) document the emergence of entrepreneurial firms that are redeveloping brownfield sites without public-sector intervention. They find these private ventures favor sites in high-value locations, under private ownership, and larger parcels. Such case studies do not estimate the price discounts associated with contamination, nor do they put contamination in perspective with the other conditions that may cause redevelopment to fail.

Three studies examine the price discounts associated with contamination. McGrath found redevelopment occurring on polluted sites and with "discounts in land value due to contamination risk [that] . . . are consistent with the limited cost data available. The industrial land market is highly competitive in the City of Chicago . . . and it appears that the market has successfully valued and capitalized the contamination liability" (1995, 18). Tracking sales over a two-and-a-half-year period at the Port of Baltimore, Howland (2000) found price discounts on contaminated parcels, which, when discounted, were as likely to sell as "clean" parcels. Page and Rabinowitz (1993) found land price reductions of 10 to 50 percent on four industrial projects spanning three states.

Greenberg et al. (2000) studied brownfields in New Jersey, and in a survey of municipal tax assessors, identified barriers to redevelopment aside from land contamination. These barriers included state and local regulations (aside from those related to brownfields), unsafe neighborhood conditions (e.g., crime, stray animals), industrial decline, more attractive adjacent areas, lack of schools and poor transportation access.

The contribution of the current study is that we can determine the extent to which contamination halts redevelopment, the range of the price discounts associated with contamination, the role contamination plays in deterring land sales and subsequent redevelopment, and the relative importance of contamination with respect to other potential barriers to central-city redevelopment.

Baltimore Versus Other Industrial Cities

Baltimore is typical of other industrial cities in the Northeast. It is similarly experiencing structural change, with a declining share of its work force in manufacturing and a growing share in service employment. In comparison with other metropolitan areas where brownfield issues have received attention, Baltimore's regional manufacturing sector has shown relatively greater decline than the Chicago, Detroit, Philadelphia, Boston, Cleveland, Atlanta and Pittsburgh

Figure 5.1   Manufacturing Employment Change

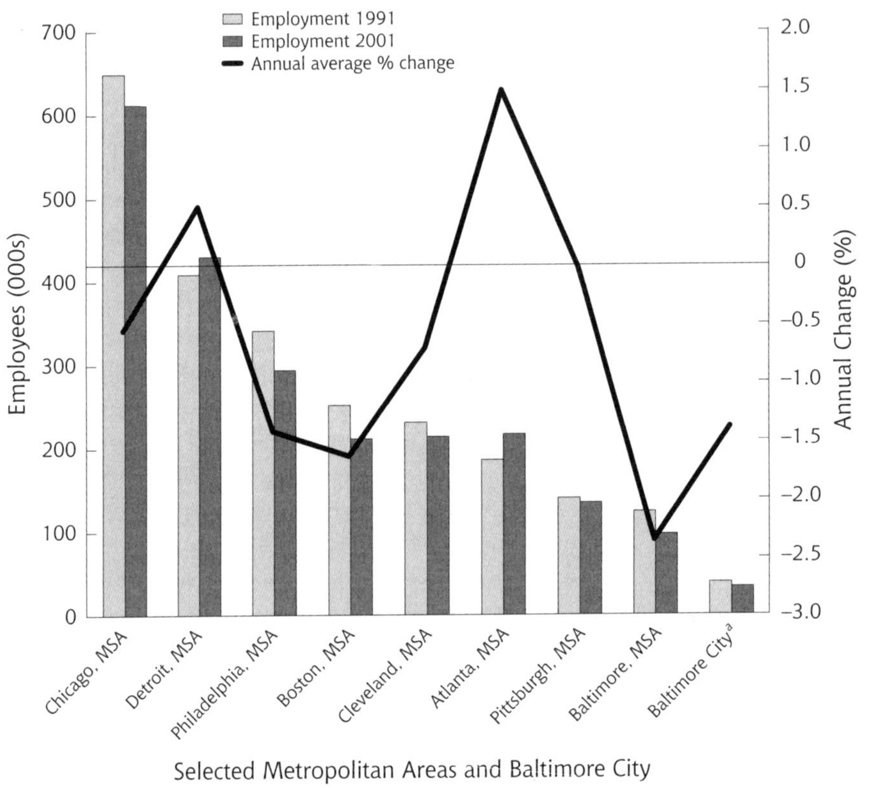

Selected Metropolitan Areas and Baltimore City

---

a. The city data is based on County Business Patterns data for 1991 to 1997.

Sources: U.S. Department of Labor, Bureau of Labor Statistics, 1991 to 2001, and County Business Patterns, 1991 to 1997.

metropolitan statistical areas (MSAs), and a more dramatic decline than the city of Baltimore (see Figure 5.1). From 1991 to 2001 the region experienced an annual average manufacturing employment loss of 1.3 percent. From 1991 to 1997 the Baltimore region lost 22,700 jobs, with 23 percent of the regional job loss concentrated in the city core.[3]

Early History of Carroll Camden

Using Sanborn maps, industrial activity in the Carroll Camden district can be traced back to the mid-1890s. The 1890 maps indicate the presence of glass, brick and ironworks activities. Waterpower from Jones Falls, proximity to a port and the presence of rail lines were critical attractions.[4] During the following 10

---

3. County Business Patterns, 1991 and 1997.

4. The site is adjacent to the B&O roundhouse and was one of the earliest sites in the U.S. to have access to train transport.

years, the district grew in population and area. The Baltimore Consolidated Gas Co. built a coal and gas plant. Machine shops and coal bins were established to support the United Railway and Electric Company. Bartlett and Hayward ran a foundry, and the area became home to distilleries, a varnish and color works, a paper box company and a glass manufacturer. By 1915 industrial activity expanded to above Washington Boulevard and along Jones Falls with a freight depot; a brass and copper company; cattle, swine and sheep sheds; and fancy leather goods manufacturing. By 1951 steel and iron foundries, lumberyards, household products manufacturers, scrap metal yards and warehouses operated in Carroll Camden (Sanborn Map Co. 1890, 1901, 1915, 1953). Our study area includes approximately 5,580 acres and 740 industrial parcels. From March 2, 1990, to November, 2, 2000, 161 parcels (22 percent of the total) went on the market and 16 (2 percent) were for sale as of November 2000. There were no sizeable parcels that sat idle and were not on the market over the period.[5]

Quantitative Data and Sales Transactions

The Baltimore Development Corporation (BDC) provided us with initial boundaries, defined by one of the city's "enterprise zones" and the study area of the BDC. This zone proved to be too small; the number of sales (fewer than 10) was not sufficient for valid analysis. A drive-through revealed that "industrial type/use" parcels and buildings extended well beyond the enterprise zone and BDC study area. Thus, we expanded the study area as shown in Figure 5.2.

The base map was created from the Baltimore City Department of Public Works (DPW) parcel point file. We obtained data for real estate transactions from six sources. First, sales and price data from 1990 to 2000 came from the Baltimore DPW property tax records. These data were supplemented and cross-checked with information from the BDC, the State Department of Assessment and Taxation data (SDAT), COSTAR and the MacKenzie Group—a commercial real estate broker. Whereas DPW and SDAT data sources contain information on properties that sold, COSTAR, a database maintained by the real estate industry, contains information on commercial parcels currently for sale through real estate brokers. COSTAR records contain contact information, asking prices, descriptive data regarding unique features of the sites, and previous sales information for sites currently on the market. BDC provided information on a few parcels for sale by owner. The MacKenzie Group added the time a parcel remained on the market prior to sale, and where missing, the MacKenzie data were supplemented with time on the market information obtained through personal interviews and phone calls to sellers and brokers.

From these sources, a data set was created with all industrial parcels in the study area. This includes industrial parcels never on the market after 1990, those currently for sale, and those that sold between January 1990 and January 2000. We geocoded owner, address, sales price, date of sale, sales history, time

5. Based on interviews with Richard Escalante, planner with the Baltimore Development Corporation (BDC) for the Carroll Camden area; Evans Paull, BDC Brownfields coordinator; and The MacKenzie Group, a local real estate company.

Figure 5.2   Camden Carroll Study Area

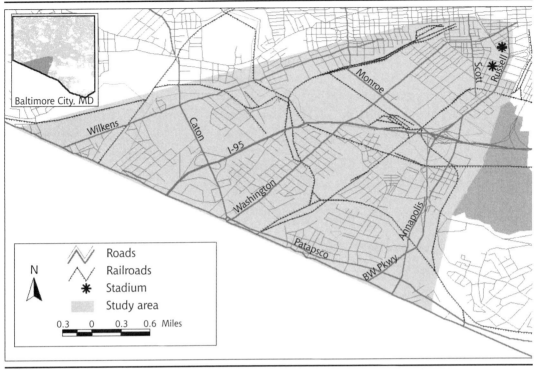

Source: Urban Studies and Planning Program, University of Maryland at College Park, 2001

on the market of last sale, acreage, unique features of the site, improved or unimproved, and accessibility to the highway. The final result is 750 identified industrial records within the boundaries shown in Figure 5.2. The final number of parcels that went on the market over the decade is 161. This includes sales through brokers and by owner. The sales price is missing on 38 parcels.

Environmental Information

To capture environmental conditions on each of our industrial properties, we looked to three sources: the U.S. EPA; Sanborn atlases; and the State of Maryland Department of the Environment (MDE). We collected substantial qualitative information on environmental conditions on each site and developed a broad ranking system for the potential contamination level. The categories are (1) receipt of a MDE No Further Requirements Determination;[6] (2) no evident contamination; (3) adjacent to a contaminated parcel; (4) potential historical contamination; and (5) confirmed contamination.

The Sanborn Fire Insurance Atlases were the primary source for identifying potential historical contamination, as there are few alternative sources of

6. The MDE performs a data screening to decide whether conditions at a property pose a risk to human health or the environment. Based on the results of the data screening, MDE determines whether there will be further requirements at the property. MDE and EPA Region III signed a memorandum of agreement that provides participants with certain protections from federal action after MDE issues a No Further Requirements Determination or a Certificate of Completion.

historical land use. A review of Sanborn atlases for southwest Baltimore City was conducted for 1890, 1915, 1951 corrected Sanborn, and 1953. The atlases provided excellent information regarding original site boundaries, historical activities on each parcel, and the layout of activities within the site. We relied on these maps because there is frequently a connection between the level and type of contamination and the kind of manufacturing activity (steel manufacture, transformers, chemical manufacture, etc.). Companies specializing in historical contamination and liability issues commonly utilize Sanborns.

Qualitative Data

We conducted a series of extended interviews to determine the factors that are barriers to property sale and industrial redevelopment. Interviews were held with real estate agents and/or property owners for every parcel that had been on the market for two years or more or that had been on the market and withdrawn without sale. In addition, we conducted four in-person interviews with private firms that purchased or sold contaminated parcels. In all cases, the land purchasers were using the property for their own businesses.[7] We interviewed city officials to identify parcels that were idle and not on the market,[8] and we conducted site visits for every sold and for-sale parcel.

We also conducted an in-depth case study of the Koppers site, which was identified by the city as their most difficult brownfield redevelopment case. We selected the most problematic case to explore the boundary of the brownfield redevelopment experience.

Results

From March 2, 1990, to November 2, 2000, 161 properties, for a total of 379 acres, went on the market, 144 properties sold, and at least one was listed for sale and then pulled off the market when it did not sell. Sixteen parcels were on the market as of November 2, 2000. Most of this market activity occurred in the last years of the decade. Only 16 of the 144 parcels sold prior to 1995.[9] Not all 16 sales are represented on Figure 5.3 because data are missing on 38 of the sales that occurred over the decade.

Of the 144 sales, 19 parcels were known to be contaminated, and there was historical information to suspect that 23 additional properties were

---

7. The typical profile of the purchaser is an entrepreneur who is using the property to operate his or her own business and who self-financed the deal.

8. Interviews were conducted with local real estate brokers Chuck Franklin, Robert Milhauser, Kate McDonald, David Tufaro and Bill Miller; with Evans Paull and Richard Escalante of the Baltimore Development Corporation; telephone or in-person interviews were conducted with the sellers, purchasers, developers and/or brokers for the 15 parcels that had been on the market for two years or more. Visits were made to each site. In addition, four interviews were held with purchasers and/or sellers of contaminated sites.

9. Fewer sales prior to 1995 may be the result of data inadequacies. After 1996 we had two sources of sales data, the DPW records and the SDAT data. Therefore, we could catch sales in one database missed by the other. Prior to 1996 we relied on only the DPW database. Thus, if the DPW failed to catch a sale prior to 1996, we did not catch it.

contaminated. Table 5.1 shows how these sales break down by level of contamination and period of sale.

While the majority of sales were clean sites, 13 percent of the sales were parcels with confirmed contamination. Only 2 percent of the parcels with suspected or known contamination went through the voluntary cleanup program (VCP). We suspect that the majority of properties do not go through the VCP program for two reasons: first, the process involves delays, which can prove costly to a business; second, most properties are used by the purchaser for their own industrial use, therefore, they are not seeking legal protection from future lawsuits. When the property is purchased for resale, there is a price premium to be gained by the "developer" for receipt of a No Further Requirements letter, and

Figure 5.3   Sales Price for Sold Properties in Carroll Camden, 1990–2000

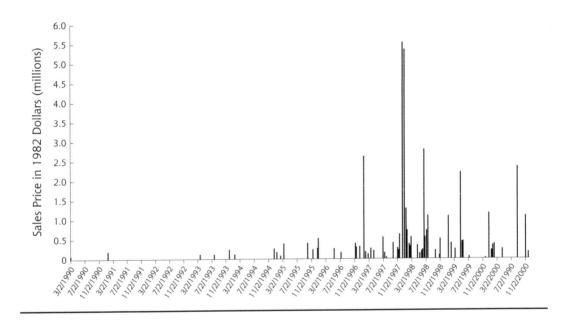

Table 5.1   Sales by Category of Contamination

	1990–1993	1994–1996	1997–2000	Total Sales	Percent of All Sales
MDE No Further Requirements letter	0	1	2	3	2
No evident contamination	5	13	53	71	49
Adjacent to contaminated property	1	6	21	28	19
Potential historical contamination	4	2	17	23	16
Confirmed contamination	2	2	15	19	13
Total	12	24	108	144	100

it protects the seller from lawsuits by the buyer. Thus, we suspect that properties purchased for resale are taken through the VCP process.

Contrary to the prevailing wisdom, there is an active market for parcels known to be and suspected of being contaminated, with prices adjusted to accommodate the costs associated with owning a polluted site (Figures 5.4 and 5.5). The land market is working with discounts for property known to be, suspected to be, and adjacent to contaminated parcels. For the decade as a whole, the data show a 60 percent price discount for parcels known to be contaminated; a 31 percent discount for parcels suspected of contamination because of their historical use; an 8 percent discount for parcels adjacent to contaminated parcels; and a 14 percent discount for parcels that went through the Maryland VCP (see Figure 5.4). The 60 percent discount for contaminated parcels represents (1) delays associated with testing and finding an acceptable remediation technique; (2) the costs and time delays associated with cleanup; (3) the reduction in demand because of the difficulty of obtaining bank credit; and (4) the additional risk associated with owning a polluted parcel.

Not surprisingly, there were fewer transactions of contaminated than clean parcels (Table 5.1). While there is substantial missing data on the amount of time parcels sat on the market, clearly parcels that went through Maryland VCP and are adjacent to contaminated parcels spent the longest period on the market prior to sale (Figure 5.5). Participation in the Maryland VCP denotes the purchaser received with the land either a letter of no further requirements determination, indicating that no additional cleanup was required based on the future use, or a certificate of completion, showing that all state-required cleanup is complete. In both cases, subsequent purchasers can rely on those documents to indicate no further cleanup is needed. Properties adjacent to contaminated parcels and

Figure 5.4 **Average Sales Price per Acre, by Level of Contamination, for All Sales in Carroll Camden, 1990–2000**

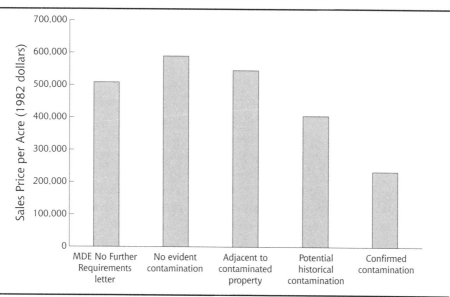

Figure 5.5   Average Time on the Market, of Sold and For Sale Properties in Carroll Camden, 1990–2000

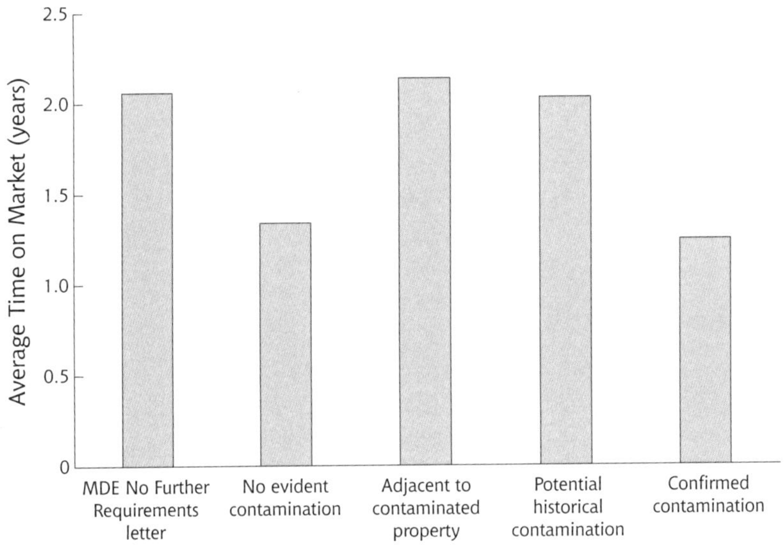

parcels with evidence of historical contamination were on the market longer than properties known to be contaminated. This may be because purchasers of parcels with known contamination were, out of necessity, using their own funds to finance the purchase.[10]

When the decade is broken down into three equal periods, there is evidence that during the 1990s, industrial land purchasers and sellers adapted to the complications raised by contamination. In the first two periods of the decade, 1990–1993 and 1994–1997, there were few sales of contaminated parcels—in fact, there were few sales at all. Those parcels with suspected or proven contamination sat on the market for long periods of time, and the few sales did not reflect price discounts for contamination. However, in the last period of the decade, 1998–2000, the overall market was stronger. A downward adjustment in prices—a reflection of the increased expense and risks of contamination—led to an increase in the number of sales (Figures 5.6 and 5.7).

In the third period, parcels that went through the Maryland VCP were discounted 17 percent off the sale price of clean parcels; parcels adjacent to contaminated parcels were discounted by 24 percent; parcels with an indication of historical contamination were discounted by 34 percent; and parcels known to be contaminated were discounted by 65 percent. Purchasers, sellers and financial backers appeared to be gaining confidence in how to assess risks and cleanup technologies, and were adjusting asking and offer prices to accommodate this risk.

---

10. All the purchasers of contaminated parcels that we interviewed used their own funds. They could not get a bank loan.

Figure 5.6   Number of Transactions in Carroll Camden, by Time Period and by Category of Contamination, 1990–2000

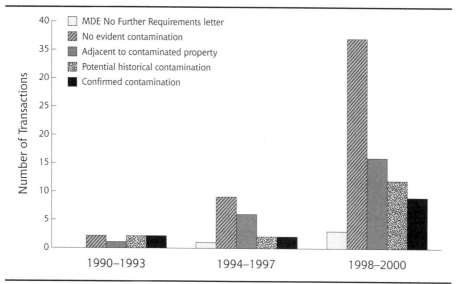

Figure 5.7   Average Sales Price per Acre in Carroll Camden, by Time Period and by Category of Contamination, 1990–2000

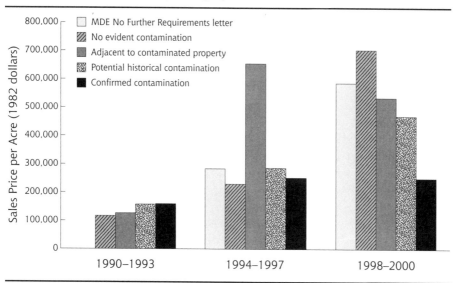

The 16 parcels on the market in November 2000 reflect the same discounted price pattern for contamination (Figure 5.8). In this case, however, the parcels adjacent to and suspected to be contaminated because of historical use had been on the market longer than clean parcels. As of November 2, 2000, clean parcels had been on the market an average of 1.5 years, adjacent to contaminated parcels on the market 3.3 years, and the parcels suspected of contamination for historical reasons sat on the market for an average of 3.1 years (Figure 5.9).

Figure 5.8 **Asking Price per Acre of Industrial Property, by Evidence of Contamination, November 2, 2000**

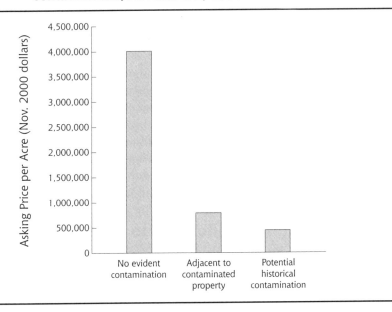

Figure 5.9 **Years on the Market, For Sale Parcels, by Category of Contamination, November 2000**

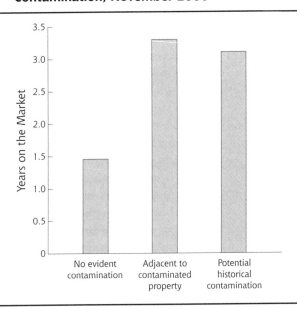

Barriers to Sale and Redevelopment

An examination of parcels that languished for long periods on the market and those that sold quickly can reveal the barriers to industrial land sales. Table 5.2 compares the parcels that took more than two years to sell and parcels that sold within one year. Contamination did not appear to be a deterrent to sale. The

Table 5.2   Characteristics of Parcels on the Market More than Two Years and Less than One Year

	Languishers (more than 2 years)		Quick Sellers (less than 1 year)
	For Sale	Sold	Sold
Number of parcels	8	9	16
Asking/sales price per acre	$798,319	$825,937	$313,920
Size (acres)	2.92	2.73	1.7
Extent of contamination (%)			
MDE	0	22	0
No evident contamination	25	11	37
Adjacent to contamination	25	22	6
Historical contamination	50	44	31
Contamination	0	0	25
Unimproved (%)	13	0	13
Accessibility			
On the main road	0	70	25
One turn to the main road	50	20	62
Two turns to the main road	50	10	6
Three or more turns to the main road	0	0	13

quick sellers had a higher probability of being contaminated than the languishers. The striking feature of this comparison is that quick sellers had an average price per acre of approximately $314,000 as opposed to the sales price of about $826,000 per acre for parcels that took two or more years to sell. Parcels that were on the market as of November 2000 for more than two years have an average asking price of about $798,000 per acre. One barrier to redevelopment appears to be that some sellers misperceive the value of their property. Real estate agents surmise that owners of these overpriced parcels were holding out for the city government to purchase the site at the higher price—which was the case in the property purchased by the government for the Camden Yards baseball stadium and the PSI NET football stadium. Howland (2000, 418) similarly found price to be a statistically significant determinant of time on the market, for both contaminated and clean sites, in southeast Baltimore.

In contrast to the findings of Meyers and Lyons (2000) and previous research in Baltimore's Canton Industrial District (Howland 2000), small parcel size does not appear to be a factor in the speed of sale in Carroll Camden, where the quick sellers were, on average, smaller than the languishers. In older industrial areas, unimproved land is often an advantage, because obsolete buildings must be removed before redevelopment can occur. But, there is little difference in the proportion of unimproved parcels between the quick sellers and languishers. In fact, there is little unimproved land in the Carroll Camden area. This district's long industrial history has left behind extensive and often substantial still-standing structures.

There is no indication that quick sellers and languishers are concentrated in specific locations. Figure 5.10 (the quick sellers) and Figure 5.11 (the languishers) show that both are spread over the whole industrial area. Table 5.2 indicates the parcel's accessibility. Seventy percent of languishers were located on one of the district's main roads, and none of them fell into the most inaccessible category, a location that required three or more turns before reaching a main road. This variable does not measure the quality or width of the roads.

There are several shortcomings in our more quantitative analysis. The degree of contamination and costs of cleanup are only crudely measured. Landowners were not willing to share their cleanup costs with us, and it turned out to be impossible to quantify the seriousness of the contamination. First, for example, how do you compare serious contamination concentrated on one portion of the site with less serious contaminants spread over the site, without actual cleanup costs? Second, there are features that affect sales price other than the presence of contamination and distance from the main highway. For instance, the shape of the lot, the adjacent uses incompatible with industrial uses, and obsolescence of the frontage road are a few of the factors that affect industrial prices. To capture some of the nuance not available in quantitative data, we conducted a series of interviews to determine the factors that are barriers to parcel sales and industrial redevelopment.

Figure 5.10   Parcels Sold in Less than One Year, 1990–2000

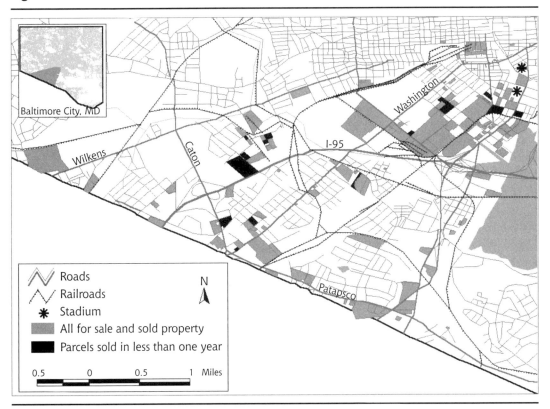

Source: Urban Studies and Planning Program, University of Maryland at College Park, 2001

Interviews were held with real estate agents, property owners whose parcels have been on the market for long periods, those who purchased contaminated parcels and city officials. These interviews highlighted a number of obstacles to redevelopment, including small, odd-shaped sites, the expense of removing unusable structures, obsolete road size and configurations, inadequate water, sewer and telecommunications infrastructure, existing land uses incompatible with industry, and the difficulty of changing the land use from industrial to residential, because housing prices in Baltimore do not compensate for cleanup costs. These interviews were conducted independently of our in-depth case study of contaminated site that has proven problematic for the city.

The Koppers site was selected as a case study to put the findings of our quantitative analysis in context of the literature findings that highlight the barrier that contamination plays in hindering central-city redevelopment. The Koppers site was identified by the city as their most problematic brownfield redevelopment project.

The Koppers Site

One of the most high-profile problem sites in Carroll Camden is the 11-acre Koppers property located in Pigtown, which takes its name from the days when pigs were herded through the streets to slaughter. Pigtown is a neighborhood in

Figure 5.11   Parcels Sold in Two Years or More, 1990–2000

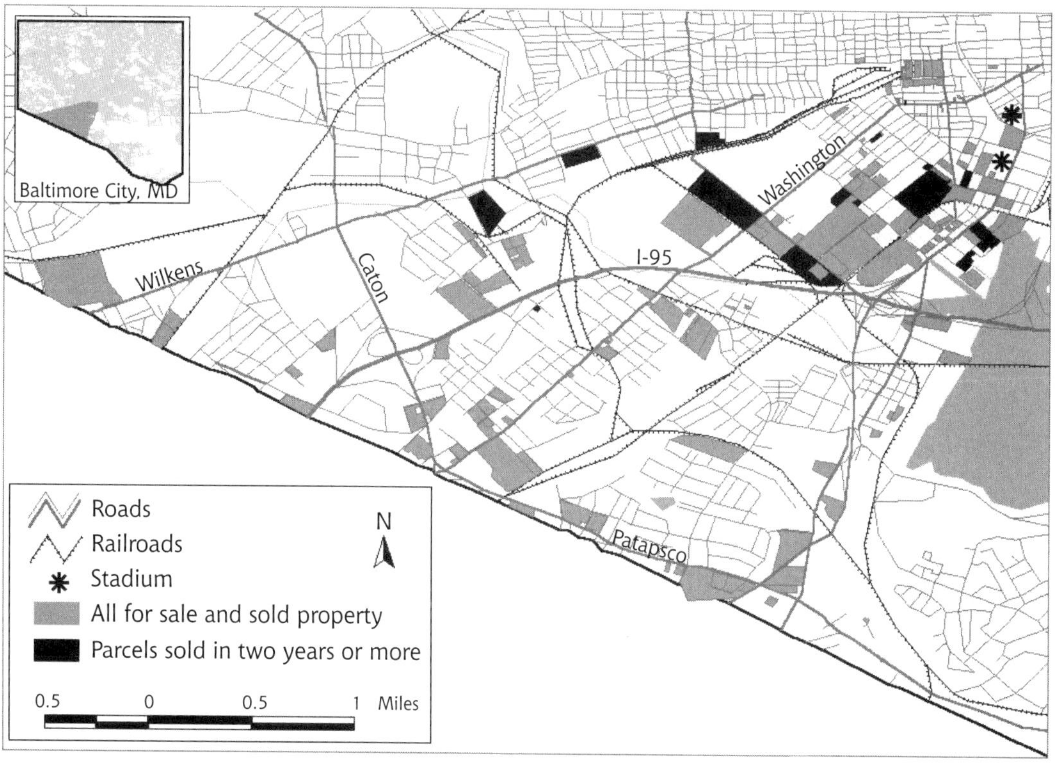

decline, with all of the attendant social problems, including housing abandonment, high crime and poverty rates, and a shift from homeowners to renters. From 1901 to 1915 the site belonged to Bartlett-Hayward and Co., Engineers and Founders, and was operated as a blacksmithing operation. In 1953 it was transferred to Koppers Company, a division of Bartlett-Hayward. Koppers Co. is a metalworking, chemical, construction and engineering business that made carriages for rail cars, rail engines, cannons and smaller munitions. Koppers vacated their Baltimore location in 1986, and the property became an eyesore after a nine-alarm fire in 1986 consumed the old company warehouse and ripped through nearby homes.

The city purchased the site in 1993 for $1.5 million and determined that middle-income housing should be built on the property. The Koppers parcel is in a Federal Empowerment Zone. Thus, home purchasers would be eligible for a number of subsidies, including the city's Housing Ventures Fund, which provides $5,000 toward the down payment or settlement, and the state's Community Development Administration low-interest mortgage program.

In 1993 the city put the concept of a residential development on the site out for bid. The city agreed to clean the site, setting aside $1.4 million for this purpose. Residents of the surrounding community worked with city officials to establish guidelines for the new homes. They lobbied hard for a residential development that would bring customers and new life to the depressed commercial development along Washington Boulevard and would infuse new energy into a neighborhood teetering on poverty. Ryland Homes won the bid with their proposal to build middle-income housing in the $100,000 per unit range.

The site was contaminated with PCBs, cadmium, lead, oil, polycyclic aromatic hydrocarbons (PAHs) and asbestos, and underground storage tanks and foundations. After a $1.9 million cleanup, which included the removal of storage tanks and some foundations, in 1997 the city entered the site into the State of Maryland's VCP with the intent of being able to provide a determination that no further cleanup is required. MDE found that additional action was necessary to address PAH levels, which were elevated enough to be harmful to children with long-term exposure (MDE 2001).

In March 1998 Ryland Homes decided to abandon their plans to redevelop this site and released their option to purchase it. The company cited continuing environmental concerns as the reason (Nubgart 1998, L1). Equally and perhaps even more important, Ryland developers noticed that houses in adjacent neighborhoods were selling in the $79,000 range with sluggish sales activity. More than likely, the economics of the project began to convince Ryland that even at $100,000 per unit, the project would be a tough sell (Nubgart 1998, L1).

In 1998 the city again put the project out to bid. Although in early estimates four developers would submit proposals in the city's new round of bid requests (Gunts 1998a and 1998b), only one housing proposal was received. The bid came from Metroventures, proposing Scotts Landing, an $18.6 million community with 144 townhouses priced at no more than $105,000. In September 1998 the city awarded the project to Metroventures, who planned middle-income housing for employees working nearby at the University of Maryland at Baltimore, the University of Maryland Medical Center and Baltimore City.

As of January 2004 the project had yet to break ground because Metroventures had not received a No Further Requirements letter. On July 11, 2000, the Maryland Department of Housing and Community Development reported correspondence from MDE "noting that the remediation plan needs to comply with the current MDE guidelines for residential development of brownfield sites," and at present the plans do not meet residential standards (Maryland Department of Housing and Community Development 2000, 2–3).

The delays at the old Koppers site can be attributed to a number of factors. First, the city's aspirations of shifting the site from an industrial to residential use increased cleanup costs beyond what had been required in the surrounding area, which has remained industrial and was cleaned up by private interests. Residential uses require higher cleanup standards, which add to the project cost. When these higher costs are combined with a weak southwest Baltimore housing market, the economics of the project do not work, even with extensive government subsidy. According to current estimates, there are 12,259 abandoned houses and 24,259 additional unoccupied houses (well-kept but without tenants) in Baltimore and 1,152 abandoned and an additional 1,483 unoccupied houses in the southwest area of the city (McMahon 2001). Moreover, in addition to the increased and originally hidden cleanup costs, project delays are contributing to the escalating estimated new-housing sales prices at the Koppers site. The original sales price of $79,000 has risen to $125,000 per unit. The housing surplus in the neighborhoods surrounding the old Koppers site undermines the profitability of this new residential development and makes it even more difficult to justify the climbing costs and development delays.

Second, contamination on the site was not as serious before the city took over the site, and the city underestimated the site cleanup costs. Neither Ryland Homes nor Metroventures foresaw the cleanup complications that would arise and contribute to rising costs. Third, during the development period, there were staff changes in Maryland's Department of the Environment. New personnel imposed new cleanup standards, which have added to delays and costs.

Other Barriers to Resale

Aside from the problems encountered at the Koppers site, where the city is attempting to shift land use from industrial to residential, local property and business owners and real estate agents describe four additional barriers to a revitalized industrial area: incompatible surrounding land uses; obsolescent road patterns; inadequate water, sewer and telecommunications infrastructure; and outmoded structures. As a turn-of-the-century industrial city, Baltimore still has residential city blocks integrated with industrial activities. Without the benefit of walking access to work, these blocks have lost their desirability as residential locations. Land values are low, housing conditions poor and vacancy rates high. Heavy truck traffic and dirty industrial activities (such as a waste management facility) further depress the desirability of these areas for housing. Heavy industry, of the type located in Carroll Camden and many other turn-of-the-century industrial cities, is incompatible with residential activity—even in the current smart growth environment, which favors the integration of land uses. Buyers of industrial sites are reluctant to purchase land in proximity to residential areas for fear commercial trucks will hit playing children, because heavy truck traffic in off-hours stirs neighborhood complaints, and because rates of theft and vandalism are relatively high.

Lack of modern truck access also inhibits industrial land sales, particularly in areas where the road width and pattern are incompatible with today's trucking. The current street pattern was laid out for multistory, rail-oriented manufacturing and small-scale trucking. Rail dependence has declined, displaced by container trucking. Without modern truck access, industrial parcels are difficult to sell.

In spite of the widespread view that one advantage of an inner-city site is the ready access to infrastructure, a common complaint among property owners is that water, sewer and telecommunications facilities are outdated and inadequate.[11] In the Carroll Camden area, land sellers and recent purchasers, as well as operating businesses, complained that water and sewer facilities need updating and expanding and that modern telecommunications linkages are missing.

Finally, several additional parcels that have failed to sell contain obsolete buildings that are expensive to demolish. In one case, a refrigerated storehouse could not be cleared without significant demolition costs. However, in the final analysis, such properties are languishing on the market because the seller's asking price is out of line with demolition costs and the property's productive capacity.

Conclusion

The Carroll Camden Industrial District is typical of older industrial districts across the northeastern U.S. Our tracking of property sales over the past decade shows that sellers and purchasers have accommodated contamination by lowering prices. Over the decade, parcels with known contamination sold at a 60 percent discount, parcels with historical reasons to suspect contamination sold at a 31 percent discount, and parcels adjacent to a contaminated site sold at a 8 percent discount. Parcels that went through the Maryland VCP were discounted by 14 percent. Tracking the pattern over the 1990s reveals that only from 1997 to 2000 did the market show a willingness to mediate transactions of contaminated parcels. During this later period, contaminated parcels were more likely to sell, spent less time on the market prior to sale, and demonstrated price discounts consistent with liability, cleanup costs and time delays. The majority of contaminated sites did not go through the Maryland VCP.

---

11. DSL-OIT connections to speed data and information access.

In the emphasis of environmental contamination as a barrier to redevelopment, we may have overlooked other obstacles to central-city redevelopment in industrial districts. In Carroll Camden, these include cleanup costs that raise expenditures beyond what the residential market can bear in a weak housing market, outdated road configurations, which make truck access and egress difficult, antiquated infrastructure and inadequate telecommunication linkages, a mixture of incompatible and adjacent residential and industrial land uses, and obsolete uses that are expensive to demolish (and where sellers are unwilling to lower the cost sufficiently to compensate). Fortunately, most of these are barriers over which policy makers and city government have control.

Acknowledgments

I am grateful to the Lincoln Institute of Land Policy for financial support and to Margaret Dewar of the University of Michigan, who took the initiative to write the proposal to Lincoln. Ann Piesen meticulously assembled the data and prepared the maps, and Richard Escalante and Evans Paull of the Baltimore Development Corporation assisted with data and made helpful comments on earlier drafts. I am also grateful to Chuck Franklin of the MacKenzie Group, David Tufaro of Terra Nova, and Bill Miller of KLNB, as well as the Carroll Camden businesses that granted interviews. Shari Wilson of the MDE made valuable comments on an earlier draft. I alone am responsible for any remaining errors.

References

Bartsch, Charles. 1996. Paying for our industrial past. *Commentary* (Winter): 14–23.

Bartsch, Charles and Elizabeth Collaton. 1996. *Coming clean for economic development.* Washington, DC: Northeast-Midwest Institute. September.

De Sousa, Christopher. 2000. Brownfield redevelopment versus greenfield development: A private sector perspective on the costs and risks associated with brownfield redevelopment in the greater Toronto area. *Journal of Environmental Planning and Management* (43)6:831–853.

———. 2001. Contaminated sites: The Canadian situation in an international context. *Journal of Environmental Management* (62):131–154.

Duff, L. B. 1994. Groundwater contamination and property transfer. *Maryland Bar Journal* 27(1): 25–28.

Greenberg, Michael, Karen Lowrie, Laura Solitare and Latoya Duncan. 2000. Brownfields, TOADS, and the struggle for neighborhood development. *Urban Affairs Review* 35(5): 717–733.

Green Leigh, N. 1994. Focus: Environmental constraints to brownfield redevelopment. *Economic Development Quarterly* 8(4):325–328.

Gunts, Edward. 1998a. City eyes proposal for Barre Station. *Baltimore Sun*, June 2.

———. 1998b. Company to build housing east of B & O Museum. *Baltimore Sun*, September 1.

International City Managers Association (ICMA). 1998. *Beyond city limits, best practices from ICMA's 1998 brownfield peer exchanges.* Washington, DC: International City Managers Association.

Hernandez, Angelo. 2000. Economic development officer, Land Acquisition/Disposition Section, Baltimore Department of Housing and Community Development, Baltimore. Interview by author, September 13, Baltimore, and November 19 (by telephone).

Howland, Marie. 2000. The impact of contamination on the Canton/southeast Baltimore land market. *Journal of the American Planning Association* 66(4):411–420.

Karimian, Shawn. 2000. Director, Baltimore Department of Housing and Community Development, Baltimore, Department of Construction. Interview by author, September 13, Baltimore.

Maryland Department of the Environment (MDE). 2001. Barre Station/Camden Crossing project chronology. January.

Maryland Department of Housing and Community Development. 2000. Memo to Art Ray, Maryland Department of the Environment, from Michelle Wright, Maryland DHCD. December 20.

McGrath, Daniel T. 1995. *An investigation into the impact of hazardous waste contamination liability on urban industrial land redevelopment in the city of Chicago.* Chicago: Great Cities Institute, University of Illinois.

McMahon, Patrick. 2001. Personal memo to Marie Howland on OSOSW and Citywide Abandonment. February 8. Neighborhood Design Center, Baltimore.

Meyers, Peter B., and Thomas S. Lyons. 2000. Lessons from private sector brownfield redevelopers. *Journal of the American Planning Association* 66(1):46–57.

Nubgart, Robert. 1998. Clean polluted site too risky. *Baltimore Sun*, March 29, L1.

Page, W., and H. Rabinowitz. 1993. Groundwater contamination: Its effects on property values and cities. *Journal of the American Planning Association* 59:473–481.

———. 1994. Potential for redevelopment of contaminated brownfield sites. *Economic Development Quarterly* 8(4):353–363.

Paull, Evans. 2001. Brownfields Coordinator, Baltimore Development Corporation. Telephone interview by author, January 19.

Pepper, E. M. 1997. *Lessons from the field.* Washington, DC: Northeast-Midwest Institute.

Russ, Tom. 2000. Spotts, Stevens and McCoy. Interview by author, November 11, Towson, MD.

Sanborn Map Company, Fire Insurance Maps, Baltimore City. 1890, 1901, 1915, 1953. Chicago: Sanborn Map Company.

Schriner, J. 1998. Brownfields still too risky. *Industry Week* (March 2): 18.

Spotts, Stevens and McCoy, Inc. 1992. Environmental assessment report at 250 Scott St., Baltimore, Maryland for Department of Housing and Community Development, Baltimore. February 14.

Staley, Samuel R. 1996. Environmental policy and urban revitalization: The role of lender liability. *Capital University Law Review* 25(1):51–75.

State of Maryland. 1997. *Brownfields—Voluntary Cleanup and Revitalization Program*, Senate Bill 340.

Swartz, R. O. 1994. Michigan's approach to urban redevelopment involving contaminated properties. *Economic Development Quarterly* 8(4):329–337.

U.S. Environmental Protection Agency. 1997. Brownfields economic redevelopment initiative. Washington, DC: U.S. EPA, Solid Waste and Emergency Response.

Wernstedt, Kris and Robert Hersh. 1998. Urban land use and Superfund cleanups. *Journal of Urban Affairs* 20(4):459–474.

Yount, K. R. 1997. The organizational contexts of decisions to invest in environmentally risky urban properties. *Journal of Economic Issues* 31(2):367–373.

Yount, K. R. and P. B. Meyer. 1994. Bankers, developers, and new investment in brownfield sites: Environmental concerns and the social psychology of risk. *Economic Development Quarterly* 8(4):338–344.

6 | Survey of State-Level Policies to Address Urban Vacant Land and Property Reuse

Nancey Green Leigh

Vacant land represents both a significant problem and an attractive opportunity for many central cities. Despite the need to better understand its positive and negative aspects, there have been few attempts to do so. In 1997 Accordino and Johnson (2000) surveyed cities' perceptions of their vacant land and abandoned structures and found that they were viewed as a serious problem in the Northeast, South and Midwest, but not in the West.[1] A year later, Pagano and Bowman (2000) undertook the first effort in 30 years to actually quantify vacant land in U.S. cities.[2] This survey found that, on average, 15 percent of a city's land remains vacant. But, while both surveys help to clarify the issue and city responses to it, neither was comprehensive. In order to understand the full scope of the problems—and opportunities—associated with vacant land and abandoned structures, we need systematic and ongoing data collection.[3]

---

1. Accordino and Johnson's 1997 survey also found that city officials deemed aggressive building code enforcement the most effective technique to address vacant and abandoned land and structures, followed by the use of tax foreclosure (used by 60 percent of the surveyed cities). Survey respondents ranked tax foreclosure lower in effectiveness due to difficulties posed by state regulations. Ranked third in effectiveness by respondents was eminent domain (employed by 42 percent of the cities). Cosmetic improvements were rated of similar utility to eminent domain, and 43 percent of cities used this tool. Cosmetic improvements named by respondents included "lawn mowing, exterior façade painting, and in some cities, placing curtains in front windows and installing porch lights" (308). Cities typically charged the expense of the improvements as a lien against the recipient property.

2. The lack of an official definition or survey of vacant and abandoned land and properties complicates efforts to understand the extent of the problem. Pagano and Bowman observe that the vacant land label is given to "many different types of unutilized or underutilized parcels—perimeter agricultural or uncultivated land; recently razed land; derelict land; land with abandoned buildings and structures; brownfields; greenfields" (2000, 2). Vacant land within cities may even include small or irregular greenfield parcels left over from earlier development, or parcels of land difficult to build on such as those on steep grades or flood plains.

3. No uniform standard exists for the length of time property must go unoccupied in order to be considered abandoned. A 1998 survey of cities found the definitions ranged from 60 to 120 days or longer. The U.S. General Accounting Office applies the term to "a building or lot that has been vacant for two years or more" (Accordino and Johnson 1997).

The current set of tools being applied at the local level is insufficient to measure vacant urban land and abandoned structures in many cities. But addressing the issue is not the responsibility only of localities; in many cases, the ability to overcome the problems associated with vacant properties, and to put them back into productive use, requires legislative powers that are found only at the state level. These powers include, for example, the use of eminent domain, the implementation of financing tools such as tax-increment financing, state level sign-off of brownfield remediation plans, and the creation of land banks.

Several states have already successfully legislated reforms to support urban vacant land redevelopment. This chapter reviews these state-level policies, and then provides a model state agenda for urban land reform, which, if pursued, would provide cities with the resources they need to turn problem properties into tax-generating assets.

State-Enabled Approaches to Vacant Land and Abandoned Structures

Various state legislative and programmatic approaches have either directly or indirectly facilitated the redevelopment of vacant and abandoned structures. These strategies fall into three broad categories: property-specific tools; redevelopment programs; and redevelopment finance tools. Table 6.1 provides an inventory of the various approaches undertaken by the 50 states.

Property-Specific Approaches

Five strategies can contribute directly to property redevelopment. Three of these tools focus on the acquisition and disposal of property: tax lien foreclosures; eminent domain powers and condemnation/acquisition of blighted properties; and land banking. Two other approaches seek to prevent the problem in the first place: the levying of split-rate taxation; and the adoption of building rehabilitation codes.

Tax Lien Foreclosures

Properties that become tax delinquent reduce public revenues and contribute to neighborhood deterioration. Alexander (2000b) observes that the failure to pay property taxes typically results from property owners' loss of income in depressed economic conditions; public protest over property tax rates that are perceived to be too high; and owners' efforts to maximize the income they receive from their property by neglecting tax payments. This last cause is more typical of property owners who are investors and plan to eventually abandon their property, and is most common in major urban areas experiencing suburban flight (Alexander 2000b). A major issue in cities all across the nation, tax delinquency can be viewed as an "early warning system to municipalities that there are market problems with particular properties . . . [it is] a reliable but unintentional signal to governments of emerging problems" (Keating and Sjoquist 2001, 5).

With the tax lien foreclosure process, cities can move to put back into productive use tax-delinquent vacant land and abandoned structures. The effectiveness of this action is greatly influenced at the state level by the system that has been legally authorized for the enforcement of property tax collection. These systems vary from state to state because, historically, states retain great autonomy over their individual methods of property tax collection and enforcement (Alexander 2000b, 28). State laws set the parameters for how local governments deal with their tax-delinquent properties, either helping or hindering the process. Massachusetts, for example, has set no specific deadlines for owner notification or response to foreclosure, and the foreclosure process can take years. Florida, Georgia, Maryland, Michigan and Texas, by contrast, all have adopted legislative reforms in recent years that improve cities' abilities to expeditiously foreclose on properties and put them back into productive use. Michigan's 1999 legislation shortens the process to one and a half years and creates insurable property titles through judicial action (Fannie Mae Foundation 2001).

Alexander focuses on the events that trigger a legal requirement to give notice of a property's foreclosure. Central is the right of redemption: the option for the tax-delinquent property owner to pay off the taxes to retain or reclaim the property. There are three categories of enforcement procedures: (1) "one event, such as a public sale or transfer of the property to the government, with no redemption; (2) one event, but it is followed by a redemption period; (3) two separate events . . . in which the initial event is the sale of the property, and the second event is the termination of the right of redemption" (2000a, 28–29). Alexander observes that the third category presents the most problems to governments as they seek to meet constitutional due-process requirements established in the 1983 Supreme Court case of *Mennonite Board of Missions v Adams*.[4]

States can also be divided into three categories according to whether they (1) allow lien enforcement and property sale without a judicial process; (2) require judicial involvement at the sale or termination of the redemption period; or (3) permit enforcement of property tax liens through a judicial or nonjudicial process. In 2000 nine states fell into the third category and the remaining states were almost evenly split between the first two categories (Alexander 2000a). According to Alexander, a judicial tax enforcement proceeding, which relies on the court system, is superior for several reasons. It provides a permanent public record and an opportunity for a hearing, which currently is unavailable under most tax lien enforcement systems. Further, the judicial order of sale and issuance of a final tax deed that results from the judicial process establishes the

---

4. In this case, an Elkhart County, IN, lender challenged the adequacy of notice to it during a routine tax foreclosure during which a notice of pending sale had been published once a week for three weeks in accordance with state law before the property was sold. The U.S. Supreme Court, which had previously deferred to state autonomy on property tax collection, ruled that the Fourteenth Amendment guarantee of due process required the government to provide notice to the mortgagee of a pending foreclosure sale. Alexander writes, "the court concluded that a party holding a 'legally protected property interest' whose name and address are 'reasonably ascertainable' based upon 'reasonably diligent efforts' is entitled to notice 'reasonably calculated' to inform it of the proceeding" (2000a, 27). This ruling rendered questionable most property tax lien and sale procedures throughout the country.

Table 6.1 State Tools and Programs to Promote Urban Vacant Land and Abandoned Property Reuse

	Property Specific Tools				Redevelopment Programs				Redevelopment Finance Tools		
	Tax Lien Foreclosure	Eminent Domain	Promoting Split-Rate Tax Legislation	Rehabilitation Codes	Enterprise Zone	Brownfield Voluntary Cleanup Programs	Infill Smart Growth Legislation	Urban Renewal	Development Authority	Tax Increment Financing	Business Improvement District
New England											
Connecticut	■	■			■	■	■	■	■	■	■
Maine	■	■			■	■	■	■	■	■	■
Massachusetts	■	■				■		■	■	■	■
New Hampshire	■	■				■			■	■	■
Rhode Island	■	■			■	■	■		■	■	
Vermont	■	■			■	■	■			■	■
Middle Atlantic											
New Jersey	■	■		■	■	■	■	■	■	■	■
New York	■	■	■		■	■		■		■	■
Pennsylvania	■	■	■		■	■	■		■	■	■
East North Central											
Illinois	■	■			■	■		■	■	■	■
Indiana	■	■			■	■		■	■	■	■
Michigan	■	■			■	■	■	■	■	■	
Ohio	■	■			■	■		■	■	■	
Wisconsin	■	■			■	■	■	■	■	■	
West North Central											
Iowa	■	■			■	■		■	■	■	■
Kansas	■	■ *			■	■		■	■	■	■
Minnesota	■	■			■	■		■	■	■	■
Missouri	■	■			■	■		■	■	■	■
Nebraska	■	■ *			■	■		■	■	■	■
N. Dakota	■	■			■			■		■	
S. Dakota	■	■			■			■	■	■	
East South Central											
Alabama	■	■			■	■		■	■	■	■
Kentucky	■	■			■	■		■	■	■	■
Mississippi	■	■			■	■		■	■	■	■
Tennessee	■	■			■	■	■	■		■	■

Northeast

Midwest

South Atlantic									
Delaware	■	■		■	■		■	■	■
Florida	■	■		■	■	■	■	■	■
Georgia	■	■		■	■		■	■	■
Maryland	■	■	■	■	■	■	■	■	■
N. Carolina	■	■	■	■	■		■		■
S. Carolina	■	■*		■	■	■			■
Virginia	■	■	■	■	■	■	■	■	■
West Virginia	■	■		■	■	■	■	■	■
West South Central									
Arkansas	■	■		■	■	■	■	■	■
Louisiana	■	■		■	■	■	■	■	■
Oklahoma	■	■		■	■	■	■	■	■
Texas	■	■		■	■	■	■	■	■
Mountain									
Arizona	■	■		■	■	■	■	■	■
Colorado	■	■*		■	■	■	■	■	■
Idaho	■	■		■	■		■	■	■
Montana	■	■		■	■		■	■	■
Nevada	■	■		■	■		■	■	■
New Mexico	■	■		■	■	■	■	■	■
Utah	■	■*		■	■	■		■	■
Wyoming	■	■		■	■		■	■	
Pacific									
Alaska	■	■			■		■		■
California	■	■			■		■	■	■
Hawaii	■	■			■		■		
Oregon	■	■			■	■	■	■	■
Washington	■	■			■	■	■	■	■

Note: Legislation was reviewed as of 2002. Legislative Web sites were reviewed using the following criteria: (1) urban renewal or revitalization program; (2) tax increment financing or district; (3) enterprise zone; and (4) industrial, downtown or redevelopment authority. Search terms used to determine smart growth initiatives included *smart growth and infill, redevelopment, revitalization, vacant land and abandoned property*. Only those programs that explicitly stated infill, redevelopment or vacant/abandoned land were included.

* States for which more than one condition must be met to legally declare blight.

foundation upon which subsequent title insurance and property transfer can be made. In other words, the process produces a marketable property title that an insurance company would be willing to insure. In this way, the proceeding resolves one of the major roadblocks to transferring and financing properties that cities seek to redevelop.

Tax lien enforcement systems vary also in the length of the redemption period and the amount of interest and penalties that are levied upon tax-delinquent properties. In recent years higher penalties (averaging 10 percent annually) and interest rates (16–18 percent) have been imposed as a means of discouraging property owners from delaying their tax payments. However, these increased penalties and fines can increase the rate of property abandonment. Alexander (2000b) advocates expediting the foreclosure process, in part to hold down fine accruals. He also supports reforming the tax lien enforcement system to ensure its constitutionality and reduce the number of tax-delinquent properties and time they remain so to decrease their negative impact on urban revitalization (2000a). Guaranteeing the constitutionality of the process will aid particularly in the efforts of cities seeking to relieve financial pressures through the bulk sale and securitization of large numbers of tax-delinquent properties. His prescription for reform addresses a number of problems in existing foreclosure processes, including their excessive length of time (sometimes seven years), the multiplicity of entities often involved, and the due process problems exposed by the Mennonite ruling on foreclosure notices given by publication. There should be a single enforcement proceeding that is as short as possible. The length of time (i.e., one or two years) that is established from the initial tax delinquency to loss of all property rights (the redemption period) should be shifted from post-sale to pre-sale of the property. The entire proceeding must be kept within the control of a single entity, and there should be a title examination to reveal the interests affected by the sale. Finally, notice to such interests should be by certified mail, and public notice should be mailed to, and posted on, the property.

Michigan recently overhauled its property tax foreclosure process. In 1999 the state passed legislation (Public Act 123), commonly referred to as the Certification of Abandoned Property for Accelerated Foreclosure Act, that streamlines the tax reversion system "from a process which could last as many as seven years to a two-year foreclosure process, with title transferring to the county treasurer of the State of Michigan, depending on the option chosen by each county" (Kildee 2001). Foreclosures on abandoned property could take place in as little as one year. Already, the city of Flint is in the process of developing a new governmental system and land disposition plan that take advantage of the revised system to address the estimated 12 percent of its housing stock that is abandoned (Kildee 2001).

Eminent Domain and Condemnation/Acquisition of Blighted Properties

Eminent domain—in which the owner of the condemned property is provided "just compensation" for its taking—is a police power for the public good: government takes private property through condemnation proceedings, during which the property owner has the right of due process. Every state has at least one statute establishing how the eminent domain power may be exercised at the local level. State procedures vary widely, however. In some states, the government is required to negotiate with the property owner before instituting eminent domain proceedings. Elsewhere, the government may institute proceedings without prior notice.[5]

Traditionally, eminent domain has been utilized to facilitate transportation and the provision of water and other utilities, but its use to establish public parks, preserve places of historic interest and promote beautification has substantial precedent. Municipalities—often through their economic development or redevelopment entities—can also utilize eminent domain to retake blighted property for the purpose of urban revitalization. Eminent domain has been critical in revitalization efforts, but here it receives some of its most vehement criticism. Property owners complain about insufficient compensation for the taking, or that condemned parcels may not actually be blighted. They might protest that a taking was actually a simple transfer of property rights from one private landholder to another for development, and not for the expressed reason of economic development and/or revitalization.

In reviewing recent eminent domain court cases, Jennings (2001/2002) concludes that it remains unclear if the cases reflect new resistance to the process or simply the need for legal clarifications. He cautions all sides to keep in mind that a public purpose must be demonstrated. He writes further that "turning over the authority for condemnation to a private developer with an economic interest that results from condemnation may cause . . . the eminent domain authority and process [to be] questioned." Consequently, he continues, "governmental bodies must be careful to establish the generic public benefit in addition to individual benefit [of condemnation]" (236–237). Finally, takings always require process and compensation no matter how small and uncontroversial they are.

It should be noted that the use of eminent domain in property condemnation remains a widely practiced and viable means of land acquisition for a number of public-use purposes. In addition, many courts are leery of infringing upon the powers of the legislature to regulate eminent domain and will abstain from judgments that may curtail or redefine this tool. Local governments' ability to apply eminent domain effectively to acquire vacant and abandoned land for redevelopment purposes, however, may require reform of often complex and cumbersome state laws.

The determination of blight is a fundamental criterion that a condemnor must establish prior to targeting land for acquisition through eminent domain. Some courts have determined that even the *potential* for blight on a property is valid grounds for a taking, although this is not common. In 45 of the 50 states, only one condition of blight is required to take property through eminent domain. Five states (Colorado, Kansas, Nebraska, South Carolina and Utah) require more than one criterion to consider a property blighted, which include such factors as: deteriorated or deteriorating structures; predominance of

---

5. The power of eminent domain is not limited to states, cities and political bodies. In many states, public utilities and even pipeline companies have the power to expropriate private property.

defective or inadequate street layout; unsanitary or unsafe conditions; unusual topography; environmental contamination of buildings or property (Colorado C.R.S.A. Sec. 31-25-103); age; dilapidation; obsolescence; deterioration; illegal use of individual structures; excessive vacancies; deleterious land use or layout (South Carolina SC ST Sec. 31-10-20); and many others. Nebraska also requires that unemployment in the designated area reach at least 120 percent of the state or national average, and that the average age of the residential or commercial units in the area is at least 40 years (Neb. Rev. St. Sec. 58-209.01).

Increasingly, cities suffering from large-scale blight are taking proactive stances to address the problem. These cities are using the state-empowered tools of eminent domain and tax lien foreclosures. Three examples are profiled below.

- *Chicago.* The Chicago Abandoned Property Program (CAPP), administered through the Department of Housing, provides a means for developers to acquire and restore abandoned buildings, or to demolish buildings and reuse the land. CAPP focuses on one- to four-unit brick buildings, which are unoccupied, dangerous/hazardous, have unpaid real estate tax and water bills for two years, and whose owner(s) fails to appear in court.

- *Philadelphia.* The Neighborhood Transformation Initiative (NTI), a program begun by Mayor John F. Street, is a five-year, $295 million plan to revive distressed communities in the city. When completed, the effort will have demolished 14,000 vacant buildings, rehabilitated 4,500 distressed homes, and constructed a total of 2,000 new housing units. The city will assist community development corporations in acquiring vacant properties and potentially provide development financing as well. The bill funding the initiative was passed by the city council and signed into law by Mayor Street on March 13, 2002.

- *Baltimore.* In January 2002 Mayor Martin O'Malley launched an anti-blight initiative targeting as many as 5,000 vacant properties for acquisition through foreclosure or condemnation. Targeted properties include entire city blocks, which will be cleared and offered to private companies for residential and commercial redevelopment or redesigned as open space. Though the city will take, rather than purchase, the titles to the properties, the cost of these actions is expected to reach $5 million, with the potential for millions more spent on demolishing structures over the course of the program. City officials believe private-sector help will be necessary to fully fund the program (Siegel and Epstein 2002).

Land Banking

Local governments generally establish land bank authorities to address urban blight and promote redevelopment. Such authorities acquire tax-delinquent properties with the goal of returning them to productive use. Typically they are nonprofit entities empowered by state (or local) governments to waive or forgive back taxes owed on a property, to acquire and manage land, often in anticipation of a future use, and to sell or give it to nonprofit or for-profit groups. Land banks provide a flexible and manageable mechanism for infill development. The assemblage of small, individual parcels into larger blocks under common ownership can enhance the development potential of each parcel, which otherwise would not be of sufficient size to attract investment by most developers. This strategy, however, is not without drawbacks. Piece-by-piece acquisition of land can be time-consuming and expensive, especially if a property owner refuses to sell or holds out for more money. Prices for parcels being sought for the land bank may escalate if word gets out about the land bank's plans. In addition, parcels may be occupied by derelict or damaged buildings that require either extensive and costly remodeling or demolition to facilitate development.

The Municipal Research and Services Center (1997) recently identified several potential policy issues arising from land banking:

■ Land assembly can be very expensive, particularly if unanticipated costs arise associated with environmental cleanup, title encumbrances and similar expenses;

■ Land banking can require considerable capital investment in the early stages of the program, before property is resold. If state or federal seed money or loan money is not available, strong citizen support may be required for a bond approval or a unique situation (such as Cleveland's tax delinquency holdings);

■ While the land is under local government ownership, it is removed from the tax roles. (Of course, it may not be producing tax revenue anyway if the property is in default.) Property maintenance also will be needed until the property is resold. A community may be able to generate revenue to offset these costs by leasing the property for some interim use; and

■ Land banking may not be popular with the real estate industry, particularly with those who might profit from land speculation.

In addition to these challenges, it may be difficult to carry out land assembly and banking on a significant scale without some use of eminent domain. If these powers are used, it will be important to demonstrate a valid public purpose and to proceed with acquisitions based on an adopted plan.

Cities with far-sighted vision can circumvent some of the pitfalls of land banking by acquiring and improving small parcels of vacant land in an organized manner that creates large clusters for development if and when the need arises. Partnering with counties to acquire targeted land blocks also benefits cities looking to spur local development. Tools to accomplish such acquisition include tax defaults, donations and barter with other agencies. Once a package of assembled lots is accumulated, a municipality can offer the land to a developer for purchase, or transfer it to a development corporation for long-term action. By involving the private sector in negotiation and sales of assembled properties, at attractive prices with minimal risk, cities can reduce the perceived threat of public land banking to private developers, who often see local governments as competing land speculators in urban markets.

Atlanta and Cleveland show how state involvement can smooth the way. Both cities' state legislatures passed land bank laws in the early 1990s that enabled their land banks to take the lead in acquiring and disposing of tax-delinquent properties. In Cleveland's case, the city has partnered with other county and local agencies to acquire property. A majority of delinquent, foreclosed properties in the area not sold at auction are received by Cleveland's land bank, with an average of 900 lots per year transferred to the city. Cleveland pays foreclosure costs from the city's share of real estate excise tax fees, and property taxes on the parcels are forgiven. Unbuildable property is sold to adjacent landowners, while the city holds on to other parcels to sell for future development.

Split-Rate Taxation

Split-rate or two-rate property taxation is little used in the U.S.; its advocates, however, argue that, when fully implemented, it will encourage construction activity (Plassmann and Tideman 2000). Split-rate property taxation entails dividing the taxation into two parts: one for the land and the other for the improvements (i.e., buildings) on the property. Relatively higher tax rates on land than on buildings serve to spur owner investment in buildings and to suppress holding undeveloped and unused land. This combination of incentives and disincentives leads many urban planners to conclude that the split-rate tax encourages infill redevelopment and discourages suburban sprawl (Fulton 2003). Pennsylvania—the state that most actively uses split-rate taxation—recently passed enabling legislation to extend split-tax authorization not only to its first- and second-class cities,[6] but also to boroughs and school districts. As of 1999, the program was in use in more than 15 Pennsylvania cities (Schwartz 1999), and many other states are looking into this strategy for urban vacant land development (Hartzok 1997).

Advocates of the split-rate tax find their inspiration from Henry George's land value tax. George saw the land value tax as a mechanism to provide incentives to those who were using land productively, while penalizing those who held on to high-value land that was not being used in an economically productive fashion. Thus, those interested in promoting the productive use of urban land under contemporary circumstances see the split-rate tax as a promising policy tool. Furthermore, the land value tax is attractive to fiscal scholars because it can be revenue neutral (i.e., it would not change total tax collections). Unlike a tax on the fruits of productive activity (e.g., buildings), the land tax does not distort behavior; that is, a tax on buildings can reduce the number of buildings, while a tax on land cannot reduce the supply of land.

While the tax is gaining more popular attention from those interested in the reuse of urban land, scholarly evaluations of split-rate tax experiments have been limited. An economic analysis by Oates and Schwab (1997) presents a complicated and nuanced understanding of the Pittsburgh experience. It evaluated the impact of the city's two-rate tax system that was implemented in 1979–1980 after

---

6. First-class cities have populations of over 1 million; second-class cities have populations of over 250,000 (Pennsylvania General Assembly 2003).

the significant economic restructuring that took place in Pittsburgh and many of the country's older manufacturing cities. The city's population had fallen by more than 40 percent from 1950 to 1980; it was the only one of 15 cities in the Oates and Schwab study that experienced "a large and significant increase in levels of building activity in the 1980s" (1997, 2). Can the two-rate tax system explain these increases? Oates and Schwab consider this question, taking into account the other public policy initiatives of the time.

On the one hand, they argue, the higher tax rate on land did not have an impact on development decisions. On the other hand, because of the tax's neutrality, "we would *expect* it to have no effect on any decision. This is its very appeal: it does not distort economic choices" (Oates and Schwab 1997, 18). Thus, they find the greater economic activity entirely consistent with the two-rate tax system because the city was able to avoid alternative taxes that do not have the advantage of neutrality. The lesser city tax on buildings, which one would expect to affect development decisions, probably influenced the increase in construction activity. Their study, however, does not deal with the question of density of development, which is of interest to the anti-sprawl advocates.

Despite the recognition that Pittsburgh has received for its experimentation with the split-rate tax, it is in the midst of making changes to the tax structure, due to the city's recent budget gaps. According to a series of articles in the *Pittsburgh Gazette*[7] the city has been facing a fiscal crisis since the mid-1990s, and is now faced with a very limited set of political and fiscal choices. These include putting the city's finances under the control of the state, cutting services, and/or raising revenues through higher parking and garbage collection fees and increasing the commuter tax. These sorts of taxes are very different from the two-rate tax in their neutrality; they are exactly the type that influence development decisions and that economists such as Oates and Schwab want to avoid.

There is no set rate differential for the two parts of the split-rate tax system. The rates differ considerably among Pennsylvania's cities. For example, in Pittsburgh improvements on property were taxed at one-sixth the tax on the property itself, and in Harrisburg the economic revitalization of the city has been attributed to a land tax three times that of the improvements on the land. The highest spread between the land and building tax is found in the small town of Aliquippa, which taxes land at 16 times the rate of buildings. Pittsburgh eventually repealed its split-rate tax, "after a controversial property tax reassessment process and an approaching mayoral election made it politically untenable" (Catts 2002).

Building Code Reform

The enforcement of traditional building codes has proven a major barrier to the renovation and reuse of vacant buildings. Complex and frequently outdated codes were often written for new construction and are not appropriate for rehabilitation. State and localities have begun to rewrite their building codes to

---

7. See Wereschagin (2004); Semuels (2004); McNulty (2003); Pittsburgh in crisis (2003); Burnham (2002); and Special report (2001).

facilitate reinvestment in existing buildings. The U.S. Department of Housing and Urban Development (HUD 2001) recently profiled these state and local movements and created a handbook for others to use in revising their codes. HUD also published "Nationally Applicable Recommended Rehabilitation Provisions (NARRP)" in 1997, which was adapted from New Jersey's innovative Rehabilitation Subcode. NARRP is intended to serve as a model rehabilitation code and rests on two principles:

> Predictability and proportionality. HUD's model provides predictability because rehabilitation requirements for a particular project are clear from the beginning. NARRP [also] ensures that code requirements are proportional to the extent of work, making rehabilitation more affordable. NARRP borrows four concepts from New Jersey's Rehabilitation Subcode:
>
> - Six categories of work: repair, renovation, alteration, reconstruction, addition, and change of occupancy;
>
> - Work area: the portion of the building affected by repair or alteration;
>
> - Supplemental requirements: additional requirements, such as installing fire sprinklers, triggered by extensive work areas;
>
> - Four hazard scales: provide predictability by clearly relating specific requirements to specific increased hazards in the existing buildings.
>
> (U.S. HUD 2002)

Research on New Jersey's subcode shows that spending on rehabilitation increased significantly in five cities that were studied after the code went into effect. Further, the Rehabilitation Subcode has been estimated to reduce the cost of redeveloping old buildings under the old code by 10 to 40 percent (Smart Growth America 2002). Other states that have adopted rehabilitation codes include Maine, Maryland, Michigan, New York and Rhode Island, and California and Connecticut are considering legislation. At the city level, Wilmington, Delaware, adopted its own rehabilitation code (Smart Growth America 2002).

Redevelopment Programs

Property-specific approaches are not the only way states can face the challenge of vacant or deteriorated property. More general redevelopment initiatives can also play a role. Here we consider several less site-specific types of state programs that can help promote redevelopment, including voluntary cleanup programs for brownfields, smart growth initiatives, enterprise zones and several other innovative activities.

Brownfield Voluntary Cleanup Programs

Previous activities on abandoned properties (particularly for commercial or industrial purposes) frequently contaminated them, which can hamper their redevelopment. The resulting barrier for reuse of these sites (called brownfields) emerged as a major issue for economic revitalization after the 1980 passage of the Comprehensive Environmental Response, Compensation, and Liability Act (CERCLA), also known as the Superfund law. Knowledge and suspicion of a site's contamination can bar site redevelopment even on contiguous parcels. This de facto disqualification historically has resulted from the liability that owners of a contaminated site assume under the CERCLA law, whether or not they were the actual pollutors, and the high costs—which are not always fully calculable at the outset—that can be required to clean up sites for reuse. The resulting "environmental redlining" or "brownlining" of areas that are effectively excluded from redevelopment can significantly dim the economic prospects of whole populations residing near a brownfields site, as well as hurt a municipality's tax base (Leigh 1994).

In response, states have begun to address barriers to brownfield reuse through the design of voluntary cleanup programs (VCPs), thereby "demonstrating that there are many different ways to reach the common goal of site cleanup and reuse" (Northeast-Midwest Institute 2002, 2). Key elements of state programs include variable cleanup standards, engineering and institutional controls, and liability relief from third-party actions and from public actions. All states except North Dakota and South Dakota have adopted a VCP. These programs "vary in terms of comprehensiveness, incentives, level of state liability relief granted, and overall effectiveness. They regulate differently and emphasize different types of reuse, whether industrial, commercial, housing, or open space. Some states are well positioned to take advantage of federal initiatives, while others are not" (Northeast-Midwest Institute 2002, 2). In addition, 14 states have signed memoranda of understanding (MOAs) with the U.S. Environmental Protection Agency (EPA) that provide assurances to brownfield redevelopers that by meeting the state's remediation requirements they will avoid subsequent federal liability or EPA enforcement action.

Pennsylvania's Land Recycling Program, for example, has been an important vehicle for redeveloping the state's brownfields, as well as promoting more efficient urban land markets. The Land Recycling Program is the state's version of a VCP defined in a three-bill legislative package. The program modified state standards for cleanup and simplified the brownfield review process. It includes an Industrial Sites Reuse Program that gives grants to communities, nonprofits and economic development organizations. It also makes low interest loans to businesses for the cost of environmental studies and implementation of cleanup programs (Pennsylvania Land Recycling Program n.d.). The program facilitates brownfield redevelopment by providing liability relief to owners and developers of a former industrial site, as well as financiers, lenders, fiduciaries and economic development agencies who use one of three designated cleanup options (Scott 1997).

On January 11, 2002, President George W. Bush signed the Small Business Liability Relief and Brownfields Revitalization Act, which is seen as a major step forward in overcoming the barriers to brownfield redevelopment that federal regulations created for cities and states. Federal money now can be spent for cleanup as well as site assessment (previously only the latter was allowed). The law allows funding for the previously excluded category of LUSTs (leaking underground storage tanks). It further provides liability relief for minimally polluting small businesses, contiguous property owners, prospective purchasers and innocent landowners that demonstrate due diligence (Wright and Powers 2002). Overall, the law increases the value of state VCPs because it exempts from further federal enforcement those property owners who voluntarily enter qualified programs.

Smart Growth Infill Strategies

"Strengthen and direct development toward existing communities" is listed as one of the guiding principles of smart growth, according to the EPA and the Smart Growth Network (2002). Designed to discourage sprawl and encourage reinvestment in inner cities, smart growth has taken hold as a major policy focus. Consequently, the introduction of smart growth legislation has risen exponentially in the past five years. According to the American Planning Association (2002), eight states issued legislative task force reports on smart growth between 1999 and 2001; there were only 10 reports from 1990 to 1998. With such activity has come significant legislation, several components of which address infill development and have significant potential to reduce the number of central-city vacant land and abandoned structures. Much of the legislation remains elementary, directed toward activities such as creating advisory committees and panels or simply announcing support for smart growth and urban infill initiatives. While these efforts are noteworthy, we focus here on implemented programs that are working and potentially adaptable to other regions and states for addressing urban vacant land.

One of the oldest and most recognized programs, the Oregon Land Use Planning Act (ORS 197) was enacted in 1973. This legislation required cities and counties to develop and adopt comprehensive plans. Urban growth boundaries (UGBs) were designed to focus development activity within certain confines. As an incentive for development within the UGB, urban infrastructure would be provided. In December 1997 the State of Oregon adopted legislation promoting compact, mixed-use, pedestrian-friendly development. State investments would become available to those cities and counties supporting urban redevelopment initiatives.

Since 1992 New Jersey has emerged as a leader in smart growth–based infill projects. Most notable has been the New Jersey State Development and Redevelopment Plan, which packages revitalization elements focused on comprehensive planning; public infrastructure investments; economic development; urban revitalization; housing; historic, cultural and scenic resources and open land; brownfields; and design (NJOSP 2001).

Arizona has enacted legislation to promote infill development through its Growing Smarter legislation, which was first adopted in 1998 and updated to Growing Smarter Plus in 2000. Both versions promote infill development through the identification of appropriate locations and special incentives, such as expedited zoning and processing, waiver of municipal fees, and relief from development standards (Arizona Department of Commerce 2002). By December 31, 2001, Arizona counties and cities with populations of more than 75,000 were required to have a valid comprehensive plan in place, while municipalities with populations between 2,500 and 74,999 had until the end of 2002 to comply. Communities that do not comply may lose state funding for certain projects.

Maine also recently passed legislation related to infill development under the smart growth umbrella. Chapter 776 limits state investments to growth areas designated in adopted comprehensive plans. In addition, the state provides incentives to local governments whose comprehensive plans conform with state policies for smart growth. Specifically, the Municipal Investment Trust Fund supports local governments with comprehensive downtown revitalization efforts. Other states that have enacted infill-focused legislation include Connecticut, Rhode Island, Tennessee, Vermont, Washington and Wisconsin (Nelson 1999).

These smart growth legislative initiatives have begun to influence the redevelopment of urban vacant land. Such programs are often combined with state financing tools to promote the implementation of the infill development.

Enterprise Zones

Separate from, and preceding, the 1994 federal Empowerment Zone/Enterprise Community legislation of the Clinton administration, states have enacted enterprise zones to concentrate redevelopment efforts in areas of distress, decay and blight. The enterprise zones, borrowed from experiments in Hong Kong and Singapore (Wolf 1990), were first introduced in the U.S. in the early 1980s. By 2000 nearly 40 states had implemented some form of enterprise zone legislation. While the zones typically offer job credits, sales tax exemption, property tax reductions or abatements and other financing mechanisms, they vary widely in design and geographic targeting. Enterprise zones do not always focus on vacant property reclamation. In their case study of six states with enterprise zone programs (California, Florida, New Jersey, New York, Pennsylvania and Virginia), Greenbaum and Heinz (2000) observe that the zones do not necessarily target the most blighted areas, particularly when they require that areas show development potential. In fact, the emphasis of these programs appears to be more on providing jobs for local residents than on capital investments by businesses in the zones to raise property values and reduce vacancies. New Jersey incentives, for example, were found to have no effect on property values in a 1996 study by Boarnet and Bogart. Likewise, Greenbaum and Heinz (2000) found there was a small impact in moderately distressed cities, but not in those with severe blight. Nevertheless, New Jersey's enterprise zone program has won national awards.

Other Innovative Programs

There are a number of less familiar but nonetheless promising programs recently created to address the problem of urban vacant land and abandoned property. Michigan's Urban Homesteading on Vacant Land Act (Act 129, of 1999), intended to bring such land back into the tax register more quickly, offers tax-delinquent properties for $1. As part of the legislation, local governments may operate or contract with nonprofit organizations to administer the program. Act 131 (1999), also allows for state housing development authorities to create loan or grant programs to facilitate the homesteading process. Minnesota Urban and Rural Homesteading Program and Portland, Oregon, have similar homesteading programs.

Implemented by a city, but enabled by a state-level tool, the Neighborhood in Bloom program in Richmond, Virginia, addresses severe problems of vacant land and tax delinquency in six neighborhoods. The program, established in 1999, seeks to strengthen the link between code enforcement/nuisance abatement programs and the city of Richmond's housing rehabilitation and development programs and resources (International City/County Management Association 2002). For financing, the program draws on the state-level Virginia Derelict Structures Fund, begun in 1997 (Code of Virginia, secs. 36-152 to 36-156). Through this fund, the state gives grants to local governments for the acquisition, demolition, removal, rehabilitation or repair of derelict structures (ICCMA 2002, 23 n. 30). Priority is given to projects that include areas or structures that have a planned reuse, are part of drug-blight removal plans, or are in officially designated redevelopment or conservation districts, historic districts, or enterprise and empowerment zones. In this fashion state financial resources seamlessly support city redevelopment activity.

State legislators have moved in another innovative direction by requiring state governments to consider locating their facilities in downtown centers. This legislation parallels that of federal Executive Order no. 12072, which, seeking to "strengthen our nation's cities," requires federal agencies to first consider central business districts when locating offices (Fitzgerald and Leigh 2002). Pennsylvania has enacted such legislation in the Downtown Location Law (HB969) (Zausner 1998); Maine's smart growth legislation also urges that state office facilities and schools be located within designated growth areas (State of Maine 2000).

Financing Tools for Infill Development

Traditional financial mechanisms for alleviating blight and slums also implicitly aid efforts to promote infill development and reuse vacant land. Some of the most widely used financing tools are urban renewal development authorities, tax increment financing and business improvement districts (BIDs).

Development Authorities

In the late 1970s, following the end of federal funding for urban renewal programs, a majority of the states passed some type of legislation supporting urban renewal programs (Table 6.1). The intent of most of these programs is to "eliminate and redevelop substandard, decadent, or blighted open areas for industrial, commercial, business, residential, recreational, educational, hospital or other purposes" (Mass. DHCD). They take on a variety of shapes and often include the establishment of redevelopment agencies or authorities, redevelopment plans and strategies to implement them. These strategies might include rehabilitation codes; assembly and disposal of land including use of eminent domain; relocation of businesses and residents; demolition and rehabilitation of substandard structures; revitalization initiatives; the issuance of bonds; borrowing and investing money; and the receipt of grants, loans and gifts.

Development authorities are key implementing vehicles for urban renewal programs. They typically are able to levy and collect taxes, issue bonds, and receive public and private grants to promote improved economic development and living standards. These groups can be considered quasi-municipal corporations that are authorized by state legislation to improve a specific area's development (Municipal Research and Services Center 2002). They do not have to be focused on inner cities or downtowns, and, in fact, many development authorities have a larger (countywide or multicounty) concern. However, they typically concentrate on defined areas of cities in particular need of redevelopment efforts. In Georgia, for example, downtown development authorities are created by a municipality that defines the areas of focus within the city; appoints initial directors; prepares and approves a resolution that documents the need for the authority; and files specific documentation requirements with the appropriate state entities. Georgia downtown development authorities purchase and dispose of property; use eminent domain powers; finance projects by loans, grants, leases and revenue bonds and receive government grants, loans and other financial assistance; prepare redevelopment plans; and act as an actual redevelopment agency under state law (Georgia Municipal Association 2002).

Tax Increment Financing

Tax increment financing (TIF) is a tool often used to generate the funds necessary for redevelopment of a district in need, whether it is from an urban renewal plan or another area deemed worthy of revitalization by a local government. Forty-eight states and the District of Columbia possess enabling legislation to offer TIF (Table 6.1). TIFs allow a portion of the tax revenues generated by new development to be either directly reinvested in the special district created or leveraged with bonds. While there have been some failures with regard to poor planning, successful TIF programs can be found throughout the country. One of the most well-documented, for example, has been Chicago's program, with over $2 billion in revenue for reinvestment and the creation of more than 28,000 jobs (Local Initiative Support Corporation 2001). Minneapolis's Neighborhood Revitalization Program (NRP) also successfully uses TIFs. In response to concerns about growing crime and blight, in 1990 the Minnesota State Legislature and the Minneapolis City Council dedicated $20 million a year for 20 years to fund housing and economic development activities in the city's 81 neighborhoods. The program is unique in that it is funded through TIF revenues generated from profitable downtown development projects. As of 2000, $176.2 million had been allocated toward the implementation of more than 1,400 projects and programs (Minneapolis Neighborhood Revitalization Program 2000). TIFs are not, however, without their detractors. Critics contend that localities do not always discriminate carefully enough when making TIF financing available, and argue that TIFs are too often used for projects that would have been developed without public subsidy. But used prudently, TIFs can be a valuable tool for local governments to finance redevelopment without using existing revenues or proposing new taxes to pay for it.

Business Improvement Districts

Business improvement districts are city subdivisions that subject all property owners or businesses in a delineated area to additional tax assessments that are used to fund various district improvements. They were created by state legislatures to remedy particular public policy challenges that were either being ignored or beyond the ability of existing governmental entities to ameliorate. Revenue from taxes raised from BIDs is used to pay for services supplemental to those provided by city government (Seliga 2001). It typically finances physical improvements, traditional municipal services, social services and business services (Briffault 1999).

The laws governing BID formation vary considerably from state to state, but the creation of a BID generally involves formal actions by both the city government and the private sector. The rules may even differ within one state. Several states, including California, Pennsylvania and Texas, provide more than one means of creating BIDs and similar bodies. Generally, statutes authorizing BID formation contain specific language detailing fund collection procedures, services to be provided, the composition of the governing board and methods to facilitate government involvement.[8] Briffault (1999) counted more than 1,000 BIDs in the U.S. in 1999, including over 40 in New York City; 54 in Wisconsin; 35 in New Jersey; 16 in San Diego; and one or more in cities as diverse as Anchorage, Baltimore, Buffalo, Dallas, Denver, Houston, Los Angeles, Memphis, Philadelphia, St. Louis, Seattle and Washington, DC. The number of BIDs has likely continued to grow since 1999. While the two most prominent—New York City's Times Square and Philadelphia's Center City District—are located in the midtown and downtown areas of these cities, many BIDs have been established along small commercial strips in large metropolitan areas, and have also been created in suburbs and even small towns (Briffault 1999).

BIDs are not an entirely new concept. Finance tools such as special assessments and the more specifically targeted special purpose district have long provided means to manage and fund public-sector activities outside the purview of most municipal governments.[9] BIDs combine aspects of both the special assessment finance tool and the special purpose district, but extend these older

---

8. Emerging from legal structures and concepts that go back more than a century, the specific form of the BID is a relatively recent phenomenon. Most BIDs were created after 1980, with the majority of those coming after 1990, though the first modern BID in the U.S. was apparently the 1975 Downtown Development District of New Orleans (Briffault 1999).

9. Colorado has a true alphabet soup of assessment types. The acronyms SID, LID, GID, PID and BID refer to types of districts Colorado counties and municipalities can use to finance many kinds of public infrastructure. Special improvement districts (SIDs) and general improvement districts (GIDs) are organized by a municipality under two sets of state codes, while local improvement districts (LIDs) and public improvement districts (PIDs) are organized by a county using two others. In Colorado, BIDs are hybrid entities organized by a municipality under still another state directive (Wisor and Crawford 2001).

mechanisms well beyond their traditional uses. BIDs differ from special assessments in that their monies are used primarily to finance municipal services in older, established areas rather than to fund infrastructure for newly built, growing districts. BIDs may offer a broader utility as well. As Mitchell notes, "although most BIDs do not engage in traditional economic development activities, there are several that do, leading to the consideration that BIDs are another alternative organizational mechanism to encourage economic growth within communities (joining tax increment financing districts, enterprises zones, and other such programs)" (2001, 121).

Model State Agenda for Vacant Land and Abandoned Property Reform

There is an impressive, but scattered, array of programs and policies at the state level to tackle the nationwide problem of urban vacant land and abandoned structures that impede redevelopment. Here we outline the essential components of a model state agenda for vacant land and abandoned property reform.

All states need better information regarding location, condition, ownership and other related characteristics. Quite simply, no state or region will successfully address the problem of vacant land and abandoned structures unless it can quantify and monitor them. Currently, no state keeps a consistent and updated inventory of such properties. Consequently, the model agenda begins by recommending state support of an inventory, which would entail statewide uniform and regular data input on vacant land and abandoned structures in a geographic information system. While there will be many issues to resolve when establishing such a system—such as how to officially define what is vacant or abandoned, and linking the inventory to existing land use and property data collection—it remains vital that states have current, accessible and transparent information publicly available.

At the same time, the broad redevelopment programs and the general redevelopment and financing tools reviewed here represent a useful toolbox of mechanisms by which to promote the reuse of vacant land and abandoned properties. The two youngest of these vehicles most directly impact redevelopment. Brownfield voluntary cleanup programs specifically remove barriers to the reuse of contaminated properties, while infill-directed smart growth legislation seeks on a regional basis to curb further greenfield development and to channel development toward underutilized urban parcels.[10] As Table 6.1 demonstrates, nearly all states now have some form of brownfield VCP, but only 19 boast smart growth legislation with a specific infill focus. Thus, the second element of a state

---

10. The EPA supports a variety of state-level activities that can be used as state models. For example, EPA Region 1 has the Brownfields Targeted Site Assessment Program, which assists in the redevelopment of contaminated sites by municipalities. Public or nonprofit groups that are interested in redeveloping a brownfield site can have a site assessment done, thereby minimizing uncertainities related to the real or perceived site contamination. http://www.rkmc.com/article.asp?articleId=40.

agenda must be a two-pronged approach to expedite cleanup of centrally located contaminated parcels and simultaneously construct incentives and disincentives to redirect growth away from metropolitan fringes and toward urban cores.

Development authorities and tax increment financing, along with the bonding capability upon which their economic development efforts depend, are important financial strategies for supporting vacant land and abandoned structures redevelopment. In practice, however, none of these tools has been exclusively used for depressed urban areas. Because the tools leverage limited resources, the ideal state agenda for vacant property would concentrate their use in depressed inner cities, and limit their use in stronger urban areas and greenfields. That is, states should focus their financial tools on locations that are overlooked by market financing. Enterprise zones, in this regard, *are* specifically targeted on depressed urban areas, but a review of their implementation has revealed that they do not necessarily target the most blighted neighborhoods. Further, they tend to emphasize job creation over capital improvements. Enterprise zone programs, therefore, should be supplemented by focus area programs, which would target funds for community revitalization in areas with the most significant blight and large-scale incidence of vacant land and abandoned structures, and provide greater financial incentives to developers to work in these areas.

Of the four property-specific tools reviewed, meanwhile, two are used by all states and two are used by less than a handful. All states have some type of tax lien foreclosure process as well as authorized eminent domain. However, the current form of these systems remains a key impediment to cities' effective and quick resolution of their problems of vacant and tax-delinquent property. The model state agenda calls, therefore, for a reformed judicial tax-lien foreclosure system, which features a single enforcement proceeding that takes as little time as possible; a shift from post-sale to pre-sale in the length of time from initial tax delinquency to loss of all property rights; a single entity that controls the entire proceedings; mandatory title examination; and notice to all property interests. Such a system would maximize municipalities' ability to resolve their problems in a manner that will not be subject to legal contest. Once municipalities address their large backlog, the ongoing use of this reformed judicial tax-lien foreclosure system will ensure that the problem of vacant and abandoned properties never reaches the scale that currently plagues many large cities. At the same time, with such a reformed system in place, city-level land banks can be created to facilitate the assembly and resale of vacant parcels.

All states have eminent domain powers, but only a handful have strict standards for declaring blight. It remains to be seen whether public criticism of what is perceived to be the misuse of eminent domain (e.g., defining a property as blighted because its current business does not produce as much income as it might) may affect cities' ability to use this tool. For the model state agenda, state encouragement of the judicious use of eminent domain by community land trusts remains a promising approach for redeveloping the most blighted urban neighborhoods.

Finally, the two property-specific tools that are used the least have great promise for the redevelopment of vacant land and abandoned properties and should be part of the model state agenda. Split-rate taxation encourages reinvestment in structures and discourages the speculative and nonproductive holding of vacant land. Likewise, rehabilitation codes significantly increase the feasibility of reusing old, abandoned structures. While theses are typically municipal-level fiscal and regulatory reforms, they often require state legislative action. Beyond adopting new legislation and initiating new programs, it also will be necessary for states to educate municipalities and developers, as well as other appropriate members of the public and private sectors, to the availability of these tools. One discovery of this research has been that existing programs are underutilized. Although many have been in place for years, they have not yet been embraced as opportunities to promote redevelopment.

In the end, state governments have a strong stake in facilitating the reuse of their cities' vacant land, and they have motivated partners in local governments as well as in the real estate, financial and property-owning communities. The national level of urban vacant land redevelopment will be enhanced if all states become aware of, and adapt to their best use, the legislative reforms and approaches identified in the model state agenda.

Acknowledgments

This chapter is excerpted with permission from "The State Role in Urban Land Redevelopment," a discussion paper prepared for The Brookings Institution Center on Urban and Metropolitan Policy and CEOs for Cities (April 2003). The research assistance of Lynn Patterson and Alex Pearlstein of the Georgia Institute of Technology City and Regional Planning Program is gratefully acknowledged, as are Rosalind Greenstein's insights on split-rate taxation and the views of Henry George.

References

Accordino, John and Gary T. Johnson. 2000. Addressing the vacant land and abandoned property problem. *Journal of Urban* Affairs 22(3):301–315.

Alexander, Frank S. 2000a. Constitutional questions about tax lien foreclosures. *Government Finance Review* (June): 27–31.

———. 2000b. Tax liens, tax sales, and due process. *Indiana Law Journal* 75:747–807.

———. 2002. Planning for Smart Growth 2002 State of the States. http://www.planning.org/growingsmart/states2002.htm.

Arizona Department of Commerce. 2002. Growing Smarter Legislation. http://www.azcommerce.com/CommunityPlanning/GSLegis.htm.

Boarnet, Marlon G. and William T. Bogart. 1996. Enterprise zones and employment: Evidence from New Jersey. *Journal of Urban Economics* 40:198–215.

Briffault, Richard. 1999. A government for our time? Business Improvement Districts and urban governance. *Columbia Law Review* (March): 365–468.

Burnham, James B. 2002. Pittsburgh's fiscal crisis: No more rabbits in the hat. *Pittsburgh Post-Gazette*, October 20. http://www.post-gazette.com/forum/comm/20021020edburn1020p1.asp.

Catts, Timothy. N.d. Pittsburg, Philadelphia mull past and future of property tax reform. *The Progress Report*. http://www.progress.org/philly08.htm.

Fannie Mae Foundation. 2001. State policies are critical to local responses on tax delinquent properties. *Housing Facts & Findings* 3(1):10.

Fitzgerald, Joan and Nancey Green Leigh. 2002. The reuse of office and industrial property in city and suburb. *Economic revitalization: Cases and strategies for city and suburb*. Thousand Oaks, CA: Sage Publications.

Fulton, William. 2003. Creating a land boom. *Governing* (August). http://www.governing.com/articles/8econ.htm.

Georgia Municipal Association. 2002. Downtown development authorities. http://www.gmanet.com/general/default.asp?pagetype=askgma_dda&menuid=AskGMAID.

Greenbaum, Robert and John Engberg Heinz. 2000. An evaluation of state enterprise zone policies. *Policy Studies Review* 17(2/3):29–47.

Hartzok, Alanna. 1997. Pennsylvania's success with split-rate tax reform. *American Journal of Economics and Sociology* 56(2):205–215.

International City/County Management Association (ICCMA). The revitalization of vacant properties. *Document Number* 10000162. *Document Year* 2002; *Project Year* 2001.

Jennings, Marianne M. 2001/2002. Eminent domain is not what it used to be. *Real Estate Law Journal*. 30 (Winter): 232–239.

Keating, Larry, and David Sjoquist. 2001. Bottom fishing: Emerging policy regarding tax delinquent properties. *Housing Facts & Findings*, Fannie Mae Foundation 3(1).

Kildee, Dan. 2001. Tax reversion implementation and land disposition planning, Genessee County, Michigan. Mimeo.

Leigh, Nancey Green. 1994. Introduction to environmental constraints in brownfied redevelopment. *Economic Development Quarterly* 8(4):325–328.

Local Initiative Support Corporation (LISC). 2001. National survey of urban economic and community development models. http://www.liscnet.org/resources/econdev/best_practices/ent_zone_model.shtml.

Massachusetts Department of Housing and Community Development (Mass. DHCD). 2003. *Urban renewal program fact sheet.* www.state.ma.us/dhcd/publications/fact_sheets/ch121b.pdf.

McNulty, Timothy. 2003. Pittsburgh begs state for help with fiscal crisis. *Pittsburgh Post-Gazette*, November 11. http://www.post-gazette.com/neigh_city/20031111murphy1111pl.asp.

Minneapolis Neighborhood Revitalization Program. 2000. *A program of the people, by the people, and for the people: Progress report 2000.*

Mitchell, Jerry. 2001. Business improvement districts and the "new" revitalization of downtown. *Economic Development Quarterly* 15(2):115–123.

Municipal Research and Services Center of Washington. 1997. *Infill development: Strategies for shaping livable neighborhoods.* Report no. 38 (June). http://www.mrsc.org/Publications/textfill.aspx#E19E.

———. *Public corporations/public development authorities.* 2002. http://www.mrsc.org/Subjects/Econ/ed-pda.aspx.

Nelson, A.C. 1999. Economic development and smart growth. *News and Views*, American Planning Association Economic Development Division. October.

New Jersey Office of State Planning (NJOSP). 2001. New Jersey State Development and Redevelopment Plan. http://www.state.nj.us/dca/osg/plan/plan.html.

Northeast-Midwest Institute. 2002. Brownfield basics: An issue primer. www.nemw.org.

Oates, Wallace E., and Robert M. Schwab. 1997. The impact of urban land taxation: The Pittsburgh experience. *National Tax Journal* 50(1):1–21.

Oregon Department of Land Conservation and Development. 2001. 1999–2001 Biennial Report to the Seventy-First Legislative Assembly. http://www.lcd.state.or.us/legislative/TextRpt2001.rtf.

Pagano, Michael A. and Ann O'M. Bowman. 2000. *Vacant land in cities: An urban resource.* Washington, DC: The Brookings Institution.

Pennsylvania General Assembly Local Government Commission. October 2003. Municipalities—How they change. *Pennsylvania Legislator's Municipal Deskbook* 21. http://www.lgc.state.pa.us/deskbook03/Basics05.pdf.

Pennsylvania Land Recycling Program. N.d. *A clear road to development.* Publication no. 2530-BK-DEP2310. http://www.dep.state.pa.us/dep/deputate/airwaste/wm/landrecy/facts/roadsign.pdf.

Pittsburgh in crisis: State receivership? 2003. *Pittsburgh Tribune-Review*, August 23. http://www.pittsburghlive.com/x/search/s_151166.html.

Plassman, Florenz and T. Nicolaus Tideman. 2000. A Markov Chain Monte Carlo analysis of the effect of two-rate property taxes on construction. *Journal of Urban Economics* 47(2):216–247.

Schwartz, Stewart. 1999. Split-rate tax promotes smart growth. *Getting Smart Newsletter*, Smart Growth Network 2(4). http://www.washingtonregion.net/html/article.html.

Scott, Michael J. 1997. Pennsylvania's land recycling program. *State Innovations.* Lexington, KY: Council of State Governments (December).

Seliga, Joseph. 2001. Democratic solutions to urban problems. 25 *Hamline Law Review* 1 (Fall): 22–68.

Semuels, Alana. 2004. City's parking tax elevated to "sinful" level. *Pittsburgh Post-Gazette*, January 21. http://post-gazette.com/pg/04021/263844.stm.

Siegel, Eric and Gady A. Epstein. 2002. Mayor seeks control over 5,000 houses. *Baltimore Sun*, January 27, 1A.

Smart Growth America. 2002. Rehabilitation codes. http://www.smartgrowthamerica.org.

Smart Growth Network. 2002. What is smart growth? http://www.smartgrowth.org/sgn/partpublist.asp?part=16.

Special report: Pittsburgh in crisis. 2001. *Pittsburgh Tribune-Review.* http://www.pittsburghlive.com/x/tribune-review/specialreports/pghincrisis/index.html.

State of Maine. 2000. Final report of the task force on state office building location, other state growth-related capital investments and patterns of development. January. http://www.state.me.us/legis/opla/sprawl.PDF.

U.S. Department of Housing and Urban Development, Office of Policy Development and Research. 1997. Nationally applicable recommended rehabilitation provisions (NARRP). May.

———. 1999. An assessment of state brownfield initiatives. March.

———. 2001. Smart codes in your community: A guide to building rehabilitation codes. August.

———. 2002. Smart codes spur reinvestment. http://www.huduser.org/periodicals/rrr/rrr_02_2002/0202_2.html.

Wereschagin, Mike. 2004. County proposes assessment fixes. *Pittsburgh Tribune-Review*, April 24. http://www.pittsburghlive.com/x/search/s_190403.html.

Wisor, Dee P. and Kimberley K. Crawford. 2001. Improvement districts for Colorado counties, cities and cowns. *Colorado Lawyer* (January): 53–59.

Wolf, Michael Alan. 1990. Enterprise zones: A decade of diversity. *Financing economic development*, Richard Bingham, Edward Hill, and Sammis White, eds. Thousand Oaks, CA: Sage Publications.

Wright, Andrew G. and Mary Buckner Powers. 2002. Reclamation. *Engineering News-Record* 248(6).

Zausner, Robert. 1998. Proposed measure could give downtowns a boost. *Central Penn Business Journal* (Harrisburg), May 13.

Statutes and Laws

C.R.S.A. Sec. 31-25-103. Colorado Revised Statutes Annotated Title 31. Government: Municipal Powers and Functions of Cities and Towns, Article 25. Public Improvements, Part 1. Urban Renewal, Section 103—Definitions.

K.S.A. Sec. 17-4760. Definitions Kansas Statutes Annotated, Chapter 17. Corporations, Article 47. Urban Renewal Law, Act of 1955 and Amendments, Section 60. Definitions.

Neb. Rev. St. Sec. 58-209.01 Nebraska Revised Statutes of 1943, Chapter 58. Money and Financing. Article 2. Nebraska Investment Finance Authority. Section 09.01. Blighted area, defined.

SC ST Sec. 31-10-20 Code 1976 Sec. 31-10-20. Code of Laws of South Carolina 1976 Annotated, Title 31.

Housing and Redevelopment, Chapter 10. Community Development Law, Section 20, Definitions.

Utah Code, 1953, Title 17B. Limited Purpose Local Government Entities, Chapter 4. Redevelopment Agencies Act, Part 6. Blight determination in redevelopment project areas, 17B-4-604. Conditions on board determination of blight. Conditions of blight caused by the developer.

7 Environmental Devolution and Local Capacity

Brownfield Implementation in Four Distressed Cities in New Jersey

Sarah S. Gardner

S ince the 1980s, when President Ronald Reagan launched his New Federalism initiative, devolution has defined the cutting edge of environmental policy. Implementation and enforcement of the Clean Air and Clean
Water Acts has been largely delegated to the states. Successive administrations
since Reagan have hailed market-based initiatives, public-private partnerships
and local solutions as the best answers to environmental regulation and reform.
Proponents of devolution argue that in addition to reducing government expenditure and streamlining political processes, decentralizing authority moves government closer to the people and thereby fosters citizen participation in public
life.[1] States-rights conservatives on the right and community activists on the
left both support the policy. According to John Donahue, the broad appeal of
devolution has contributed to "something as close to consensus as American
politics ever sees" (1997, 4).

Brownfield initiatives represent the greatest crystallization to date of this
vision of environmental devolution. States have delegated to municipalities
responsibility for identifying sites, attracting developers, determining cleanup
levels, methods of remediation and reuse. Locally managed and market-driven,
brownfield programs promise to solve a public problem with limited public
investment of cash and minimal governmental intrusion into local affairs.

To address the additional responsibilities delegated to them by devolutionary policies, municipalities require a variety of resources, including funds, staff,
legal and technical expertise, and a mature civic culture. Social scientists have
expanded the traditional notion of capital to capture other necessary requirements for high-quality production of goods and services. To help labor economists understand variations in earned wages, Becker (1976) conceptualized

---

1. See, for example, Ackerman and Stewart (1988); Anderson and Hill (1997); Butler and Macey
(1996); Ceplo and Yandle (1997); Cimitile et al. (1995); Commoner (1990); Crews (1996); John (1994);
Kilgore and Sylvester (1995); Kincaid (1999); Lund (1995); Muller and Fix (1980); O'Connor (1999);
Rabe (1997); Ringquist (1993); Schoenbrod (1997); Stewart (1988); Stroup (1996); and Thompson (1997).

human capital as nonmaterial assets—knowledge, skills, health or values—accumulated through individual or family investment. He argued that those who accumulate more and better human capital earn higher lifetime wages.

Over the past decade, political scientists have highlighted the importance of a number of different forms of capital, including social capital (Putnam 1993, 2000; Gittell and Thompson 2001), civic capacity (Stone et al. 2001), political capital (Fuchs, Minnite and Shapiro 1999; Fuchs, Shapiro and Minnite 2001) and administrative capacity (Stone 1989, 179). Foster (2000) identifies eight forms of capital requisite for effective governance, including historical, structural, legal, socioeconomic, developmental, civic, corporate and political capital. Each of these forms of capital contributes to the efficacy of local political processes by providing the material or human resources necessary to forge cross-sector networks, increase citizen involvement and focus political efforts; in short, to form policy coalitions, "working alliances among different interests" that can secure the cooperation needed from other public and private actors to manage a specific policy area (Mollenkopf 1992, 38). Because these different forms of capital have the similar effect of enhancing local governance, they may be gathered under the common rubric of *local capacity*, which may be defined concisely as capital resources—civic, governmental or private—for the initiation and implementation of public policy initiatives. High levels of social capital, civic capacity, structural capital and so on all serve to augment local capacity.[2]

This chapter argues that local capacity plays an important role in the implementation of devolutionary programs, particularly when other facilitating factors (such as a strong market) are absent. Devolution is not an inherently good or bad approach to policy; the problem with devolving responsibility to local governments is that programmatic outcomes depend on the capacity of the city to implement and administer policy initiatives. Economically thriving cities with high real estate values, strong economies, functioning growth regimes[3] and effective local governments have the resources to meet the challenge of devolution. Economically depressed cities steeped in conflict and corruption generally do not. Local capacity can help compensate for economic and structural disadvantage. Distressed municipalities with high local capacity in one or another form are able to craft effective brownfield programs, whereas those with low local capacity are likely to fail.

The significance of local capacity in the implementation of brownfield programs may be illumined through an examination of four socioeconomically and environmentally distressed cities in New Jersey: Newark, Trenton, Camden and Paterson. Newark has a viable real estate market, is ruled by a growth machine,

---

2. Foster (2000) expresses a similar concept as *regional capital*.

3. An urban regime is "the informal arrangement by which public bodies and private interests function together in order to be able to make and carry out governing decision" (Stone 1989, 6). This "informal arrangement of civic cooperation" is contingent on the institutional capacities of groups and the resources that groups control (Stone 1989, 232, 240). A growth regime is similar to a growth machine (Logan and Molotch 1987) in that the business community wields the greatest influence, but whereas the focus of the growth machine is limited to property development, the growth regime's focus includes all forms of economic development.

and has made comparatively scant use of such state incentives as the Hazardous Discharge Site Remediation Fund and Redevelopment Agreements. The other three cities have been largely unsuccessful at attracting private developers. High levels of local capacity among neighborhood actors in Camden and motivated local officials in Trenton have helped these cities compensate for the lack of a market. Paterson has neither a market nor strong civic or governing capacity, and there the brownfield program has floundered.

Four Cities in Distress

Camden, Newark, Paterson and Trenton are cities in crisis. New Jersey municipalities are especially reliant on property taxes, from which they receive 52 percent of their total revenue, compared with 27 percent nationally, a fact that has resulted in striking wealth gaps, especially between cities and the suburbs (Regan 2003, 1). The municipal tax rate in New Jersey's eight cities is on average more than twice the statewide norm, but their tax resources are less than half the statewide average (Orfield and Luce 2003, 4). Burdened by structural poverty, aging infrastructure and a decrepit housing stock, all four cities rank in the top 10 of New Jersey's Municipal Distress Index—a composite score of economic, social, fiscal and infrastructure distress (Table 7.1). Rusk (1995) included three (Camden, Newark and Trenton) in his definition of "point of no return cities." Each has a disproportionate number of tax-free facilities, including tax-free zones created by the New Jersey Urban Enterprise Zone, and in Camden and Newark, tax-free zones created through the U.S. Department of Housing and Urban Development's Enterprise Community Program. Lacking the tax revenue to provide even the most basic services, all four exist in a state of "deindustrialized dependency," relying on federal and state subsidies for their survival (Burchell 1984; Perry 1987, 113).

Camden is the poorest city in the Northeast and the fifth poorest city in the nation, "nine square miles of people on welfare and the homeless," according to the city's planning chief. It suffers from the highest population decline, the highest unemployment rate, the highest poverty rate, the highest crime rate and the highest state equalized tax rate of New Jersey's cities. It is the most violent place in the state, with the highest homicide rate, which is 10 times higher than the state average. Camden is often described as under siege by drug dealers who outgun the beleaguered police department—there are about 200 open-air drug markets in the small city (Wilson 1997, 36). Social conditions in Camden are closer to those of a developing nation than the U.S.: the infant mortality rate is double the national average; the school district has one of the highest dropout rates in the nation; and domestic abuse rates are the highest in the country (Hester 1999, B1). Public health is poor; a high proportion of city residents lack medical insurance and suffer from chronic illness, especially asthma and diabetes. Camden has few businesses and lacks a critical mass of middle-income residents, who might otherwise create demand for retail goods and services and increase property values (Smith and Thompson 2001). About 82 percent of the

Table 7.1. Socioeconomic Data

	New Jersey	Camden	Newark	Paterson	Trenton
Demographic Indicators					
Population (1998)	8,115,011	83,546	267,823	148,212	84,494
% Change since 1990	4.7	−4.5	−2.7	5.2	−4.7
% Black (1990)	14.6	56.4	58.5	36.0	49.3
% White (1990)	79.5	19.0	28.6	41.2	42.2
% Hispanic (1990)	12.4	31.2	26.1	41.0	14.1
Economic Indicators					
Municipal Distress Index rank	N/A	1	5	7	2
Per capita income (1989)	$18,714	$7,276	$9,424	$10,518	$11,018
% Below poverty level (1989)	8.7	36.6	26.3	18.5	18.1
Unemployment rate (%) (1997)	4.6	13.9	11.0	10.5	9.7
% Substandard housing units (1990)	4.1	15.4	14.9	14.3	8.0

Sources: 2000 County and City Extra: Annual Metro, City, and County Data Book; New Jersey Municipal Distress Index (1997) (NJOSP).

population depends on some form of public assistance, and one in three residents lives in poverty (Wilson 1997; USEPA 1997). Twenty-five percent of the population is comprised of school-aged children (five to 17 years old), and about 70 percent of the city's elderly citizens are categorized as extremely low income.

Because of the shortage of tax-paying residents and the preponderance of tax-delinquent property, Camden is in perpetual financial crisis. Camden's ratable base declined steadily through the 1990s, and the city has the highest tax rate and the smallest tax base per capita of any municipality in New Jersey, as well as one of the highest tax delinquency rates (New Jersey 2001). There are nearly as many acres of vacant property as there are in productive manufacturing (USEPA Region 2 1997), and almost half the assessed value of property is exempt from taxation (New Jersey 2001). Retail sales have shown no growth in two decades, and the once-busy shopping district is now a vacant open space of expanding parking lots because about two-thirds of the buildings have been leveled and never replaced. Today, the largest employers in the city are a county trash incinerator, a county sewage treatment plant, a state prison and a county jail. Camden is the major government center for South Jersey and houses several county, state and federal government offices. No bank has opened a branch in Camden for 40 years, but an informal economy of drugs and prostitution is thriving. Public investment in Camden has provided jobs, but it has also eroded the property tax base, the sole source of income for New Jersey municipalities. The state funds more than 70 percent of the municipal budget (over $3 billion in the past 10 years) and 89 percent of the school budget (N.J. Dept. of Treasury 1996). The Community Development Block Grant Program provides the city with $3 to $4 million annually for neighborhood revitalization, economic development, elimination of slums and blight and assistance to low- and moderate-income families.

Although Camden is in worse financial shape than the other three cities, all have experienced the same trends to varying degrees (Table 7.1). The state's capital, Trenton, suffers from a poverty rate of 18 percent. The unemployment rate is over 7 percent, which is double the state and national rates, and the median per capita income is $11,089. In addition to jobs, the city also lacks open space, recreation areas and housing. Trenton has a minuscule tax base: 89 percent of the owner-occupied homes are valued at less than $99,999, and the city receives 97 percent of its municipal revenue from the state. Trenton has a high concentration of contaminated sites, and the city's residents have high rates of infant mortality and childhood lead poisoning.

Paterson is the only city of the four with an increasing population: the 2000 population was 149,222, up from 140,891 in 1990, due to an influx of immigrants. The ethnic composition according to the 2000 census was 35 percent white, 35 percent African American and 50 percent Hispanic. About 18.5 percent of the city's population lives below the poverty level. Ninety-three percent of the housing is at risk for lead paint (Kanter 2000, A1). The 2001 unemployment rate was 8.8 percent, compared to the statewide rate of 4.2 percent. A majority of the workforce (67 percent) is employed in manufacture and services; the major employers are hospitals, city government and industry. Finance, insurance and real estate account for an additional 7 percent of the jobs (PEDC 1998). Drugs and prostitution are highly visible in the city's poorer neighborhoods. The public schools, badly managed, were taken over by the state in August 1991. Property values are higher in Paterson than the other three cities, and it receives the smallest proportion—55.6 percent—of municipal revenue from the state.

Until recently, Newark was a disaster area, with a per capita income in 1990 of only $9,424 and rates of tuberculosis, AIDS and infant mortality paralleling those of the third world (Schulgasser 2002a). It is New Jersey's largest city and the most densely populated city in the U.S. after New York City and Jersey City. Racially it is one of America's most hypersegregated cities (Massey and Denton 1993). Almost 70 percent of its land is owned by the government, nonprofit corporations or religious institutions, and is thus exempt from property taxes. Newark has zealously pursued ratables to fatten its chronically inadequate tax base and to compensate for the declining percentage of aid from Washington; this approach has paid off. In recent years, Newark has been undergoing a renaissance of sorts, with substantial commercial and residential development in the city's Central Business District and Ironbound neighborhood and elsewhere. Recovery is far from complete, but among the four cities in this study, Newark is the only one to attract private investment, a sign of hope.

The cities' social and economic straits are matched by their environmental condition. Overwhelmingly comprised of devalued property, polluting facilities and brownfields, they are among the most blighted municipalities in the state, sharing a total of 779 known contaminated sites and an unknown number of additional brownfield sites. This is not uncharacteristic for New Jersey. The most densely populated of the 50 states, New Jersey leads the nation in the number of Superfund sites and boasts more than 8,000 contaminated sites, at least one in each municipality. Every resident of the Garden State lives within

10 miles of a toxic dump (New York Times 2002). It was to address these conditions that New Jersey governor Christine Whitman enacted the Brownfield and Contaminated Site Remediation Act (BCSRA) in 1998, which promised to "help protect the public health and environment, conserve open space, improve the economy, create jobs, and revitalize cities and neighborhoods" (N.J. State Senate 1997).

New Jersey's Brownfield Program

New Jersey's brownfield program has won several National Phoenix Awards, an honor for outstanding brownfields projects that serve as national models of innovation, and is widely hailed by policy makers and practitioners as one of the strongest in the country. The BCSRA, which expanded and enhanced a Voluntary Cleanup Program operative since 1992, aims to accomplish three much-needed functions. First, it encourages the voluntary cleanup of contaminated property in urban areas, thus redressing the health hazards and other problems that stem from urban blight. Although cities are free to take on the task of cleaning polluted sites themselves, almost none can afford to. Like other state-level brownfield programs, the BCSRA seeks to attract businesses and industries through a range of financial incentives and liability relief, which often amounts to giving away properties to whomever will redevelop them. This furthers the initiative's second goal: urban economic revitalization through private investment. Contaminated sites represent not only health hazards, but also lost jobs and tax revenues; the BCSRA seeks to remedy both environmental and economic distress. Finally, the BCSRA aims to protect open space by making it more cost effective for businesses and industries to locate in cities instead of suburban or rural areas.

The BCSRA pursues these goals by granting private and municipal owners of brownfield sites authority over site selection, cleanup standards, remedy selection and redevelopment plans. The program offers technical assistance from the state, but little oversight (Ellerbusch 2000, 23), and does not impose specific cleanup standards or remedies.[4] Funds for actual cleanup—the most costly part of the process—are not available. To attract private investment in the rehabilitation of contaminated property within depressed real estate markets, the program offers financial incentives such as grants for site assessment, loans and reimbursements for site remediation and property tax reductions.

Although there have been some notable successes building public-private partnerships to remediate brownfields in New Jersey, this activity has been limited. With few exceptions, none of the major cities has been successful in attracting business investment to their contaminated sites. This is because New

---

4. Indeed, the State DEP does not specifically track the brownfield program's progress and does not keep data on the number of sites redeveloped. An official in the brownfield program answered my inquiry with, "If anyone tells you the number of brownfield sites remediated and redeveloped, it would be a lie. We don't keep track."

Jersey's brownfield program assumes that the robust conditions that might foster local economic development are already in place and delegates responsibility for promoting growth to the invisible hand of the market.[5]

Brownfields and the Market

All brownfield sites are not created equal. Any comparative analysis of brownfield redevelopment must clarify what type of site is being analyzed (Wright and Davlin 1998). Tier I sites, which tend to be large, former industrial or commercial properties, are those in which market values exceed the costs of remediation. Tier I sites are often on major thoroughfares in suburbs or edge cities. Redevelopment of these sites is usually driven by market forces, and public subsidy is likely unnecessary. They are especially suitable for industry, big box retail or major residential developments. One oft-cited example is the 127-acre former Lily Tulip factory in Holmdel, New Jersey, whose location and vast size made it prime for a major development. The factory was demolished in 1999 and is being rebuilt by a group of Boston investors into The Commons, a mixed-use project that includes assisted-living senior housing, a nursing home, offices, retail space including several big box stores and an office complex (Garbarine 1999; Van Develde 2002).

Tier II sites have less redevelopment potential and more complications including higher cleanup costs than Tier I sites. They are usually located in urban commercial or industrial zones along transportation corridors. The profitability of Tier II sites is uncertain: market value may slightly exceed or fall short of the purchase price and cleanup costs. These locales usually remain idle without concentrated government intervention to address the barrier and reduce risk. The Edison Crossroads Redevelopment project is an example of a Tier II site. Located along Route 1, a commercial corridor, this 30-acre former steel manufacturing site with soil and groundwater contamination was smaller than the Lily Tulip property and required extensive remedial work, including ongoing groundwater monitoring. The developers entered into a redevelopment agreement with the N.J. Commerce and Economic Growth Commission to recoup up to 75 percent of the cleanup costs. In 2000 it opened as a big box retail shopping center, winning a Phoenix Award.

Least developable are Tier III sites, which tend to be smaller properties in urban areas, often in or near residential neighborhoods, where the cleanup costs far exceed the value of the land after remediation. The market model of redevelopment fails these sites, and without public intervention and subsidy, they have no redevelopment prospects. The Magic Marker site in Trenton is a typical Tier III brownfield. It is relatively small (7.5 acres) and located in a

---

5. For a discussion of the political processes that led to the particular configuration of the BCSRA, which favors the needs of suburbs over those of cities and relaxes environmental standards to attract business interests, see Gardner (2001, 69–119).

densely populated, low-income residential neighborhood across from an elementary school. The property includes an industrial building previously used for lead acid battery manufacturing, the source of much of the contamination and continuing malodor. Although the first cleanup of the site occurred in 1997 as a USEPA Emergency Removal Action, it is still not fully remediated, and there is no private developer interest in the property, which the city owns through foreclosure. Published reports—official bulletins, newspaper stories and academic articles—tend to showcase Tier I site success stories, but Tier III sites are more abundant, particularly in major cities.

This highlights a shortcoming of a market-driven strategy: the municipalities that most desperately need redevelopment are the ones that are least likely to attract available investment. New Jersey's old industrial cities are at a huge redevelopment disadvantage compared to suburbs and edge cities. Virtually all the land available for development in urban centers is contaminated, while the New Jersey suburbs still have greenfields, which are more appealing to developers because site preparation is considerably less expensive and less complicated. Further, urban brownfield sites are often smaller and almost always less accessible to commercial traffic than suburban brownfield sites. Cities also have higher property tax rates than suburban towns.

One way of approaching brownfields might be to prioritize sites to clean based on such factors as health and environmental risk or neighborhood blight. But New Jersey's market-driven program results in the cleanup of sites with the most profit potential, which are the Tier I sites, the low-hanging fruit. This system reinforces spatial inequality, both between and within cities, by neglecting the neediest cases. Most of the 779 brownfields in Camden, Trenton, Paterson and even Newark are Tier III sites, because of both the level of contamination and the location.[6]

Government intervention is necessary to compensate for market failures at Tier III sites. Cities wanting to take advantage of the incentives offered by New Jersey's brownfield program have had to operate on their own initiative. Under the terms of the BCSRA, municipalities may apply for Hazardous Discharge Site Remediation Fund (HDSRF) grants to begin the remedial process by conducting preliminary assessments and site investigations (PA/SIs) and in some cases remedial investigations (RIs). Securing these funds is the first step toward overcoming market obstacles and building a redevelopment regime by fostering community organizations and durable cross-sector networks. Even with a growth machine in place, this process is a complex, multifaceted, long-term

---

6. Research has shown that the municipalities in New Jersey with the most severe brownfield problems, the most Superfund sites and the poorest populations also have the lowest proportion of white residents (Greenberg and Cidon 1997; Greenberg et al. 2000). Given such conditions, it might be argued that a market-based policy amounts to environmental discrimination, based not on locating toxic facilities in poor and minority neighborhoods, but rather on failing to clean them up. The fact that the BCSRA was not designed explicitly to help the state's cities may be an example of what Bobo and Smith call "laissez-faire racism," which they define as "a situation in which overt forms of racism have receded, but institutionalized disadvantages and inequalities continue to be condoned under a free market ideology" (Bobo and Smith 1998, 1).

and expensive enterprise requiring dedicated policy entrepreneurs to maintain momentum through the inevitable hurdles along the way and to coordinate the efforts of multiple public and private actors. There are many opportunities for the process to break down. Shepherding brownfield remediation and redevelopment projects from PA/SI to fruition requires a nonmaterial resource that many distressed cities have in short supply—local capacity.

Local Capacity and Programmatic Efficacy

Local capacity is a function of the presence of one or more varieties of capital directed toward fostering public policy initiatives. Social capital contributes to local capacity indirectly. Putnam found that dense social networks lead to a high degree of civic participation and strong democratic processes, but as Heffron notes, the "energies locked up in social capital are not always accessible or cast in a form that makes them useful to policymakers" (2000, 255). However, by creating a culture of trust and association, social capital fosters community economic development through "aggregat[ing] and leverag[ing] other development assets" (Gittell and Thompson 2001, 133). A more direct influence on local capacity is political capital: interpersonal bonds acquired through participation in voluntary organizations that engage in political activity, including mobilizing around issues, contacting local officials and voting (Fuchs, Minnite and Shapiro 1999; Fuchs, Shapiro and Minnite 2001). Political capital affects a "community's ability to negotiate, set the terms of that negotiation, define what the neighborhood will look like, and control resources" (Turner 1999, 16). Fuchs and her collaborators find that political capital can be acquired apart from social capital, and social capital in the community can be used to create political capital (Fuchs, Shapiro and Minnite 2001).

Whereas social capital and political capital are resources attached to individuals and communities, civic capacity is a resource used by local regimes. Civic capacity is a product of civil society, the range of institutions outside of government that play a role in public life. These include nonprofit organizations, community associations and religious institutions. Civic capacity represents "intentional effort," not simply happenstance, the "conscious creation of actors seeking to establish a context in which extraordinary problem solving can occur" (Stone 2001, 156).

If civic capacity is a measure of the quality of local, politically oriented voluntary association, governing or administrative capacity is a measure of the quality of operations within the public sector. Governing capacity is the ability of the local administration to govern: to carry out the public good, to address problems, to apply for grants, to obtain assistance and to produce results.

Each of these forms of local capacity plays a vital role in ensuring that local governance meets the challenges of devolutionary policies. Social and political capital foster the public-private partnerships critical to urban development (Bogart 2003). Stone found that in cities with low levels of civic capacity, concerns remained diffuse and scattered and never materialized into concerted action for community goals; whereas in cities with relatively high levels of civic capacity, actors were able to mobilize to address community problems.

Local capacity facilitates the identification of problem spaces, coordination of shared goals and mobilization of resources (Stone et al. 2001). It is essential for the success of devolutionary programs. The delegation of environmental responsibilities to municipal governments does not produce results unless the city has the requisite local capacity to generate the material and human resources necessary for program initiation, implementation, management and maintenance. Although local capacity alone cannot convert a Tier III brownfield site into a Tier I site, it can compensate significantly for the absence of the market incentives on which a program such as the BCSRA depends.

Local Capacity and Brownfield Redevelopment

The effect of local capacity may be seen in the variation among New Jersey's distressed cities with regard to their progress in implementing the brownfield program. Demographically, all have concentrated poverty and a sizable proportion of low-income minority populations. Environmentally, all suffer from degraded environments: poor air quality, polluted waters, blighted landscapes and abundant brownfield sites. Newark is undergoing an economic upswing, but the other three are effectively no-market cities.

City leaders in Camden, Trenton and Paterson, therefore, must rely on sources of support other than private capital for brownfield remediation. There is a panoply of state and federal programs offering assistance to local governments and room for local entrepreneurship with regard to initiating public projects. But attaining local aid and promoting public works depend on the expertise, efficiency and motivation to apply for grants and other programs. Thus, the standard socioeconomic indicators are less crucial for a successful brownfield program than less quantifiable factors such as the citizens' proclivity to organize, the city's ability to mobilize outside resources, the involvement of the state, federal and business sectors, and the quality of mayoral leadership.

Table 7.2 presents data on brownfield activity in the four case-study cities. The first column lists the number of contaminated sites documented by the New Jersey Department of Environmental Protection (DEP), which is widely considered an undercount. Some of these sites are still in use (i.e., factories with contaminated soil) and, therefore, are not classified as brownfields, which refers only to abandoned or unused contaminated land. The second column aggregates the total value of grants received by each city under the HDSRF since 1992 for PA/SIs of the sites enumerated in the third column.[7] These two columns relating to the HDSRF are indicative of the effort made by each city to at least initiate

---

7. The brownfield program enacted by the BCSRA in 1998 expanded on earlier legislative initiatives, including the Industrial Sites Recovery Act of 1992, which established the HDSRF grants. For a history of site remediation legislation in New Jersey before the BCSRA, see Gardner (2001, 42–68).

Table 7.2   Contaminated Sites, Municipal Brownfield Grant Recipients and Redeveloped Sites

	Contaminated Sites	Total HDSR Funds Received ($)[a]	Sites Receiving HDSR Funds[a]	Sites Redeveloped by City (approx.)[b]	Redevelopment Agreements[c]
Camden	104	4,122,910	42	5	1
Newark	411	2,072,961	29	4	1
Trenton	97	1,666,011	24	16	1
Paterson	167	469,042	4	0	1

Sources: Known Contaminated Site List (New Jersey Department of Environmental Protection); N.J. Economic Development Authority; N.J. Commerce and Economic Growth Commission

a. Since creation of Hazardous Discharge Site Remediation Fund in 1992

b. Since Brownfield and Contaminated Site Remediation Act passed in 1998

c. Public-private redevelopment partnerships with N.J. Commerce and Economic Growth Commission

the remedial process. The next two columns indicate their success, listing the approximate number of redeveloped sites completed with public funds,[8] and the number of sites for which the cities have negotiated redevelopment agreements (RAs) with private investors—one in each municipality.[9]

The variation among the cities is not due to their comparative wealth. According to the Municipal Distress Index (1997), Paterson is the most robust of the four, yet it has made the least amount of progress. Trenton, the second worst-off city in New Jersey, has been remarkably successful in promoting brownfield remediation. And Camden, by far the direst socioeconomically of the four, has been the most active among the case study cities in applying for HDSRF grants, though not in carrying projects to fruition. It is also not due to need; there is no correlation between the number of brownfield sites in a city and the amount of grant funding received through the HDSRF program. Some wealthy suburban towns surrounding central cities have fewer brownfield sites, but receive a disproportionate amount of funding, such as Lawrence, a suburb of Trenton, and Gloucester, a suburb near Camden. The allocation of funding is not consonant with need, but with level of municipal organization. The variability in policy mobilization is a result of differing amounts of local capacity in these cities.

Newark

Brownfield redevelopment has thrived in Newark because it is governed by an energetic growth machine comprised of a land-hungry private sector and an accommodating municipal government. Newark has an estimated 700 acres of

---

8. The number of redeveloped sites is approximate because no one at either the municipal level or the state level tracks this activity. The figures were tallied after conversations with officials in each city and with officers at the New Jersey Economic Development Authority and the New Jersey Commerce and Economic Growth Commission.

9. Brownfield RAs executed in the case-study cities are Fairfield Inn and Suites, Newark Airport; Trenton Marriot Hotel and Conference Center; Camden Baseball Stadium; and a Home Depot in Paterson.

contaminated land, including 300 acres of abandoned industrial sites and thousands of small residential sites interspersed among commercial and industrial areas. Newark is enjoying a renaissance, and the real estate market is undergoing an unprecedented boom. There is a huge demand for industrial property in Newark—the city has requests for land every day, particularly around the port, the airport and the Central Business District. In some areas, industrial property is selling for up to $500,000 an acre for container storage along major thoroughfares or townhouse development in the Ironbound, double the value of 10 years ago (Jack Kennedy interview). Residential real estate values have also increased as former factories in the Ironbound district are being privately redeveloped as housing; home ownership is at a high of 24 percent (Ellerbusch 2000, 4). One example of success is the former Zipper Factory, once four acres of blight and now a development of 40 new houses. The market is so strong that the city has not had to take a proactive role in fostering site remediation and redevelopment. Newark has received grants for PA/SIs at 29 sites; many of these sites have been taken up by private investment. The city itself has redeveloped four brownfield sites since the state program began in 1998,[10] and has at least a dozen more brownfield sites in the remedial process and at least 15 more scheduled for remediation.

The shape of this progress has not always satisfied community activists. Brownfield activity has been developer driven, so it is the most profitable sites (Tier I) that are being remediated. Tier III brownfields, the small sites in residential neighborhoods that pose the greatest potential health risk and present the greatest opportunity to improve quality of life in the community, are not being addressed. This has exacerbated the dual-city phenomenon in Newark, where the poor, blighted neighborhoods are increasingly isolated from the Central Business District. Civic activists complain, moreover, that unplanned development is causing overcrowding and traffic congestion and is stressing services, and fear that brownfield sites are not being decontaminated at a level to render them safe for housing.[11] Lack of planning and vision has resulted in a hodge-podge city. Since there is no comprehensive framework, development happens project by project. According to George Sternlieb, the former director of the Center for Urban Policy Research at Rutgers University, the zoning motto in Newark has been: "Take whatever you can get, and whatever they want, give 'em and pray that they're legitimate and they're going to build something" (Drucker 1998).

---

10. This number does not include the New Jersey Performing Arts Center, a $180 million, state-financed project that began and was completed before the passage of the BCSRA.

11. Since most of Newark is built on contaminated historic fill, the city has pursued many projects that may be cleaned to low environmental standards. When asked to describe the city's vision for brownfields, Newark's city engineer said without a hint of sarcasm, "we've had lots of success locating billboards and container storage on brownfield sites along the highway" (Lazarus interview). As Steven Kehayes, state brownfield coordinator for Newark, explains, "these uses are perfect for city-owned sites, because they don't need to remediate. They can just cap [them with asphalt] and make money off them" (Kehayes interview).

Newark has a history of poor relations with community organizations, and as a result they have not been incorporated into the policy process. "The city is catering to developers who are coming in and is largely ignoring community-based organizations," complained Ray Ocasio, director of La Casa de Don Pedro, a neighborhood development organization in the West Ward. Thanks to Newark's history of neglect and corruption, a culture of mistrust pervades City Hall. One official I interviewed would not speak with me from his office phone because he feared it was tapped. The Newark Economic Development Commission, long reputed to be a center of graft and machine-style politics, was abolished by the municipal council in 2002. Tensions between public leaders and civic organizations have occasionally given rise to legal battles. A grassroots group in the Ironbound neighborhood, SPARK, went to court to compel the city to rehabilitate Riverbank Park into a usable recreational area for the neighborhood instead of building a baseball stadium. Public officials expressed disdain for civic involvement. As one engineer remarked:

> I don't want community input in redevelopment. They are a pain. They never want anything that may be a public necessity. Right now we're ripping up a community garden for a Sanitation parking lot, and the community is putting up a huge fight. But, I said, "you don't have a lease, so you're trespassing." (Butler interview 1999)

Thus, although Newark has a thriving, market-driven brownfield program, its low level of civic capacity has led to controversy and discontent. Alan Mallach, the former director of Housing and Community Development for Trenton, contrasted his city with Newark:

> Newark has urban assets that make Trenton look pathetic. It has more potential for redevelopment than any other small city in the U.S. A mind-boggling number of sites to redevelop and they don't have a problem getting investment. There's a pool of substantial corporations with some real money. But Newark has no vision. Outside of the downtown, there is poverty and squalor that make the worst thing in Trenton look benign. What is the city doing about that? They will have problems unless they dramatically rethink their modus operandi and figure out how to build a healthier city. There's hardly a distressed neighborhood in Trenton where we don't have some kind of strategy going. (Mallach interview 1999)

Trenton

Trenton is the most visionary of the four cities in the study. Its goal, articulated by Mayor Arnold Palmer, is to "once again become a working, healthy city" (Palmer 1998, 2). And, despite the lack of private-sector engagement in the city, it has made great strides toward achieving its goal. As the state capital, it is less dependent on the private sector than other cities and has proven to be highly capable of making the best of its circumstances. The governing capacity, for a city so beleaguered by socioeconomic disadvantages, is astoundingly high. Trenton "has always been a progressive city led by forward-looking people" (Cumbler 1989, 189). The city's political culture reflects decades of a civic-minded government that has seized every opportunity to improve the quality of life for residents. Benevolent city officials and city planners believe they know what is best for the neighborhoods—Trenton's vision and master plan is more comprehensive and nuanced than those of the other cities—and they have been tremendously successful at applying for state and federal grants and have a good institutional capacity for implementing programs. There are also a few strong civic associations, most notably Isles, a community development association adept at securing grants, publicizing their work and cultivating a statewide if not national reputation. The bureaucracy relies heavily on Isles to fulfill its mandate to involve the community, and the group is locally regarded as akin to an arm of city government.

Although there is strong governing and civic capacity in Trenton, the broader distribution of social capital is relatively low. Side effects of Trenton's expansive bureaucratic culture are a paternalistic political culture and an apathetic citizenry. According to the former director of Housing and Development, "there is a historical civility about political discourse in Trenton. There's a citywide codependency between the citizens and the city government. People feel that Mama Trenton will solve their problems, so individual initiative and activism are discouraged" (Mallach interview 1999).[12] Nevertheless, the city, working in conjunction with Isles, has sought to respond to the needs of its citizens. Rather than blindly pursuing commercial development, the city "looks at sites in their neighborhood context and aims to redevelop according to neighborhood needs" (Christina interview 1998). Of all the case-study cities, Trenton is the most successful at involving and working with the community in brownfields redevelopment. And despite relative apathy among residents, there is a keen sense of civic identity demonstrated by the fact that the city has three local newspapers; neither Camden nor Paterson has one.

The city's high local capacity has helped it to overcome market obstacles to redeveloping its brownfields. Trenton has more than 300 acres of potential brownfield sites and has had more redevelopment success than any city in the state. Since the brownfield act was passed, Trenton has addressed 24 sites and finished redevelopment at approximately 16. The city was able to do this despite its budgetary woes and lack of private interest by enlisting the support of the state and federal public sector, most particularly the U.S. EPA, which selected Trenton several times for its Brownfields Pilot Program and featured Trenton as a Brownfield Showcase city. EPA's current brownfield work plan for Trenton includes 61 sites. Civic associations have also been crucial. The successful community involvement at the Magic Marker brownfield site is largely attributed to Isles, whose strong ties with city government ensured that officials were receptive to a neighborhood organization, the Northwest Community Improvement Association (NCIA). Isles also sent members of NCIA to a five-month training seminar on hazardous waste and site remediation and provided technical and organizing assistance. Isles was a "godfather group to the community," according

---

12. Mallach observes that most of the city's activists are imports, including the founders of Isles, who started the group while attending graduate school at Princeton University in the 1960s.

to Mallach.[13] As a result of the local capacity built through cross-sector partnerships, a dedicated municipal administration, and a few strong civic associations, Trenton has been awarded three Phoenix Awards.

Camden

Camden's relative success in sponsoring brownfield redevelopment is due almost entirely to its civic capacity. The city's administrative capacity has long been dysfunctional, and the business sector is practically nonexistent. But Camden's community organizations, many of which are well-organized and effective, have picked up the slack and have provided continuity and momentum around issues throughout the quickly changing and often erratic mayoral regimes.

Corruption runs deep in Camden's political culture and it has been well documented for 200 years. A New Jersey state attorney in the 1800s described local officials as "the worst of Public Robbers," and a Philadelphia *Daily News* article described Camden as "a pest hole of political corruption . . . the sink into which all that is vile in politics flows" (Kirp et al. 1995, 19). According to some analysts, these words still describe Camden today. The city's three most recent mayors have upheld this tradition of corruption by ending their terms in court instead of in city hall. Milton Milan was elected in 1997 and was convicted in 2001 on 14 corruption charges; he was sentenced to seven years and three months in federal prison (Peterson 2000, 4). Milan followed Arnold Webster, who had been a school superintendent before being elected to office. He was deposed when he was convicted of accepting $20,000 in superintendent salary while serving as mayor. Webster's predecessor was Angelo Errichetti, who was sentenced to six years in prison in 1981 for accepting bribes in the Abscam corruption sting operation. After the fall of Milan, the city government was in a state of collapse and functionally bankrupt, and many residents, tired of living in intolerable conditions, called for state intervention (Record 2000). In an unprecedented move, the state of New Jersey took control of Camden city government in 2002 and installed a chief operating officer to assume many of the duties of the mayor.

Corruption cannot be blamed on individual politicians; it is endemic to the city's political culture. "We must recognize that Camden's difficulties run much deeper than a few corrupt leaders," said Rev. Heyward Wiggins, president of Camden Churches Organized for People. "Any serious attempt to set Camden on the road to recovery must address the underlying cause of Camden's condition—and that is lack of resources" (Peterson 2001, B2). A 1995 state audit of Camden found that due to "waste, incompetence and maybe worse," one in every five tax dollars is misspent. The audit recommended the state to "continue to hold that hammer over [the mayor's] head" (Philadelphia Inquirer 1995). In the following year, another audit, this one by the Department of the Treasury, described the deep-seated malaise that afflicted city government in Camden. There is widespread perception that political influence plays a large role in

---

13. Despite the community participation around the Magic Marker site, it still has not been remediated for lack of public funds and private interest.

the decisions made by city employees, that jobs are filled through nepotism or political reasons not based on merit or qualifications, and that there are many inexperienced and unqualified employees in many departments (N.J. Department of Treasury 1996).[14]

A strong community-based sector organized around planning and redevelopment has filled the void left by Camden's official administrators. Almost every Camden neighborhood is organized, and most organizations are longstanding and well-established groups that are well funded and staffed by committed professionals. Independently funded, the civic sector in Camden has more autonomy and expertise than the municipal government, functioning as "governing nonprofits" (Hula, Jackson and Orr 1997, 459). The city has generally played a reactive role to the community's proactive role. Community development organizations were the driving force behind the first two brownfield projects in Camden, the Knox Gelatin site in North Camden and the ABC Barrel site in Cooper Grant. "You have to work outside of the system to get anything accomplished here," said Frank Fulbrook, president of the Cooper Grant Neighborhood Association (Fulbrook interview 1999). His organization has helped rehabilitate brownstones in the Cooper Grant neighborhood, one of the most stable middle-class communities in the city. But relations between community activists and city administrators are seldom harmonious. Historically, municipal leaders have resented challenges to their sovereignty and have been reluctant to cooperate with community-sponsored initiatives.[15]

Camden has nearly 4,000 abandoned lots, an unknown percentage of which contain toxins that pose threats to human health. Despite its general level of disorganization, the city government has been masterful at brownfield grantsmanship, applying for and receiving many more HDSRF grants for site assessment and investigation than the other cities (see Table 7.2). It has been less successful at finding private capital to complete the work of remediation. In the words of one EPA staffer on location there, "Do we have developers interested in contaminated sites here? No way. We couldn't give shovel-ready sites away"

14. Not every city employee is incompetent. Several have diligently gone about their work during the chaos of changing mayoral regimes. Camden's chief planner, Charles Lyons, has his own method of accomplishing things in Camden: "I work as much as I can on my own and with the community. It helps that my office isn't in City Hall. If I can create enough momentum from below using the community as a force, and from above working with state and federal agencies, by the time the project gets to City Hall, I hope there will be enough momentum that the city won't screw it up" (Lyons interview 1999).

15. There are indications that under Mayor Gwendolyn Faison, and the COO, Randy Primus, city government will be more open to working with community organizations and relations will be less contentious than in the past. The recently completed master plan is one indication that the new regime intends to incorporate the community. Camden's extensive neighborhood-based master planning project was funded by a grant from the Annie E. Casey Foundation. The most recent 20 HDSRF grants to the city resulted from the neighborhood redevelopment plans organized by the City Division of Planning, which conducted more than 70 neighborhood charrettes as part of the master plan process. Waterfront South, an especially well-organized community, initiated the grant application process for all 12 brownfield sites in the neighborhood. The master plan was adopted in summer 2002 (Smith and Thompson 2001).

(Devine interview 1999). Regardless, Camden has succeeded in redeveloping five brownfield sites, and several more are in various stages of the process.

Public perception of Camden is largely negative, and some state and federal officials claim that the disorganization and mismanagement caused Camden to squander the state and federal funds it received for brownfield planning. "The city doesn't have the capacity to manage all these grants," asserts an EPA engineer working in Camden. "It's an administrative nightmare. Each one is a hassle—endless paperwork" (Devine interview 1999). One state official accused Camden of "raping the brownfield fund" by applying for grants without having a redevelopment plan in place (O'Donnell interview 1999). Although Camden may be faulted for applying for more grants than it was able to manage and for failing to have a redevelopment plan in place, one may yet recognize the virtue of a badly disadvantaged city trying to reverse its situation. In doing so, public administrators were following the lead of its civic institutions. What success the city has had in addressing its brownfields has been due solely to its civic capacity.

Paterson

Paterson's no-growth machine has neither strong civic capacity nor strong governing capacity. City government has alienated and marginalized community organizations, has a conflictual relationship with the economic development corporation, and is wracked by conflict between city hall and the city council. Paterson has never had a responsive city government. Its administration has a history of poor relations with its communities. Historically, the city did not allow for "dissent, opposition or choice" (Norwood 1974, 53), and the community leaders have always been alienated, weak and marginal to city politics. Today, no community organizations involved with planning or redevelopment has a high profile or a working relationship with city hall. The culture of mistrust has not fostered community groups: "Nobody sees nothing, nobody helps nobody, nobody trusts nobody" (Norwood 1974, 68).

Interviews with residents and city officials indicate that this anomic culture persists today (Gardner 2001, 163–187; Schulgasser 2000). Paterson is marked by a general absence of community organizations and chronic lack of community participation. According to one local activist, residents are afraid to organize, and community organization appears to be futile. "Community groups can't do anything here . . . the city runs on patronage and strong-arm tactics. There's no forum for community-based organizations" (Soo interview 2000). One respondent, who was opposing a city-led development project, feared for his life and charged the police with using intimidation tactics. After five years of misrule, Mayor Martin Barnes was indicted in 2002 on 40 counts of corruption. Deep rifts between city hall and the city council preclude any proactive initiatives coming out of city government; Paterson cannot even develop consensus around a vision, let alone move it forward (Schulgasser 2002b).

Such factionalism has hindered Paterson's ability to accomplish the cross-sector coordination involved with brownfield remediation and redevelopment.

It is not surprising that of the four cities, Paterson has the least successful brownfield program. There are about 2,000 vacant lots in Paterson, but most are small and scattered throughout the city, many in residential neighborhoods. The typical site is "about a quarter of a block large and in a residential neighborhood" (Dopirak interview 1999); some 167 are known to be contaminated, and 75 of these have been classified as brownfields.

Despite the abundance of brownfields and the risk to public health, the city has secured only four HDSRF grants for site investigation and has not succeeded in redeveloping any brownfield sites to date, although there is one development planned for a brownfield site—a redevelopment agreement with the Commerce and Economic Growth Commission—for a Home Depot. Lacking a strong real estate market like sections of Newark, or an effective governing capacity like Trenton, or organized community groups like Camden, Paterson's brownfield program has floundered.

Conclusion

The variable progress of New Jersey's brownfield program in these four cities reveals the importance of local capacity for devolutionary initiatives. Market conditions obviously are vital for the success of redevelopment efforts, but as the case of Newark shows, they are not enough. Without community involvement, Newark's growth economy has made for fractious relations between the public and civic sectors, and exacerbated inequalities within a city deeply segregated by race and wealth. In contrast, Trenton and Camden have had remarkable success pursuing development, despite the absence of private-sector interest, thanks to high levels of civic capacity in one and governing capacity in the other. Finally, Paterson, lacking the assets of a strong private, public or civic sector, has been unable to take advantage of the opportunities offered by the BCSRA.

This research demonstrates that successful local brownfield initiatives are not simply the result of the real estate value of sites as traditional economic analyses maintain, but can be explained by the amount of civic capacity in each city that is brought to bear on the brownfield problem. Cities with high local capacity can overcome market determinism to produce results. Market value cannot be discounted in brownfield analysis, but in the case of sites with little, zero or negative property value, civic capacity is the more salient variable. Indeed, even in best-case scenarios, such as Newark's Ironbound district, where the private market addresses brownfield sites, there is just as much need for civic participation and public leadership to shape development as there is in cities where there is no private interest.

Local capacity is a resource that must be fostered; it cannot be taken for granted. It is particularly scarce in disadvantaged cities; as Chupp notes, "poor, distressed neighborhoods often lack the political capital necessary for their transformation" (1999, 49), and inequality is an important corollary of market-based and locally administered programs (Miller 1981). Local capacity does not come automatically with the delegation of authority. As Doherty and Stone

(1999) observe, there are limits to the assumption that devolution will promote community participation.

For devolution to work well and equitably from the state to the local level, capacity must be devolved along with the responsibilities. Programmatic initiatives should be developed to grow local capacity by helping neighborhood organizations become actively involved in redevelopment planning, and by nurturing the development of local leaders. The U.S. Department of Housing and Urban Development's Empowerment Zone program offers a successful model (U.S. GAO 1996). It devolves capacity to cities to facilitate development of initiatives at the local level by requiring that plans be developed in the neighborhoods. Civil society might be strengthened by encouraging partnerships between voluntary institutions and public agencies (Kingsley and Gibson 1999). Finally, substantial assistance and oversight from higher levels of government is necessary to foster administrative capacity in underresourced cities.

Of course, strengthening local capacity alone will not solve the problems that distressed cities confront when faced with devolutionary policies. Communities cannot redevelop brownfields simply on the strength of their civic capacity. No amount of human capital will ensure equity across localities, or give Camden the real estate appeal of Manhattan. To fully redress environmental problems, devolutionary policies will have to offer a set of material resources to offset the new responsibilities foisted on poor communities and create a set of strong incentives to guide the hand of the market; local capacity is not a dependable policy tool and should not replace fair and carefully crafted policies. But local capacity is a crucial element in determining success, and every devolutionary initiative should factor in tools to foster it.

References

Ackerman, Bruce and Richard B. Stewart. 1988. Reforming environmental law: The case for market incentives. *Columbia Journal of Environmental Law* 13(2):171–199.

Anderson, Terry L. and Peter J. Hill. 1997. Environmental federalism: Thinking smaller. In *Environmental Federalism*, Terry L. Anderson and Peter J. Hill, eds., xi–xix. Lanham, MD: Rowman and Littlefield Publishers.

Becker, Gary. 1976. *The economic approach to human behavior*. Chicago: University of Chicago Press.

Bobo, Lawrence D. and Ryan A. Smith. 1998. From Jim Crow racism to laissez-faire racism: The transformation of racial attitudes. In *Beyond pluralism: The conception of groups and group identities in America*, Wendy F. Katkin, Ned Landsman and Andrew Tyree, eds., 182–220. Urbana: University of Illinois Press.

Bogart, William T. 2003. Civic infrastructure and the financing of community development. Discussion paper. The Brookings Institution Center on Urban and Metropolitan Policy, Washington, DC.

Burchell, Robert. 1984. *The new reality of municipal finance: The rise and fall of the intergovernmental city*. New Brunswick, NJ: Rutgers University Center for Urban Policy Research.

Butler, Henry N. and Jonathan R. Macey. 1996. *Using federalism to improve environmental policy*. Washington, DC: AEI Press.

Ceplo, Karol and Bruce Yandle. 1997. Western states and environmental federalism: An examination of institutional viability. In *Environmental federalism*, Terry L. Anderson and Peter J. Hill, eds., 225–258. Lanham, MD: Rowman and Littlefield Publishers.

Chupp, Mark. 1999. Investing in people through place: The role of social capital in transforming neighborhoods. Baltimore: Annie E. Casey Foundation, Neighborhood Transformation and Family Development Partnership.

Cimitile, Carole, Victoria Kennedy, Harry Lambright, Rosemary O'Leary and Paul Weiland. 1997. Balancing risk and finance: The challenge of implementing unfunded environmental mandates. *Public Administration Review* 57 (Jan./Feb.): 63–74.

Commoner, Barry. 1990. *Making peace with the planet*. New York: Pantheon.

Crews, Clyde Wayne. 1996. *Ten thousand commandments: A policy maker's snapshot of the federal regulatory state*. Washington, DC: Competitive Enterprise Institute.

Cumbler, John T. 1989. *A social history of economic decline: Business, politics and work in Trenton*. New Brunswick, NJ: Rutgers University Press.

Donahue, John. 1997. *Disunited states*. New York: Basic Books.

Drucker, Jesse. 1998. Newark awaits comprehensive zoning blueprint; New plan will dictate future development. *Newark Star-Ledger*, October 4, 36.

Ellerbusch, Fred. 2000. *Residential risks of brownfields redevelopment: A case study of the Ironbound neighborhood*. Newark: NJIT, UMDNJ School of Public Health, Ironbound Community Corporation.

Foster, Kathryn A. 2000. Regional capital. In *Urban-suburban interdependencies*, Rosalind Greenstein and Wim Wiewel, eds., 83–118. Cambridge, MA: Lincoln Institute of Land Policy.

Fuchs, Esther R., Lorraine Minnite and Robert Y. Shapiro. 1999. Political capital and political participation. Paper presented at the meeting of the Midwest Political Science Association, Chicago, April 15–17.

Fuchs, Esther R., Robert Y. Shapiro and Lorraine C. Minnite. 2001. Social capital, political participation, and the urban community. In *Social capital and poor communities*, Susan Saegert, J. Philip Thompson and Mark R. Warren, eds., 290–324. New York: Russell Sage Foundation.

Garbarine, Rachelle. 1999. First accord seen near on cleanup reimbursement. *New York Times*, March 21, sec. 11, p. 9.

Gardner, Sarah S. 2001. *Green visions for brownfields: The politics of site remediation and redevelopment in four New Jersey cities*. Ph.D. diss., Department of Political Science, City University of New York Graduate School and University Center, New York, NY.

Gittell, Ross and J. Philip Thompson. 2001. Making social capital work: Social capital and community economic development. In *Social capital and poor communities*, Susan Saegert, J. Philip Thompson and Mark R. Warren, eds., 290–324. New York: Russell Sage Foundation.

Greenberg, Michael and Michal Cidon. 1997. Broadening the definition of environmental equity: A framework for states and local governments. *Population Research and Policy Review* 16: 397–413.

Greenberg, Michael, Karen Lowrie, Laura Solitare and Latoya Duncan. 2000. Brownfields, TOADS, and the struggle for neighborhood redevelopment. *Urban Affairs Review* 35(5): 717–733.

Heffron, John M. 2000. Beyond community and society: The externalities of social capital building. In *Social capital as a policy resource*, John D. Montgomery and Alex Inkeles, eds., 251–268. Boston: Kluwer Academic Publishers.

Hester, Tom. 1999. State bails out Camden—With strings attached. *Newark Star-Ledger*, July 23, B1.

Hula, R., C. Jackson and M. Orr. 1997. Urban politics, governing nonprofits, and community revitalization. *Urban Affairs Review* 32(4):459–489.

John, DeWitt. 1994. *Civic environmentalism*. Washington, DC: Congressional Quarterly Press.

Kanter, Sarah. 2000. HUD launches lead paint fight. *North Jersey Herald News*, August 26, A1.

Kilgore, Ed and Kathleen Sylvester. 1995. *Blocking devolution: Why block grants are the wrong approach to devolution and three progressive alternatives*. Washington, DC: Progressive Policy Institute.

Kincaid, John. 1999. De facto devolution and urban defunding: The priority of persons over places. *Journal of Urban Affairs* 21(2):135–167.

Kingsley, G. Thomas and James O. Gibson. 1999. Civil society, the public sector, and poor communities. *The Urban Institute*, monograph. http://www.urban.org/url.cfm?ID=307053.

Kirp, David L., John P. Dwyer and Larry A. Rosenthal. 1995. *Our town: Race, housing and the soul of suburbia*. New Brunswick, NJ: Rutgers University Press.

Logan, J. and H. Molotch. 1987. *Urban fortunes: The political economy of place*. Berkeley: University of California Press.

Lund, Hertha L. 1995. Property rights legislation in the states: A review. PERC Policy Series, PS-1. Bozeman, MT: Political Economy Research Center.

Massey, Douglas S. and Nancy A. Denton. 1993. American apartheid: Segregation and the making of the underclass. Cambridge, MA: Harvard University Press.

Miller, Gary. 1981. *Cities by contract: The politics of municipal incorporation*. Cambridge, MA: MIT Press.

Mollenkopf, John H. 1992. *A phoenix in the ashes: The rise and fall of the Koch coalition in New York City politics*. Princeton: Princeton University Press.

Muller, Thomas and Michael Fix. 1980. The impact of selected federal actions on municipal outlays. In *Government regulation: Achieving social and economic balance*. Vol. 5 of Special Study on Economic Change, U.S. Congress Joint Economic Committee. Washington, DC: Government Printing Office.

New Jersey. 2001. *City of Camden multi-year recovery plan*. Trenton: Department of Community Affairs.

New Jersey Department of Treasury. 1996. *Local government budget review: City of Camden*. Office of Local Government Budget Review. Trenton: New Jersey Department of the Treasury.

New Jersey State Senate. 1997. Senate committee substitute for Senate no. 39, Senate Environmental Committee, New Jersey State Legislature, Trenton. June 5.

New York Times. 2002. Greening the Garden State. Editorial. *New York Times*, November 16, A16.

Norwood, Christopher. 1974. *About Paterson: The making and unmaking of an American city*. New York: E.P. Dutton and Co.

O'Connor, Alice. 1999. Swimming against the tide: A brief history of federal policy in poor communities. In *Urban problems and community development*, Ronald F. Ferguson and William T. Dickens, eds., 77–138. Washington, DC: Brookings Institution Press.

Orfield, Myron and Thomas Luce. 2003. *New Jersey metropatterns: A regional agenda for community and stability in New Jersey*. New Jersey Regional Coalition. http://www.regionequity.org.

Palmer, Douglas. 1998. *City of Trenton land use plan (draft)*. Trenton: Department of Housing and Development.

Paterson Economic Development Corporation (PEDC). 1998. City of Paterson brownfields work plan. Paterson: PEDC.

Perry, David C. 1987. The politics of dependency in deindustrialized America: The case of Buffalo, NY. In *The capitalist city*, Michael Peter Smith and Joe R. Feagan, eds., 113–137. New York: Basic Blackwell.

Peterson, Iver. 2000. Mayor ousted in Camden; Finance chief is appointed. *New York Times*, December 23, B4.

———. 2001. Camden church groups seek far broader state aid for city. *New York Times*, January 8, B2.

Philadelphia Inquirer. 1995. Mismanagement zone. *Philadelphia Inquirer*, December 15, A1.

Putnam, Robert D. 1993. *Making democracy work: Civic traditions in modern Italy*. Princeton: Princeton University Press.

———. 2000. *Bowling alone: The collapse and revival of American community*. New York: Simon and Schuster.

Rabe, Barry. 1997. Power to the states: The promise and pitfalls of decentralization. In *Environmental policy in the 1990s*, Norman J. Vig and Michael E. Kraft, eds., 31–52. Washington, DC: Congressional Quarterly Press.

Regan, Tracey. 2003. Study: Sprawl effects similar in cities, suburbs. *Trenton Times*, May 12, 1.

Ringquist, Evan J. 1993. *Environmental protection at the state level*. Armonk, NY: M.E. Sharpe.

Rusk, David. 1995. *Cities without suburbs*, 2nd ed.. Baltimore: Johns Hopkins University Press.

Schoenbrod, David. 1997. Why states, not EPA, should set pollution standards. In *Environmental federalism*, Terry L. Anderson and Peter J. Hill, eds., 259–270. Lanham, MD: Rowman and Littlefield Publishers.

Schulgasser, Daniel. 2000. Interview with Fran Blesso, Consulting Engineer, Department of Community Development, City of Paterson. Unpublished transcript.

———. 2002a. Six in a fix: Governing New Jersey's urban centers. Paper presented as the Urban Affairs Association annual meeting, Boston, March 21.

———. 2002b. Little trees in a big forest: Urban governance in Elizabeth and Paterson, New Jersey. Paper presented at the Urban Affairs Association 30th annual meeting, Boston, May 3–6.

Smith, Ralph and Carole Thompson. 2001. *A path forward for Camden*. A report commissioned by the Annie E. Casey Foundation for the City of Camden and its residents.

Stewart, Richard. 1988. Controlling environmental risks through economic incentives. *Columbia Journal of Environmental Law* 13(2):153–169.

Stone, Clarence. 1989. *Regime politics*. Lawrence: University Press of Kansas.

Stone, Clarence, Kathryn Doherty, Sheryl Jones and Timothy Ross. 1999. Schools and disadvantaged neighborhoods: The community development challenge. In *Urban problems and community development*, Ronald F. Ferguson and William T. Dickens, eds., 339–380. Washington, DC: Brookings Institute Press.

Stone, Clarence N., Jeffrey R. Henig, Bryan D. Jones and Carol Pierannunzi. 2001. *Building civic capacity: The politics of reforming urban schools*. Lawrence: University Press of Kansas.

Stroup, Richard L. 1996. Superfund: The shortcut that failed. PERC Policy Series, PS-5. Bozeman, MT: Political Economy Research Center.

Thompson, Barton H. 1997. Water federalism: Governmental competition and conflict over western waters. In *Environmental federalism*, Terry L. Anderson and Peter J. Hill, eds., 175–224. Lanham, MD: Rowman and Littlefield Publishers.

Turner, Robin S. 1999. Entrepreneurial neighborhood initiatives: Political capital in community development. *Economic Development Quarterly* 13:15–22.

U.S. Environmental Protection Agency. 1997. Brownfields pilot site fact sheet, Camden, NJ. Washington, DC: Office of Solid Waste and Emergency Response, USEPA.

———. 1998. Brownfield pilot site fact sheet, Newark, NJ. Washington, DC: Office of Solid Waste and Emergency Response, USEPA.

U.S. Environmental Protection Agency Region 2. 1997. *Brownfields quarterly community report* 1(3).

U.S. Government Accounting Office. 1996. *Community development: Status of urban empowerment zones*. Report to the chair of the Subcommittee on Human Resources and Intergovernmental Relations, Committee on Government Reform and Oversight, House of Representatives, Washington, DC.

Van Develde, Elaine. 2002. Former Lily Tulip site nearly filled, ready. *Independent* (Holmdel, NJ), June 26.

Wilson, Jason. 1997. Environmental inequity. *New Jersey Reporter* (March/April): 36–40.

Wright, Thomas K. and Ann Davlin 1998. Overcoming obstacles to brownfield and vacant land redevelopment. *Land Lines*, Newsletter of the Lincoln Institute of Land Policy (September): 1–3.

Interviews

Paul Butler, Department of Engineering, City of Newark. July 14, 1999, and September 23, 1999.

Michele Christina, Brownfield Coordinator, City of Trenton. December 5, 1998.

Alison Devine, USEPA IPA on location in Camden's Brownfield Office. July 15, 1999.

Anna Lisa Dopirak, Director, Department of Community Development, City of Paterson. March 30, 1999.

Frank Fulbrook, President, Cooper Grant Neighborhood Association. July 15, 1999.

Steven Kehayes, Brownfield Coordinator for City of Newark, N.J. Department of Environmental Protection. March 3, 1999.

Jack Kennedy, Coldwell Banker Commercial Realtor, Roseland, New Jersey. July 28, 2003.

Charles Lyons, Chief Planner, City of Camden. July 21, 1999.

Allen Mallach, Director, Office of Housing and Community Development, City of Trenton. March 5, 1999.

Jerry O'Donnell, Camden Brownfield Coordinator, New Jersey Department of Environmental Protection. July 2, 1999.

David Soo, Paterson Friends of the Great Falls. July 30, 1999, September 22, 1999, and March 23, 2000.

8 The Role of Community Development Corporations in Brownfield Redevelopment

Margaret Dewar and Sabina Deitrick

The mission of community development corporations (CDCs) is to rebuild low-income neighborhoods for the benefit of the residents. Their most significant achievement has been the production of affordable housing. They built or rehabilitated more than 60,000 units of housing per year from 1993 through 1997, with a total exceeding 550,000 units from the late 1960s through the late 1990s. CDCs have generated 30 percent of the assisted housing in the nation. They also built or renovated more than 71 million square feet of commercial and industrial space by the end of 1997 (NCCED 1995, 1999a; Gittell and Wilder 1999, 342–343; Bratt et al. 1998, 39).

The National Congress for Community Economic Development (NCCED, the trade association for CDCs) argues that CDCs should consider redeveloping brownfields, land that is contaminated or perceived as contaminated, in their communities. Their members express interest in redeveloping brownfields, NCCED reports, but have many questions about how to do so. Few organizations have undertaken such redevelopment (NCCED 1999b, 2).

Brownfields have strong effects on neighborhood redevelopment and, therefore, are important to CDCs. Because of loss of industry in cities, many CDC territories include derelict industrial structures and contaminated sites where members of the community once worked, but that now blight nearby residential areas. In addition, commercial services such as gas stations and dry cleaners left behind brownfield sites when they closed, and the derelict commercial areas also undermine housing investment. Due to the costs and legal issues involved, market-driven solutions often are not feasible for redevelopment of contaminated properties, especially in distressed neighborhoods suffering from lack of private investment. Brownfields pose both an obstacle and opportunity for redevelopment in these communities (Hise and Nelson 1999).

Although the NCCED urges CDCs to enter the field of brownfield redevelopment, such work may or may not advance CDC goals. In this chapter we assess the rationale for CDC activities and derive normative criteria for their involvement in brownfield redevelopment. Case studies and work with CDCs in Pittsburgh and Detroit provide information about the roles CDCs assume in brownfield redevelopment projects and the factors that contribute to their success. We then examine whether the work CDCs undertake—leading to redevelopment or not—is consistent with the normative rationale for CDC development activities.

The Rationale for Nonprofit Developers' Activities

A major purpose of urban CDC activity is to bring economic development to low-income areas to benefit the residents of those neighborhoods. The arguments for such activity focus on two principal rationales. First, CDCs should control economic resources to benefit the poor and to redirect economic opportunities to impoverished neighborhoods. Second, CDCs should deal with market barriers that interfere with private decision makers' investments in low-income areas; they should serve as leaders in reducing perceptions of risk and demonstrating the potential for profitable investment, thus spurring more economic development.

The first, and dominant, rationale is that CDCs should promote social change by controlling economic resources to create and demand solutions to the economic problems of low-income residents (Lenz 1988; Stoecker 1997a). At their root, CDC development activities should counter the harmful effects of capitalism and promote financial, social and physical neighborhood revitalization. This can be most effective, some argue, through community organizing and constituency building (Stoecker 1997b; Lenz 1988; Eisenberg 2000). Early CDCs established an anti-poverty agenda in urban neighborhoods, especially minority communities, largely abandoned by the private sector. Place-based nonprofits would redirect investment to help residents (Halpern 1995; Harrison 1974). These CDCs focused on broad community building and organizing initiatives, emphasizing business development and job training (Stoutland 1999; Murphy and Cunningham 2003; Harrison 1974). From the perspective of this rationale, private-market solutions will never intentionally help low-income neighborhoods and poor people. In Stoecker's words, "Community's tendency is to preserve neighborhood space as a use value for the service of community members, while capital's tendency is to convert neighborhood space into exchange values that can be speculated on for a profit" (1997b, 5). Conflict between community interests and market interests, therefore, is inevitable.

In practice, the social orientation of CDCs has diminished. In the 1970s federal anti-poverty programs were reduced and funding for community development decreased (Keating 1999). Both government and private funders preferred business-oriented organizations focused on economic development objectives over activist groups with social agendas (Eisenberg 2000). Arguments were made for CDCs to respond to funders' interests first, which "pressured CDCs to be more cautious and disciplined" (Murphy and Cunningham 2003, 39). Ultimately, community-articulated agendas and community-empowerment work became less important as CDCs concentrated more on successful economic activities (Rubin 1995; Stoecker 1997b) .

Thus, the shift in orientation of CDCs from comprehensive social, economic and physical activities toward mainly economic-centered ones meant that many organizations moved—or were pushed—into directions that may not support their original social mission (Blakely and Aparicio 1990). Indeed, critics have complained that CDCs abandoned their social mandate when they abandoned comprehensive community building in favor of housing and economic development (Stoecker 1997a and 2003; Eisenberg 2000). Nonetheless, others contend that CDCs did attempt to shift from their narrow economic focus to greater community-building efforts in the 1990s (Murphy and Cunningham 2003).

The second rationale supports an emphasis for CDCs in economic development and makes no argument for comprehensive community building through advocacy and organizing, although increasing residential control over economic resources remains important. According to a recent study, for instance, community economic development should improve socioeconomic equity "by ensuring that residents have the capacity to act as full partners guiding investment in their neighborhoods" (Brophy and Burnett 2003, 9). From this perspective, many viable but overlooked investment opportunities exist in poor neighborhoods (Porter 1997). The role of CDCs should be to improve inner cities as business locations for the private sector; if the private sector made new investments, the neighborhoods would be revitalized and the people who live in them would benefit. Since market failures interfere with decisions to invest, CDCs can and should work on overcoming the barriers to attract private investment (Brophy and Burnett 2003).

When economically viable investments do not exist in poor neighborhoods, subsidized redevelopment projects can create the potential for unsubsidized investments and demonstrate that the financial risk is not too high for the private sector to assume. A CDC can act as the bellwether and demonstrate market feasibility. For instance, if CDCs undertake affordable housing development, new residents create the potential for private investment in retail and, later, in more housing. Successful CDC projects can prove the viability of new housing investment and new retail development and lead to additional private-sector investment.

CDCs can also tackle many barriers to investment, such as land assembly for urban redevelopment. CDCs could be key actors in gaining control of land, which is often difficult. They can be important as well in providing accurate information about the strength of purchasing power for retail, the skills of available workers, and the nature of actual crime problems rather than perceived crime. Subsidies may be necessary to overcome market barriers, and CDCs can help in accessing these, thus reducing costs for a private developer. For example, low-income housing tax credits for nonprofits can benefit the for-profit housing developer that partners with the CDC, who can also receive funds and loans from nonprofit intermediaries to cover financing gaps between project costs and market appraisals. CDCs are capable of substantially reducing the cost of redevelopment, too, by doing the needed background research on property ownership and environmental status.

In reality, these two rationales for CDC activity are often inconsistent, although CDC leaders may espouse both at the same time (Rubin 1994). CDC involvement in brownfield redevelopment reflects this inconsistency. Brownfield redevelopment can improve lives of community residents by bettering their environment, employing residents, or providing affordable housing—much of which would be externalities from the point of view of a for-profit developer. On one hand, CDCs can play a leadership role in these redevelopments by creating conditions that attract later investment. On the other hand, CDCs may engage in brownfield projects that are detached from the neighborhood and community development; these do not benefit residents, although they may strengthen the CDC as an organization.

In trying to reconcile such conflicting aspirations for CDCs and their role in brownfield redevelopment, we offer criteria that CDC projects should meet in order to achieve each set of goals:

- Community economic development projects principally should benefit poor residents by offering employment and access to assets. Increased control of such economic assets should result.

- The projects should emerge out of community organizing and planning that identifies community priorities and sets goals for empowerment and increased capacity to bring positive change.

- A CDC's involvement in an economic development project should enable development that would not have occurred if left to the private sector.

- A CDC should identify projects that have potential for leading to other development as opportunities are created.

In addition, CDCs should not undertake projects with the same criteria as a profit-making enterprise, except in working to transfer more resources or benefits to poor residents (Rubin 1995). They should also avoid projects for which no viable market exists, where the organization must provide long-term subsidies to prevent the project's failure, and where the project drains resources from other desirable endeavors.

These are the functions that CDCs should perform, but how do they engage in brownfield redevelopment? Next, we look at the roles CDCs assume in brownfield redevelopment, then consider what conditions lead to their influencing or initiating redevelopment in these roles. Finally, we examine how CDC work with brownfields relates to the criteria for how CDCs *should* be involved. The findings are based on case studies in Pittsburgh and Detroit, on research on nonprofits' work elsewhere in brownfield redevelopment, and on the authors' experience through teaching and supervising student projects.

The Roles CDCs Assume

CDC work in Pittsburgh and Detroit and research on other CDCs and community-oriented nonprofits across the country suggest a typology of their roles in

brownfield redevelopment (see Casadei et al. 2003). This typology applies specifically to brownfield redevelopment rather than development in general because
brownfield add challenges to the development process and require expertise
beyond what most CDCs have. The roles discussed below are arranged from
least involvement in redevelopment to greatest involvement. Community-oriented nonprofits (including CDCs) have assumed different responsibilities in
development because their capacity and capabilities vary widely (Rohe et al. 2003;
Gittell and Wilder 1999) and because the demands of different redevelopment
projects also vary. The typology reflects the fact that CDCs can "learn by doing"
to increase their expertise. In any of these roles, CDC activities may or may not
be consistent with the normative criteria discussed above.

Outreach and education. CDCs and other nonprofits build community awareness about the potential for brownfields redevelopment and the ways to affect
such projects. Southwest Detroit Environmental Vision, a nonprofit formed to
improve southwest Detroit's environment, runs workshops for residents and
other community-based organizations to increase knowledge about safeguards
in brownfield redevelopment and how to build capacity for doing the redevelopment (Casadei et al. 2003). In Pennsylvania, Phoenix Land Recycling's
Brownfields Redevelopment Assistance Program offers extensive training and
education for CDC work on brownfields (Casadei et al. 2003, 67–71; Phoenix
2003b).

Facilitator. A CDC or community-based nonprofit brings its varied expertise
as an advocate for brownfields redevelopment to neighborhood improvement.
The organization builds on community planning to get new development to
fit into existing community plans or visions. The CDC may act as a catalyst, a
coordinator or a liaison (Eisenman 2003; Casadei et al. 2003). The role of facilitator requires considerable knowledge about development and brownfields, but
carries no financial or liability risks; the facilitator does not own land and has
no equity stake in the development. Southwest Detroit Environmental Vision
worked with residents for better cleanup and monitoring of the transformation
of an industrial site into a school. In Chicago the Greater Southwest Development Corporation worked on many issues to facilitate the redevelopment of a
large industrial site (Brachman 2003; Casadei et al. 2003, 80–84).

Intermediary or predeveloper. In this role, the CDC assumes a number of functions
to reduce the risks to the site's final developer that may carry significant costs and
substantial liability. The tasks include site identification, site assessment (typically
Phase I of an environmental assessment, but sometimes also Phase II), redevelopment strategies and community planning, project management and site control.
In Pittsburgh CDCs often assumed intermediary or predeveloper roles, building
on their experience in putting together development deals through multiple-
member partnerships. Because CDCs encounter brownfields as they redevelop,
but often do not have expertise in brownfield issues, a need exists for a nonprofit
to act as intermediary and brownfield redevelopment specialist, and to assist
other CDCs in handling these sites (LILP 2003). Phoenix Land Recycling has

acted as predeveloper and intermediary in numerous development projects in Pennsylvania. The Northern Indiana Center for Land Reuse is another example of a nonprofit that has acted as predeveloper in redevelopment of a major industrial site (Phoenix 2003a; Northern Indiana 2003; Casadei et al. 2003, 88–94).

Developer and codeveloper. The CDC takes a major financial stake in the partnership to redevelop a brownfield. This is the most challenging and riskiest role for CDCs unaccustomed to brownfield deals. CDCs in Pittsburgh who served as developer built their capacity through playing other roles in previous brownfields deals. Their projects involved developments in which they already had expertise, such as housing, historic preservation and business development. In Detroit the Presbyterian Village Senior Housing project encountered a brownfield where a gas station had been located, but the coalition of organizations acting as developer had the skills to deal with the cleanup. In Cleveland the Second Growth Institute functioned as developer for reuse of a former axle plant. In Philadelphia the New Kensington CDC developed a hydroponic greenhouse on a former industrial site (Keenan 2003; Salzman 2003; Casadei et al. 2003; Furr 2000).

In these varied roles, CDCs and other community-oriented nonprofits have differing levels of effectiveness in bringing about brownfield redevelopment. Case studies in Pittsburgh and Detroit reveal conditions that contribute to success in bringing about redevelopment.

Factors Contributing to CDC Effectiveness in Redeveloping Brownfields

In any of the roles CDCs assume, brownfields are difficult development projects. Beyond obstacles facing many urban redevelopment efforts—perceptions of urban markets that are often incorrect (Porter 1997), the need to assemble land from many owners, lack of land information, the obligation to relocate residents, and big city administrative hurdles—brownfields pose additional barriers. According to Fitzgerald and Leigh, these are: (1) liability concerns involving complex legal issues based on prior use and contamination; (2) lack of data on both contamination levels and remediation options; (3) high cost, which can drive projects beyond the point of financial feasibility, especially in distressed areas where property values are low; (4) insufficient time for determining environmental condition and for cleanup, which adds to costs; and (5) uncertainty, the combined result of the above, which can be the most difficult barrier (2002, 73).

Brownfield revitalization proves to be especially challenging for CDCs having modest experience with development projects. The additional expertise needed to clean up and prepare sites for redevelopment involves skill sets and networks that most CDCs do not possess. However, brownfield revitalization, as NCCED's encouragement reflects, may be financially useful for the organizations and may fall into a CDC's comprehensive strategy for community development or within its community plans. How comprehensive CDCs should strive to be remains in dispute (Vidal 1997; Gittell and Wilder 1999; Stoutland 1999; Rohe et al. 2003).

Changes in the 1990s opened the way for CDCs to become involved in brownfield redevelopment. The Environmental Protection Agency (EPA) in 1993 began to promote brownfields cleanup and redevelopment through regulatory changes and financial incentives, including brownfields pilot programs for state and local governments. At the same time, states sought ways to reform their own environmental rules, most of which had been based on stringent liability (Bartsch and Collaton 1997). In 1995 both Pennsylvania and Michigan enacted legislation to ensure liability protection, change cleanup levels to reflect reuse, and provide incentives for brownfield remediation (Urban 1996; Capstone 1998). These changes proved to be important for the redevelopment of the brownfields in our case studies, which were initiated under the amended state laws.

To examine the effectiveness of CDCs in brownfield revitalization, we studied CDCs and other nonprofits in Pittsburgh and Detroit who were involved in such remediation. The cases were chosen to examine different levels of involvement, from the outreach and education role to the developer role, in order to identify the factors that lead to CDC success (see Table 8.1). "Success" and "effectiveness" are defined here as accomplishing redevelopment, not necessarily meeting the normative criteria for CDC involvement in brownfields. The case studies are diverse in the types of properties involved as well. The Pittsburgh cases date from its industrial origins in the mid- to late nineteenth century, and the Detroit cases from the early twentieth century. Early tenants and owners show the cities' industrial roots, with production or use by companies such as Carnegie, Phipps, Alcoa, Jones & Laughlin, Crucible Steel, Studebaker, Rockwell and GM. Our cases range from a small, one-tenth-of-an-acre site of two historic buildings in an area targeted for redevelopment by the CDC to a 16-acre former Rockwell facility in Detroit, located in that city's federal Empowerment Zone (EZ). Several projects have been completed, including the Rockwell property, which has been remediated and reused (Whiteman and Sims 2001). The small project in the Lawrenceville neighborhood of Pittsburgh cleaned and reused two historic properties, housing two architecture firms. One of the properties was redesigned as a certified "green" building under the sustainable building standards of the LEED (Leadership in Energy and Environmental Design) rating system (Lowry 2000). One Pittsburgh project received funds from the EPA under its Brownfields Pilot Program. Funding for most of the projects came from multiple sources, including those at local, state and federal levels; banks and developers; and foundations and intermediaries. We examined several sites in each city that remain undeveloped to contrast the progress of the others.

The first conclusion from the case studies is that brownfield redevelopment is a new area for CDCs and represents a very different—or at least expanded—real estate project for most. CDCs that have succeeded in other kinds of redevelopment are best prepared to handle brownfield redevelopment, although none of the CDCs and other nonprofits has done brownfield redevelopment very long. The organizations were located in industrial areas or had target areas

Table 8.1   Case Studies of CDCs' Roles in Brownfield Redevelopment

Case Study	CDC Role	Outcome
Pittsburgh		
Bathhouse and Stable (Marino 2001)	Developer	Redevelopment
Lectromelt facility (Kivuva 2001b)	Facilitator	Redevelopment
Armstrong Cork (Kivuva 2001a)	No role	No change
Washington's Landing (Deitrick and Farber 2004)	Outreach and education	Redevelopment
South Side Works (City of Pittsburgh 1998)	Facilitator, intermediary	Redevelopment
Gulf Station (Capstone Seminar 1998)	Intermediary (Phase I)	No change
Detroit		
Presbyterian Village Senior Housing (Furr 2000)	Codeveloper	Redevelopment
Renaissance Global Logistics (Whiteman and Sims 2001)	Outreach and education	Redevelopment
Recycling Corporation of America (Jackson et al. 1997)	Facilitator	Partial cleanup
Wolverine Tube (Brooks et al. 2000a and 2000b)	Facilitator	No change
Empowerment Zone Contaminated Sites Task Force and Southwest Detroit Environmental Vision (Kelly and Whiteman 2000; Casadei et al. 2003)	Facilitator; outreach and education	Several sites cleaned; two sites redeveloped; no change in others
CitiPort In-Place Industrial Park (Aliberti et al. 2000)	Facilitator; outreach and education	No change

that included industrial sites. In Pittsburgh, Lawrenceville Development Corporation (now called the Lawrenceville Corporation) was previously involved in industrial site promotion and development. It was incorporated in the mid-1980s, with a focus on industrial reuse in a neighborhood designated as a state enterprise zone. Although not the developers, they performed other activities, including marketing and promoting manufacturing sites. Before the organization undertook brownfield redevelopment, its work centered on housing, historic preservation and business development. The CDC played different roles in each of the three sites studied in Lawrenceville Corporation's industrial area. It was a developer in one case, and achieved success through partnerships with city agencies and a local historic preservation agency, which had extensive knowledge of historic redevelopment and a loan fund. The project was located on historic Doughboy Square, the main priority of the neighborhood's revitalization strategy, where the CDC had already restored and renovated a historic property and built new affordable housing. The CDC was adding to its skills and capacity, rather than creating a new area of expertise.

The second conclusion is that partnerships are key to CDCs' becoming effective in brownfield redevelopment. Those partnerships include private, public and nonprofit entities in the development. Funding came from federal, state and local government sources, private capital, and nonprofits, including other developers and foundations. When one Detroit organization succeeded in cleaning up several sites, it used its nonprofit status to become a conduit for cleanup funding;

it formed a task force to facilitate decision making among government officials, neighborhood representatives, developers and lenders in order to move a site through cleanup and redevelopment (Kelly and Whiteman 2000, 14; Jackson et al. 1997). In a successful Detroit redevelopment case, the CDC partnered with private developers to construct much-needed senior housing, but used the services of a city cooperative interagency team, designed to evaluate environmental issues in development projects and recommend appropriate action in a timely way (Furr 2000). Detroit's Redevelopment of Urban Sites Team (REUS) consisted of several city agencies, available on an as-needed basis for evaluations. Again, the CDC developed new partnerships and used those partners' skills to clean and prepare a brownfield site for redevelopment.

The third conclusion is that nonprofits who use the power that a CDC's legal status confers are more successful in brownfield redevelopment. The abilities to acquire land and assemble sites, to receive grants and gifts from government agencies, foundations and businesses seeking tax write-offs, and to lead effectively were key in the cases where redevelopment occurred. In Pittsburgh CDCs often partnered with city agencies, especially the city redevelopment authority, which has the power to acquire land. One CDC director commented, "in Pittsburgh, you have to go to 15 different people to get [the deal] done" (Noszka 1999). Since many businesses do not want to spend the time to make those contacts, the CDCs saw themselves as "pulling it all together," by acquiring the properties and gaining financial backing through grants and loans from public and nonprofit sectors to redevelop the properties (Noszka 1999). In Detroit several nonprofits and CDCs felt they could not take the risk of acquiring land and leading development, because they did not have enough staff with the right skills and their strongest constituencies were leery of assuming such risk. The organizations, therefore, exhorted private corporations to do the redevelopment and worked to reduce any hurdles. The major barrier to redevelopment according to brokers and lenders, however, was lack of control of land (Aliberti et al. 2000). When the CDC was not effective in getting site control, it lost leverage with private developers. The result was that very little redevelopment occurred.

Fourth, CDC involvement as facilitators and codevelopers can make projects work better for development partners. CDCs can bring players together for a private developer, including public and other nonprofit agencies. They can fill the financing gap for projects costing more than the appraisal value by making up the loss in grants. In a Detroit case, a nonprofit developer with expertise in senior housing was initially wary of involvement with a CDC located in a fractious community. Joint planning among groups that had experienced conflict, coupled with adequate financial support from the public sector, convinced the experienced developer to join the project (Furr 2000). However, as other cases showed, the potential for CDCs to make more significant contributions to redevelopment has often not been realized. In one industrial area, the CDC was not able to take leadership in facilitating land assembly, a key obstacle to redevelopment; in another case, the nonprofit organization had insufficient capacity to use the tools at its disposal for effective development partnerships (Aliberti et al. 2000; Casadei et al. 2003).

The fifth conclusion is that CDCs with a strong community base and successful neighborhood organizing experience improve and facilitate brownfield projects by collecting informed input from neighborhood residents. A corollary to this is that linking brownfield redevelopment to larger community goals and plans improves prospects for redevelopment. CDCs often use their expertise in organizing and involving neighborhood voices in the process. Environmental projects with public funding cannot proceed without public involvement, and in many cities large-scale redevelopment projects need to meet public hearing and citizen input requirements. The nature of that input is often in dispute, as public hearings may not be the best forum for residents of distressed communities to express their views. Public participation may be used to rubber stamp decisions from downtown, rather than to seek meaningful citizen involvement in urban redevelopment (Greenberg and Lewis 2000, 2501). The public also may have the chance only to react to and comment on assessments and plans, rather than to participate in generating them (Collins and Savage 1999). CDC participation, however, can enable residents' voices to have a greater effect on the character of redevelopment and, therefore, lead to more satisfactory redevelopment.

In Detroit community-based nonprofits were able to insert citizens' views in numerous ways and result in improvements to redevelopment projects. They approached projects with the attitude that redevelopment could improve the neighborhood by controlling contamination better than derelict uses, preventing illegal dumping and blocking city decisions to locate more noxious uses in the area. "If we don't have redevelopment," said one CDC director, "we will just get dumped on—literally" (Wendler 1996). CDC leaders argued for preserving residents' access to parts of the district, for buffering and beautifying projects, for rerouting trucks away from residential areas, and for enabling very low-income residents to move to better housing away from the redevelopment (Jackson et al. 1997; Whiteman and Sims 2001). When redevelopment occurred, the organizations succeeded in getting some of what the residents wanted. However, notably lacking from the CDCs' requests were preference in hiring community residents and aid to the closest neighbors for relocating—two of the most important needs of the low-income residents.

In a Pittsburgh project, the CDC, residents and the city's Urban Redevelopment Authority of Pittsburgh engaged in a master planning process for the large former steel site, after the city proposed using it for riverboat gambling, which was opposed by South Side residents and businesses. The plan has guided over a quarter billion dollars of mixed-use development from public, nonprofit and private sources, including $6 million in U.S. Department of Housing and Urban Development brownfields loans and grant (Barnes 2002; City of Pittsburgh 1998). The neighborhood's success in planning for reuse of the LTV steel site stemmed from its ongoing neighborhood planning process, begun in 1990.

A Detroit nonprofit planned its future brownfield redevelopment work as it reached a critical juncture where funding from a major source would end. The planning process demonstrated that the organization could significantly strengthen its brownfield work by assuring that all its efforts reinforced the organization's goals for strengthening the community. Focusing on the goals the organization had developed would lead to a choice of different sites where redevelopment appeared more viable (Casadei et al. 2003).

CDC Brownfield Redevelopment Experiences and Normative Criteria for Involvement

Even if CDCs succeed in bringing about brownfield redevelopment for a range of reasons, they may or may not be acting in ways that fit the normative criteria for their involvement in brownfield redevelopment. To what extent did the cases in Pittsburgh and Detroit fit the criteria?

Did CDC brownfield redevelopment efforts lead to benefits for poor residents in control of economic assets? In Pittsburgh the record is mixed. The Lawrenceville Corporation projects have improved a previously blighted block in the neighborhood, one that residents targeted for redevelopment, and the new industrial area has employed some neighborhood residents. However, none of the projects led to increased citizen control of economic activity. In Detroit there was no increased control of economic assets. In some cases, this was not the salient goal of the organizations' activities. In other cases, what the community obtained was too modest to have an effect on residents' economic situation (Aliberti et al. 2000; Whiteman and Sims 2001).

Did the economic development projects emerge out of organizing that identified community priorities leading to empowerment and increased capacity to bring positive change? Community goals for brownfields should be established within community organizing; the brownfield redevelopment should represent an opportunity to realize residents' goals and visions. In Pittsburgh the answer is a qualified yes. The Lawrenceville CDC's brownfield involvement related to the neighborhood's goals, articulated through community organizing and planning. The projects achieved, in part, the goals of revitalizing a key area of the neighborhood and creating new jobs, some of which did go to local residents. In Detroit the answer is a qualified no. For the CDC working in the CitiPort industrial area, organizing focused on the businesses—which was necessary to make progress in strengthening the industrial park—but the CDC was never able to reconnect with the neighborhood. Although other community-based nonprofits engaged in organizing, the efforts did not link directly to the brownfield redevelopment projects, although the plans the residents generated always cited the need to clean up contaminated sites.

Did the CDC efforts make development happen that otherwise would not have under private-sector initiative, albeit with public subsidies and public endorsement? The answer is sometimes, but not often. In Pittsburgh a CDC has been the developer or codeveloper in a limited number of brownfield cases, such as the Doughboy Square historic properties, thus making projects possible only with

CDC involvement. In most instances, however, CDCs played roles in outreach and education, facilitator or intermediary with no financial risk. These roles improved the quality of the project and increased residents' participation and benefits, but development of some type would have occurred without the CDC. In Detroit the development of assisted senior housing would not have occurred without the work of the nonprofits. The brownfield section of the site, the location of a former gas station, was cleaned up as part of a larger, complex redevelopment effort. In other cases, such as the Rockwell site's redevelopment, the nonprofits' involvement contributed, with public-sector actors, to enabling redevelopment to occur that a businessperson was sure would be financially viable (Furr 2000; Whiteman and Sims 2001).

Did the CDCs undertake bellwether projects? In Pittsburgh the redevelopment of Doughboy Square and the revitalization of the block across the street, beginning with the Stable/Bathhouse project, have brought in private development projects around the square, including more historic renovations. The CDC-led project helped show that private investment could also earn a satisfactory return. In Detroit the brownfield projects demonstrated that the market for land was weak and did not help to create a market. In several situations land remained vacant even after remediation. In the case of the successful development of senior housing, other major development projects occurred nearby, but these were not influenced by the CDC project (Whiteman and Kelly 2000; Aliberti et al. 2000; Furr 2000).

Did the CDCs undertake projects that would not have been viable for the private sector with public support, and avoid projects where no viable market existed? In Pittsburgh the area where the CDC worked had burned during the 1960s riots and had received no substantial investment in the years following. The CDC investment was key. In Detroit, in the case of the senior housing project, CDCs did find the middle territory between viable private-market projects and those that the CDC could not have made work (Furr 2000). In other cases, however, the CDCs and other community-based nonprofits were not able to undertake any redevelopment. Although their efforts led to the cleanup of several large parcels, all except two of these continue to sit vacant (Casadei et al. 2003), reminders of urban renewal programs that cleared and assembled land that then sat unused for many years in the absence of a market.

Conclusion

This examination of the CDC's role in brownfield redevelopment in Pittsburgh and Detroit suggests that the organizations should undertake brownfield projects with caution. CDCs may succeed in bringing about redevelopment on brownfield sites with the aid of sophisticated real estate tactics and partnerships, and may facilitate revitalization by using community organizing skills and accessing resources provided by the nonprofit status. However, the success of such projects needs to be evaluated against the goals of the neighborhood and of the overarching desire for community betterment. Involvement in brownfields is frequently inconsistent with the rationales for CDC development activities and does not necessarily advance the movement's major aim of redistributing economic assets to poor neighborhoods and people. Our case studies suggest that when brownfield revitalization fits within overall community development goals, CDCs can play an important role in redeveloping the property according to those goals. When CDCs place brownfield redevelopment within their existing community plans or goals—whether in housing, business development, environmental improvement or targeted historic preservation—they have a greater chance of success in redevelopment that is also consistent with the normative rationale for CDC involvement. The redevelopment also is more likely to occur in ways that serve their low-income communities than projects seeking solely to redevelop a brownfield or to take advantage of new funding opportunities.

Acknowledgments

This research was funded by grants from the Lincoln Institute of Land Policy and the Office of the Vice Provost of the University of Michigan.

References

Aliberti, M., E. Daugherty, B. Hanson, N. Jung, E. Y. Kim and E. Sheneman. 2000. *Assembling an industrial future: The CitiPort revitalization plan*. Master of Urban Planning project. Urban and Regional Planning Program, University of Michigan, Ann Arbor. December.

Barnes, T. 2002. South Side to be the site of $6 million garage. *Pittsburgh Post-Gazette*, November 7, B4.

———. 2000. UPMC's sport medicine facility leads renewal at South Side steel site. *Pittsburgh Post-Gazette*, June 4, B1.

Bartsch, C. and E. Collaton. 1997. *Brownfields: Cleaning and reusing contaminated properties*. Westport, CT and London: Praeger.

Blakely, E. J. and A. Aparicio. 1990. Balancing social and economic objectives: The case of California's community development corporations. *Journal of the Community Development Society* 21(1):115–128.

Brachman, L. 2003. Greater Southwest Development Corporation. "The silver shovel" case: Brokering redevelopment as a community advocate. Case study prepared for the symposium "Reuse of Brownfields and Other Underutilized Land," Lincoln Institute of Land Policy, Cambridge, MA, January 26–28.

Bratt, R. G., A. C. Vidal, A. Schwartz, L. C. Keyes and J. Stockard. 1998. The status of non-profit-owned affordable housing: Short-term successes and long-term challenges. *Journal of the American Planning Association* 64(1):39–51.

Brooks, A., S. Gutterman, C. Kelly, M. Masson, K. Whiteman and M. Zellner. 2000a. *Background information for Phase I environmental site assessment: Hermes Automotive/Wolverine Tube site*. Master of Urban Planning project. Urban and Regional Planning Program, University of Michigan, Ann Arbor. February.

————. 2000b. *Choices for reuse of the Wolverine Tube and Chatfield/Beard brownfield sites.* Master of Urban Planning project. Urban and Regional Planning Program, University of Michigan, Ann Arbor. April.

Brophy, P. C. and K. Burnett. 2003. *Building a new framework for community development in weak market cities.* Denver: Community Development Partnership Network. April.

Capstone Seminar. 1998. *A second chance: Brownfields redevelopment in Pittsburgh.* Final project report. Graduate School of Public and International Affairs, University of Pittsburgh, PA. April.

Casadei, A., J. Eisenman, K. Koo, D. Maylie and V. Tamada. 2003. *Overcoming the brownfields challenge: Steps toward an environmental and economic rebirth of southwest Detroit.* Master of Urban Planning project. Urban and Regional Planning Program, University of Michigan, Ann Arbor. May.

City of Pittsburgh. 1998. Industrial developments: South Side. http://www.city.pgh.pa.us/ed/south_side_works.html.

Collins, T. and K. Savage. 1999. Brownfields as places. *Public Works Management and Policy* 2(3):210–219.

Deitrick, S. and S. Farber. 2004 (forthcoming). Citizen reaction to brownfield redevelopment. In *Approaches to central city revitalization*, F.W. Wagner, A.J. Mumphrey, T.E. Joder, K.M. Akundi, eds. Irvine, CA: ME Sharpe.

Eisenberg, P. 2000. Time to remove the rose-colored glasses. *Shelterforce* 110 (March/April).

Eisenman, J. 2003. Discussions with Dewar, January–May.

Fitzgerald, J. and N. G. Leigh. 2002. *Economic revitalization: Cases and strategies for city and suburb.* Thousand Oaks, CA: Sage.

Furr, J. 2000. The impact of cooperative efforts in community development. Case study prepared for project on brownfield redevelopment, University of Michigan Law School, Ann Arbor (August). Unpublished manuscript.

Gittell, R. and M. Wilder. 1999. Community development corporations: Critical factors that influence success. *Journal of Urban Affairs* 21(3):341–362.

Greenberg, M. and J. Lewis. 2000. Brownfields redevelopment, preferences and public involvement: A case study of an ethnically mixed neighborhood. *Urban Studies* 37(3):2501–2515.

Halpern, R. 1995. *Rebuilding the inner city.* New York: Columbia University Press.

Harrison, B. 1974. *Urban economic development.* Washington, DC: Urban Institute.

Hise, R. and A. Nelson. 1999. Urban brownfields: Strategies for promoting urban brownfield re-use at the state and local level. *Economic Development Review* 16(2):67–72.

Jackson, A., B. Robinson, P. Deininger, A. Tekie, T. Kutsukake and J. Paquin. 1997. *The Delray redevelopment initiative: A vision for future use.* Master of Urban Planning project. Urban and Regional Planning Program, University of Michigan, Ann Arbor. Fall.

Keating, W. D. 1999. Federal policy and poor urban neighborhoods. In *Rebuilding urban neighborhoods: Achievements, opportunities, and limits*, W.D. Keating and N. Krumholz, eds. Thousand Oaks, CA: Sage.

Keenan, M. 2003. The redevelopment of the former Eaton Axle Plant, Cleveland, Ohio. *Environmental Practice* 5(1):82–83.

Kelly, C. and K. Whiteman. 2000. *Southwest Detroit Contaminated Sites Redevelopment Task Force: History, experiences and lessons learned.* Master of Urban Planning project. Urban and Regional Planning Program, University of Michigan, Ann Arbor. December.

Kibel, P. S. 1998. The urban nexus: Open space, *brownfields*, and justice. *Boston College Environmental Affairs Law Review* 25(3):589–619.

Kivuva, J. M. 2001a. Case study of Armstrong Cork. Graduate School of Public and International Affairs, University of Pittsburgh, PA. Unpublished manuscript.

———. 2001b. Case study of Lectromelt Facility. Graduate School of Public and International Affairs, University of Pittsburgh, PA. Unpublished manuscript.

Lenz, T. J. 1988. Neighborhood development: Issues and models. *Social Policy* 18 (Spring): 24–30.

Lincoln Institute of Land Policy. 2003. Discussions at the Symposium "Reuse of Brownfields and Other Underutilized Land," Cambridge, MA, January 26–28.

Lowry, P. 2000. Three buildings here are "green," envied. *Pittsburgh Post-Gazette*, October 12, B6.

Marino, A. L. 2001. Case study of bathhouse and stable. Graduate School of Public and International Affairs, University of Pittsburgh, PA. Unpublished manuscript.

Murphy, P. W. and J. V. Cunningham. 2003. *Organizing for community controlled development: Renewing civil society*. Thousand Oaks, CA.: Sage.

National Congress for Community Economic Development (NCCED). 1995. *Taking hold*. Washington, DC: National Congress for Community Economic Development.

———. 1999a. *Coming of age: Trends and achievements of community-based development organizations*. Washington, DC: National Congress for Community Economic Development.

———. 1999b. *Reclaiming the land: Successful CDC brownfield redevelopment projects*. Washington, DC: National Congress for Community Economic Development (February).

Northern Indiana Center for Land Reuse. 2003. Northwest Indiana Forum. http://www.nwiforum.org/niclr.asp.

Noszka, N. 1999. Personal interview with Deitrick. Lawrenceville Development Corp., Pittsburgh, PA.

Parent, D. 2001. The Clark Street Technology Park: A case study of brownfields redevelopment in Detroit. Urban and Regional Planning Program, University of Michigan, Ann Arbor (March). Unpublished manuscript.

Pepper, E. M. 1997. *Lessons from the field: Unlocking economic potential with an environmental key*. Washington, DC: Northeast-Midwest Institute.

Phoenix Land Recycling Company. 2003a. http://www.phoenixland.org/index.html (accessed March 10).

———. 2003b. Brownfields Redevelopment Assistance Program. http://www.phoenixland.org/brap/index.html (accessed March 10).

Porter, M. 1997. New strategies for inner-city economic development. *Economic Development Quarterly* 11(1):11–27.

Rohe, W. M., R. G. Bratt and P. Biswas. 2003. *Evolving challenges for community development corporations: The causes and impacts of failures, downsizings and mergers*. Chapel Hill, NC: Center for Urban and Regional Studies, University of North Carolina.

Rubin, H. J. 1994. There aren't going to be any bakeries here if there is no money to afford jelly-rolls: The organic theory of community based development. *Social Problems* 41(3):401–424.

———. 1995. Renewing hope in the inner city: Conversations with community-based development practitioners. *Administration and Society* 27(1):127–160.

Salzman, S., Executive Director, New Kensington Community Development Corporation. 2003. Phone communication with A. Casadei, Philadelphia, PA. April.

Stoecker, R. 1997a. Should we . . . could we . . . change the CDC model? *Journal of Urban Affairs* 19(1):35–44.

————. 1997b. The CDC model of urban redevelopment: A critique and an alternative. *Journal of Urban Affairs* 19(1):1–22.

————. 2003. Comment on William M. Rohe and Rachel G. Bratt's "Failures, downsizing, and mergers among community development corporation": Defending community development corporations or defending community. *Housing Policy Debate* 14(1/2):47–56.

Stoutland, S. E. 1999. Community development corporations: Mission, strategy, and accomplishments. In *Urban problems and community development*, R. Ferguson and W. Dickens, eds. Washington, DC: Brookings Institution.

Toulme, N. V. and D. E. Cloud. 1991. The Fleet Factors case: A wrong turn for lender liability under Superfund. *Wake Forest Law Review* 26(1):17–21.

Urban, J. B. 1996. Life after NREPA: A look beyond environmental liability as a limit to urban redevelopment. *Wayne Law Review* 43:259–286.

Vidal, A. C. 1997. Can community development re-invent itself? The challenges of strengthening neighborhoods in the 21st century. *Journal of the American Planning Association* 63(4): 429–438.

Wendler, K., Executive Director, Southwest Detroit Business Association. 1996. Discussion with Dewar and students, Detroit, MI.

Whiteman, K. and E. Sims. 2001. Renaissance Global Logistics (former Rockwell Corporation Site) brownfield redevelopment case study. Urban and Regional Planning Program, University of Michigan, Ann Arbor (August). Unpublished manuscript.

Part 3

Innovative Uses
for Vacant Land

9 | Farming Inside Cities Through Entrepreneurial Urban Agriculture

Jerome Kaufman and Martin Bailkey

The contemporary landscape of many American cities over the last few decades shows sizable areas of vacant land left in the wake of creeping abandonment, especially in more impoverished parts of cities. Deindustrialization and decreasing urban populations have resulted in the abandonment of literally tens of thousands of residential, commercial and manufacturing structures in older United States cities. Chicago and Detroit each have an estimated 70,000 vacant lots, Philadelphia 35,000 and New Orleans 14,000. Smaller deindustrialized cities also experience the problem. In Trenton, the state capital of New Jersey, with a population of more than 85,000, for example, an estimated 18 percent of its total land is vacant.

Unlike Western European cities, which have little vacant land, many American cities find themselves with more vacant lots than can realistically be filled with new housing and businesses. Addressing this problem has become an important policy concern for municipal governments fiscally burdened by the management of thousands of tax-delinquent parcels, many acquired through foreclosure. Although city officials would prefer to redevelop these parcels with houses and stores that improve neighborhoods and generate tax dollars, the development demand for the abandoned lots is often low. Thus, there can be interest in certain vacant parcels for community open-space uses. These traditionally include neighborhood parks and playgrounds, along with less-traditional uses such as art parks (Boston Globe 2002) and memorials to the victims of inner-city violence (Rummler 1997, B3).

The past two decades have seen a slowly growing interest in using vacant land for a heretofore unconventional use, urban agriculture. Defined as the growing, processing and distributing of food and nonfood products such as flowers and trees, through intensive cultivation in and near cities (Bailkey and Nasr 1999, 6), urban agriculture is gaining recognition among some government, private and nonprofit-sector officials as a potentially viable and productive use of urban space. Perhaps the best-known urban agriculture use is that of community gardens, where small plots are cultivated by individuals or families, often in areas where residents lack yard space. A 1998 study determined that more than 6,000 community gardens existed in 38 larger American cities, with 30 percent of these gardens started after 1991, a clear indicator of their increasing popularity (Monroe-Santos 1998, 17). The idea of intensively using city land to cultivate food, beyond growing batches of tomatoes and cucumbers in home back yards, is not quixotic. It is as practical to modern needs as were the many "victory gardens" used to support domestic food objectives during World Wars I and II.

Today, employing underused land to produce food for market sale, or entrepreneurial urban agriculture, represents one subset of small-scale urban food production and is the primary focus of this chapter. Most entrepreneurial urban agriculture operations are run by nonprofit, community-based organizations, although some are private-sector ventures. For many of these nonprofits, selling to customers is only part of their intent. Other products may be consumed by the growers themselves (as is most typical of community gardens) or distributed to emergency food providers like food pantries or hot meal kitchens.

There are several reasons for the grassroots interest in entrepreneurial urban agriculture in disinvested communities. City farms can increase the amount of green space, improve the appearance of blighted neighborhoods, and supply low-income residents with fresher and more nutritious food. And, they can help revitalize poor neighborhoods economically by creating modest food-based employment, bringing more income into the pockets of residents and building greater neighborhood self-reliance.

Although there are reasons for skepticism over entrepreneurial urban agriculture—inner-city vacant land is too contaminated to grow food safely, most city-based community development organizations lack the interest and know-how to grow food for sale, the markets for selling such foods are limited, and support from city officials is sparse—there are signs of an emerging presence and constituency for market urban farming in a number of U.S. and Canadian cities. Given this skepticism and the opportunity presented by large amounts of vacant land in cities, can entrepreneurial urban agriculture projects be a viable land use for certain inner-city parcels? Some place-based organizations have sufficient knowledge, savvy and energy to take advantage of local vacant land opportunities and achieve a vision of city farming. But there is another important ingredient that must be considered—the readiness of external groups to accept and support this vision; in other words, a favorable and supportive institutional climate is required. Once entrepreneurial urban agriculture is seen positively by government officials, lending agencies and the general public, its future will be bright. If the institutional climate remains cool or indifferent, however, city farming advocates will continue to encounter difficulties in achieving their vision.

The research underlying this chapter and an earlier study by the authors (Kaufman and Bailkey 2000) uncovered local institutional contexts composed of many separate units. Some of these are networked, others not. Some are more open-minded toward innovative ideas than others. Given the lack of any sort of mandate for market or nonmarket urban agriculture, its acceptance within a particular city is largely dependent upon the personal attitudes of key players in the complex social and political environment of that community.

An Overview of Entrepreneurial Urban Agriculture

The breadth and diversity of for-market urban farming in the U.S. is best seen in the following descriptions of five organizations and projects that together represent a range of objectives, initiators and primary sponsors.

Nuestras Raices/Centro Agricola, Holyoke, Massachusetts

Expanding an existing community garden structure through entrepreneurial urban agriculture and other community-building activities characterizes this venture located in Holyoke, a city of 40,000 in western Massachusetts. Once known as the Paper City of the World, because of the many mills along the Connecticut River, Holyoke suffered from the deindustrialization process that characterized industrial centers in the Northeast. Immigrants have long comprised a significant segment of the city's population, and the influx of Hispanics that began in the 1960s has continued; they now make up 41 percent of all Holyoke residents. The Centro Agricola (Figure 9.1) represents an extension into commercial food-based programs by its parent organization, Nuestras

Figure 9.1   Centro Agricola, mural on the tavern building

All photos: Martin Bailkey

Raices (Our Roots), a nonprofit group established in 1992 to manage a single community garden in inner-city Holyoke. Today, almost 100 families from the surrounding Puerto Rican population garden on seven sites once neglected and filled with debris.[1]

In the mid-1990s the Nuestras Raices board of directors began exploring ways to direct the energy behind the community gardens into an economic development strategy. A 1996 U.S. Department of Agriculture Community Food Projects grant of $89,000 provided the seed money to plan the Centro Agricola, an umbrella designation for a number of separate endeavors centered on a single site. Subsequent appeals raised $150,000 and an additional $100,000 of in-kind donations to begin the transformation of a century-old, 2,700-square-foot former tavern into a shared-use community kitchen, designed to house small, food-based entrepreneurs and a Puerto Rican restaurant. In addition, the adjacent vacant lot at the corner of Main and Cabot Streets was acquired for $500 from the city of Holyoke, and is now the site of a 600-square-foot greenhouse set behind a landscaped plaza characteristic of rural Puerto Rican villages. Most of the renovation and new construction work for the Centro was performed by volunteer labor.

Since 1995 both Nuestras Raices and the Centro Agricola have benefited from the steady leadership of Executive Director Daniel Ross. Under Ross and his six-person staff, the tax-exempt organization has acquired hard-earned experience in fundraising and has become adept at tapping into the volunteer resources available in the communities and institutions of the Connecticut Valley. By the summer of 2003, the operating components of the Centro were the greenhouse, where 5,000 pepper and herb seedlings (including special Latino varieties) were being grown for sale to community gardeners and at the weekly Holyoke farmers' market; a bakery, producing seven varieties of artisan bread; a small catering business; adjacent office and meeting space; and (after several false starts) the restaurant. Ross and the Nuestras Raices board envision the Centro becoming fiscally self-sufficient after two years of full operation. Revenue sources would include rents and fees generated from the restaurant concession, sales from small businesses using the kitchen as an incubator, the community's use of the shared kitchen, and proceeds from the value-added processing of produce from the community gardens.

Through determination and a clear sense of mission, the Centro Agricola today represents an ongoing relationship between community gardening on once-vacant land and its logical extension into neighborhood-scaled business enterprises. Each activity reflects the cultural traditions of the local Puerto Rican community.

Growing Power, Milwaukee

Will Allen is a six-foot-seven-inch-tall African American who grew up on a Maryland farm, became a professional basketball player in Europe, and later

---

1. Many gardeners were Puerto Rican farmers who became migrant laborers in the U.S. In two separate Nuestras Raices youth gardens, and in individual plots within the seven community gardens, they now pass on their agricultural skills to local youth.

farmed 100 acres in a Milwaukee suburb. In 1993 he purchased two acres on Silver Spring Drive on the city's north side that housed five connected, badly dilapidated greenhouses, the last remnants of Milwaukee's old flower-growing district. The site soon became the center for Allen's vision to help inner-city minority youngsters gain life skills by learning the secrets of turning seeds into food (Figure 9.2). Growing Power (originally called Farm City Link) initially went through several developmental phases and partnership arrangements. Finally, in 1999, Allen stabilized the operation by joining forces with Hope Finkelstein, who pioneered the nation's first youth-based community supported agriculture (CSA) project in Madison, Wisconsin. The two served as codirectors of Growing Power until early 2003, when Finkelstein stepped down.

Today, Growing Power's mission begins with the broad aim of helping people of diverse backgrounds achieve greater food security by creating "community food centers," where residents can learn about sustainable practices to grow, process, market and distribute food. These centers will be located in cities across the U.S., but the prototype is in Milwaukee, where vegetables (from tomatoes and leafy greens to exotic varieties like Japanese kiwis), herbs and flowers are grown in the five, now restored, 3,000-square-foot greenhouses. Allen has installed a complete indoor "living machine," an elaborate aquaponics system (integrating aquaculture with hydroponics) for the farming of 2,000 tilapia fish. A series of planting beds for herbs, salads and peppers serve to filter the fish waste, eliminating the need for expensive filtration. The greenhouses also shelter

Figure 9.2   Will Allen and visitors in a Growing Power greenhouse

the processing of organic wastes by earthworms, producing an organic fertilizer known as vermicompost.

A wide variety of vegetables is produced outside the greenhouses during the growing season. The grounds are also the setting for Growing Power's larger composting system, where vegetable waste from local grocery stores becomes a source of nitrogen and carbon. Water from the greenhouse aquaponics system is added to the compost piles to inoculate them with microorganisms. Beehives are recent additions to the panoply of Growing Power food ventures; in 2002, the first year of production, the beehives produced 200 pounds of honey. Attached to the greenhouses is a community processing kitchen connected to a small roadside market selling some of the food grown on-site.

Growing Power offers a comprehensive educational program in urban agriculture targeted to both young people and adults. Each year hundreds of mostly low-income minority youngsters are taught ecological and economic interdependence through agriculture, horticulture, vermiculture and aquaculture. Many of the youth learn the steps from planting to selling by maintaining the various projects in the greenhouses—building and sustaining the worm bins used in making compost and tending to the fish systems, as well as raising and harvesting the vegetables and herbs. An offshoot of the educational program is the Youth Corps, numbering 12 youngsters ranging in age from nine to 12 from poor households. The Youth Corps aims to develop a cadre of future food-system leaders by helping the youngsters acquire a diverse set of technical and organizational skills, including landscaping, carpentry, gardening, composting and public speaking, while also earning a summer stipend.

Since 2000 Growing Power has offered annually several two-day intensive, hands-on training workshops in community food systems. Most workshop participants are adults who come from Milwaukee and other cities and rural communities. Each participant in 2003 paid a fee of $200 to learn about planning, developing, operating and sustaining community food projects and community food centers. Held in the greenhouses, with food from local farmers providing nutritious meals during the two days, each workshop averages between 30 to 40 participants, and up to 15 different trainers. Since their inception, nearly 500 people have attended the workshops, representing more than 120 groups from diverse regional, racial, ethnic and socioeconomic backgrounds. Allen estimates that the workshops have led to the initiation of more than 50 community food security projects.

Growing Power has also engaged in other outreach activities, which directly or indirectly advance community and economic objectives in central Milwaukee and for the small farmers in southeast Wisconsin. These outreach services have included helping neighborhood-based groups develop community gardens; saving one of the few fresh-produce markets serving central Milwaukee; organizing a Market Basket program to provide fresh produce at affordable prices to inner-city residents; and organizing the Rainbow Farmer's Cooperative of small area farmers, while creating new markets for their produce.

Growing Power is also establishing footholds outside of Milwaukee. Its work in Chicago, 90 miles south, was off to a promising start after just one year of organized efforts. The most ambitious of several Chicago projects (managed by Will Allen's daughter, Erika) is the creation of a community food center on city-owned land in the low-income West Garfield neighborhood on the West Side. Growing Power now has a number of sites in Chicago where baskets of food are distributed at affordable prices to inner-city residents, and a few sites on vacant parcels where community groups are learning to grow food and raise herbs for market sale.

As with most community-based organizations, Growing Power faces continuing operational challenges, in particular, acquiring sufficient funds to launch and sustain its programs. From its shaky beginnings, when it grew herbs, vegetables and flowers inside two badly run-down greenhouses, Growing Power has matured to the point where its staff now numbers seven and its volunteer base stands at well over 100. Its 2003 income reached $600,000, with 14 percent coming from fees for services. Consequently, unlike many other struggling urban agriculture operations, Growing Power is now less reliant on private foundation and government grants to survive.

Allen's vision for Growing Power has evolved concurrently with the rehabilitation of the five connected greenhouses he purchased in 1993. From its early focus on youth development—still a central part of its mission—Growing Power has expanded to new program areas in new places. Allen has been driven by the desire to challenge a commonly held perception: "Most people," he said, "think that rural areas are there to produce the food while urban areas are there to consume it.... We're trying to demonstrate that on a community level you can control the production, marketing, and distribution of food while also strengthening your community" (Wilson 2002, 62). Growing Power is clearly succeeding in challenging perceptions that place physical and mental barriers between the producers and consumers of food.

Re-Vision House Urban Farm, Boston

Fabyan Street in the Franklin Field section of Mattapan, one of Boston's poorest neighborhoods, is the site of the Re-Vision House, Inc. (RHI), Urban Farm (Figure 9.3), a notable matching of city farming benefits to other social objectives. Unlike Growing Power and Nuestras Raices, the RHI Urban Farm is not an autonomous food security or urban agriculture venture, but operates as a component unit of a service organization with goals that are not primarily food-centered.

Since 1989 Re-Vision House has served young (primarily 16–24 years of age) homeless women. Up to 24 women and their children are housed in either a short-term emergency shelter or longer-term transitional housing. Each woman is required to participate in some form of vocational or educational training. Recognizing the connections between childhood malnutrition and the combined effects of poverty, inadequate housing and food insecurity led the RHI director, Yvonne Miller-Booker, to consider linking her experiences in growing up on a farm to her organizational objectives. The result is a coordinated set of urban agriculture activities with a decidedly entrepreneurial bent, focused on both shelter residents and the surrounding community.

Figure 9.3   Re-Vision House, hoophouse and shelter (behind)

In 2003 the farm consisted of four sites for food production: a small side yard next to one of the two shelter houses; a three-story "bioshelter," created by enclosing each of the south-facing balconies of the main shelter house; a half-acre RHI-owned vacant parcel across the street; and a strip of land adjoining an existing community garden several blocks away. A 16 × 80-foot hoop-styled greenhouse is sited prominently along the Fabyan Street edge of the vacant parcel and is primarily used to grow seedlings and high-value mesclun salad mix year-round. The bioshelter houses the aquaculture system through which several varieties of tilapia fish are grown in a 2,500-gallon tank, under the care of shelter residents supervised by a full-time aquaculture manager. In addition to fish, the system also supports the growing of basil used in the production of fresh pesto. Elsewhere, an on-site beehive produces a small amount of honey.

The urban agriculture plans and expectations of RHI are ambitious. Its Urban Farm is at the center of a three-pronged strategy to (1) create a community-supported market farm providing fresh produce, fish and flowers to shelter and neighborhood residents; (2) develop a set of nutrition education, assessment and monitoring activities, and incorporate them into the care of shelter families; and (3) directly involve homeless women in the farm operation through job training internships. Such internships build the skills and confidence needed to expand work opportunities for these women, and to provide direct links to environment- or agriculture-based careers.

The specific activities of the market farm include operating a weekly farm-stand on Fabyan Street, growing vegetable seedlings for local gardeners, and producing tilapia fish for shelter residents and local restaurants. A portion of the vegetables grown goes to shelter residents. The rest is sold to low-income community residents through a community-supported agriculture operation and farmstand, to other city residents through farmers' markets, and to high-end markets, such as restaurants. In 2000 the Urban Farm began to supply Icarus Restaurant in Boston's South End with a mesclun salad mix. This arrangement has been successful enough for the restaurant to ask for more produce and for other establishments to seek a similar arrangement with RHI. The current RHI growing sites lack the capacity to supply more restaurants, but the farm hopes to expand onto at least five acres of the former Boston State Hospital nearby. In September 2003 RHI was part of a team submitting one of two competing community-based proposals to build much-needed housing and create new economic opportunities for Mattapan residents on the vacant state-owned property.

The CSA operation, a partnership with the Massachusetts Audubon Society's Drumlin Organic Farm in the suburb of Lincoln, represents a major development for the RHI Urban Farm. In 2003 the CSA had 65 members, half of whom were low-income Franklin Field residents purchasing shares at one-third of the regular price. RHI would like to expand the number of shareholders to 100 Boston households, while keeping the proportion of Franklin Field shareholders at 50 percent.

During the 2003 growing season, the longtime farm director, Judy Lieberman, was aided by a full-time program assistant and aquaculture manager and by additional seasonal help. In terms of revenue, the Urban Farm is not yet self-sufficient (although this may be achieved if the state hospital site becomes available). Lieberman hoped to earn a total of $25,000 in 2003, based on estimates of $12,000 from the CSA, $5,000 from the sale of seedlings, $5,000 from farmers' market and other produce sales, and $3,000 from Icarus Restaurant. Most of the project's $200,000 budget for the year was supported by several public and private grants. Since most of the grants supporting the farm are for only one year, the staff expends a great deal of energy seeking new funding sources.

Village Farms, Buffalo[2]

For three years (1998–2001) the Buffalo division of Village Farms, L.P., the largest hydroponic greenhouse operator in the U.S., represented the rare, large-scale entrepreneurial urban agriculture venture developed by a private-sector corporation and managed to maximize profits. Any social benefits to the local community resulting from this operation were "trickle-down" and not actively pursued as an objective that compromises profits. Although this profit approach, along with its size, made Village Farms/Buffalo something of an anomaly in urban farming, its use of innovative technologies and the example it set for

---

2. Much of this material on Village Farms was drawn from earlier research by Hope Wohl, under contract to the Pennsylvania Horticultural Society (Hope Wohl Associates 2000).

reusing contaminated industrial land for food production warrant its inclusion in this overview.

Village Farms/Buffalo was an 18-acre greenhouse facility (on a 35-acre site that also included a 42,000-square-foot packing operation) that produced vine-ripened tomatoes for sale to area supermarkets and distributors using state-of-the-art hydroponic techniques. As do many large urban redevelopment projects, Village Farms represented a partnership between a private corporation looking for a site to establish a specific business and state and local governments actively recruiting businesses, especially those promising to bring new life to abandoned areas. In this case, the abandoned site was the former Republic Steel mill in a heavily industrial area along the Buffalo River, southeast of downtown.

In the mid-1990s the parent corporation of what is now Village Farms, L.P., was looking to expand its existing local tomato-growing operations beyond the capacity of its small greenhouse north of the city. The city of Buffalo (through the Buffalo Economic Renaissance Corporation), New York State (through a $400,000 interest subsidy grant), and local utilities offered several incentives to recruit Village Farms to the Republic Steel site. These incentives were critical, given the high start-up costs involved in an undertaking of such size. By the time operations began in 1998, Village Farms had taken advantage of the site's location within both a federal enterprise zone and a city economic development zone. The latter designation allowed Village Farms to receive significant reductions in electric and natural gas rates, a seven-year, 100 percent tax abatement agreement, and other tax credits based on generated employment. The city also paid for the remediation of the oil-contaminated site (at a cost of $860,000) and bought the land, subsequently leasing it to Village Farms. Given these incentives, the primary expense for the venture was $13 million in greenhouse construction costs, out of an overall start-up and development cost of $20 million.

Village Farms/Buffalo utilized a second-hand, aluminum-and-steel greenhouse purchased at a foreclosure sale in Pennsylvania. The operation employed a Dutch technology where individual tomato plants are grown in porous, rock wool blocks of varying densities. Saplings planted in December were harvested beginning in mid-March. Production would peak in June, with the cycle starting again in December with new saplings. Computers monitored the flow of nutrients to the plants, as well as climatic conditions in the greenhouse. Bees pollinated the plants, and biocontrol measures (i.e., "helpful" insects) were used to control unwanted pests, minimizing pesticide use. Approximately 175,000 plants were grown, yielding 8 million pounds of tomatoes annually. These were sold directly to regional supermarket chains in the Northeast and Canada. Marketing agreements initially guaranteed the purchase of all greenhouse production. After operations began, there were indications that Village Farms forced some local tomato growers to leave the business (Meyer 1998, 1A), although other growers became Village Farms employees.

Initially, Village Farms/Buffalo was considered a success. Its privately held parent corporation was pleased with initial revenues and investigated replicating the operation in other cities. The city of Buffalo saw Village Farms as an example of how economic development zones can succeed and as an exemplary use of abandoned industrial land for an innovative, nonpolluting business producing an in-demand product. The project was recognized by the Environmental Protection Agency (EPA), New York Governor George Pataki and the *New York Times* as a model reuse of industrial brownfields (Revkin 1998, A1). One area where initial expectations were never met was the amount of local employment generated. The peak level of 180 jobs was below the 250–300 initially envisioned. Although pickers and packagers resided in Buffalo, the majority of management and administrative staff lived outside of the city. Citing the high price of natural gas, Village Farms/Buffalo stopped planting in Fall 2001, leaving a staff of four to distribute tomatoes shipped to Buffalo from other Village Farms sites in the U.S.

While Village Farms/Buffalo was for several years an efficiently run operation and an impressive example of food production on underutilized urban land, it should not be compared directly with other urban agriculture projects presented in this overview as grassroots ventures with benefits directed at a particular community. The goals and objectives of Village Farms were clearly different.

The Greensgrow Philadelphia Project

The Greensgrow Philadelphia Project occupies a three-quarter-acre site at Cumberland and Almond Streets in the North Philadelphia neighborhood of New Kensington, where a steel galvanizing plant stood until 1988. In 1997 Greensgrow's founding partners, Mary Seton Corboy and Tom Sereduk, spent $30,000 to construct an extensive hydroponic system directly on the broken concrete (the site had been cleared of zinc and lead by the EPA). Small plugs of different gourmet lettuces were then grown in plastic rain gutters, irrigated by water pumped from four 500-gallon reservoirs (Figure 9.4). In 1998, their first operating year, Corboy and Sereduk (both former chefs) sold lettuce to 15 local restaurants, earning $18,000. The next year, bolstered by a $50,000 Sustainable Development Challenge Grant from the regional EPA office, they physically upgraded the operation and began hiring workers through Philadelphia's welfare-to-work program. The Greensgrow product line was expanded from lettuces to heirloom tomatoes, culinary herbs and cut flowers that, along with lettuce, brought in $32,000 for 1999.

In 2000 Sereduk left and Corboy became Greensgrow's sole owner. The next three years saw Greensgrow seeking new directions. It became more integrated in the local organic agriculture movement and had an even greater focus on outreach and demonstration than it had with the "open-gate" neighborhood policy of its first years. By 2000 Corboy had acquired a 6,000-square-foot greenhouse to grow annuals, perennials and hanging baskets. Together with the Philadelphia Fair Food Project, Greensgrow is developing the Neighborhood Urban Agriculture Coalition, the goals of which include promoting urban agriculture as a form of community development for low-income Philadelphia neighborhoods, and giving small rural farmers access to the urban market. To this end, a CSA program was begun in 2002, with presubscribed shareholders coming to Greensgrow on Thursday afternoons to receive weekly baskets of

Figure 9.4   **Greensgrow, hydroponic lettuce crop**

freshly harvested food and flowers. Although Greensgrow's total 2002 gross revenues exceeded $100,000, Corboy struggles to maintain the project's viability by matching production with changes in the organic food market, and in the face of limited sources of outside funding. Nevertheless, Greensgrow's most notable achievement has been to sustain an essentially radical experiment in urban food production by working within the regulatory and neighborhood power structures of its local institutional context.

Greensgrow is connected to the long-standing grassroots interest in community gardens and neighborhood greening found throughout Philadelphia. Hundreds of individual sites, many in low-income neighborhoods, evoke William Penn's original image of the "Greene Countrie Towne." The idea of turning vacant lots into community-managed green space took hold in Philadelphia in the mid-1960s, with the creation of 60 small parks through a HUD beautification grant. This action tied into the city's aggressive urban renewal policy by establishing a land bank of tax-delinquent vacant properties for future redevelopment. The vacant land situation in today's Philadelphia forms the context in which local entrepreneurial urban agriculture occurs. There are close to 35,000 vacant lots in the city, and recent government actions reflect a belief that inner-city redevelopment in Philadelphia will result in vibrant, albeit less-populated, neighborhoods, leaving many opportunities for open-space creation on unbuilt parcels. Consequently, the future development of urban agriculture is largely tied to the city's evolving management of vacant land.

Philadelphia Green, a community program created by the Pennsylvania Horticultural Society (PHS) in the mid-1970s, has consistently viewed the city's vacant land opportunities as a logical way to further its mission to establish and manage urban green space. Since 1996 this goal has been realized in the neighborhood where Greensgrow is located, through Philadelphia Green's association with the New Kensington Community Development Corporation (NKCDC). Prior to this partnership, NKCDC had incorporated the opportunities presented by the 1,100 vacant parcels within its target area into a self-directed planning process, which had an explicit open-space management component (Bonham et al. 2002; Kromer 2000). This attracted the attention of Philadelphia Green, which had been asked by the city's Office of Housing and Community Development (OHCD) to undertake a neighborhood-based vacant land pilot project that specifically used CDCs as the primary facilitator.[3] The Greensgrow project grew directly out of this public/private land management partnership. Partly surrounded by rowhouses, its location was initially designated by NKCDC for future housing. In 1997, seeing no demand for the site from developers, NKCDC helped facilitate lease negotiations with its owner on behalf of Corboy and Sereduk.

Despite the modest awareness of urban agriculture in Philadelphia (city farming activities, including Greensgrow, have been profiled in the city's two daily newspapers), acquiring the needed land can be difficult. This is due to bureaucratic complexity and the way in which city agencies managing vacant land have traditionally guarded their own interests under a management structure developed incrementally over the last half century. For this reason, the strategic approach of locating urban agriculture within the framework of neighborhood-scaled vacant land management, as with that between OHCD, NKCDC and PHS, makes sense. In other words, first document the problematic situation of vacant land, then advocate urban agriculture as one of several possible solutions.

Overcoming Obstacles to Entrepreneurial Urban Agriculture

Surmounting the obstacles to market farming on underused city land involves practicality, persistence, a certain amount of luck and, perhaps most important, the ability and willingness to be flexible and improvisational in initiating and managing projects. (Although this section emphasizes entrepreneurial urban agriculture, some of the stated obstacles and the suggestions offered to address them apply equally to other forms of city farming, such as nonmarket community gardens.)

---

3. An assessment report on the New Kensington pilot project was produced by the Pennsylvania Horticultural Society (1999), which has also played a valuable role in examining entrepreneurial urban agriculture as a viable land use in Philadelphia.

What can be done to encourage support for entrepreneurial urban agriculture in this broader context? Its future depends in large part on the level of understanding and acceptance it can garner from key institutions—local governments, local foundations, community development corporations, neighborhood organizations and key state and federal government agencies. Yet, most representatives of potentially supportive organizations are generally unaware of the benefits of such projects or are skeptical about their durability and lasting significance. A critical entry point for advocates, then, is to convince doubters that the commonly perceived liabilities to city farming can be reduced, if not overcome. At the same time, the community benefits that result from city farming must be illuminated more clearly.

Certain barriers to entrepreneurial urban agriculture are more prevalent than others. Six of these, and approaches to overcome them, are listed below.

1. Entrepreneurial urban agriculture projects are difficult to site on vacant city lots due to excessive contamination.

Individuals often will express their concerns over the safety of food harvested from former residential sites tainted with lead and cadmium, or from commercial or industrial land harboring more dangerous contaminants. Minimizing the risk of growing food in urban soils, thus, becomes a common goal of urban agriculture managers. A variety of straightforward, low-tech methods can accomplish this. Some operations employ raised beds: a simple matter of building retaining walls of masonry or wood, generally 18 inches or higher, then filling the bed with imported topsoil and amendments of humus or compost. An effective, low-cost (and colorful) alternative are the round, plastic wading pools sometimes used in rooftop gardens (Figure 9.5). Other urban farms practice inground cultivation following careful soil preparation, by adding compost, for example, and through periodic soil testing afterward.

For certain crops, such as tomatoes, lettuces and sprouts, that can grow in a soil-free medium, hydroponics or cultivation in flat plastic trays is appropriate. Although the concept has proven effective, constructing a hydroponic system can become technically complicated, as with Village Farms/Buffalo. The cutting-edge nature of urban agriculture derives, in part, from the practical need to employ both traditional (greenhouses) and nontraditional (aquaculture, vermiculture, hydroponics and indoor growing) means of producing food at modest scales that are less land-dependent and can extend the conventional growing season into the colder months.

The relative ease with which raised beds can be created and the possibility of adapting a proposed activity to the capability of the site (deciding, for example, to grow nonedible marketable plants, such as street trees or cut flowers) mean that site contamination, while an issue of concern, is a surmountable problem. The bureaucratic complications and high costs involved in remediating a site can be avoided by simply choosing another, cleaner location. This can represent a logical option in cities with an abundance of vacant parcels. In areas that were once heavily industrial, however, the perception that many former industrial sites are beyond remediation can carry over to less-contaminated residential or

Figure 9.5   Plastic wading pools used for garden beds, Chicago

commercial land. For example, in Newark the widespread evidence of northern New Jersey's industrial past makes it difficult to argue that not all vacant parcels in the city are highly toxic and that safe and healthy food can be grown on at least some sites. In general, an increased knowledge of brownfields and the relevant legal issues and of the current parameters of environmental remediation (such as flexible cleanup standards to match different envisioned uses) allows for better decisions about whether or not to establish a food-growing operation on a particular site.

A longer-term vision guides current research into the properties of certain plant species to absorb soil contaminants, a process known as phytoremediation. This transforms the contamination issue into a relatively low-risk situation. In the late 1990s the EPA formed a phytoremediation research consortium comprised of state and federal agencies and private corporations. Meanwhile, biochemists at the University of Pennsylvania were investigating the properties of one particular plant, *Arabidopsis thaliana,* that allow it to efficiently absorb cadmium, arsenic and mercury from the soil of toxic sites (Jaffe 1999, C1).

2. Entrepreneurial urban agriculture projects located in crime-ridden neighborhoods are undermined by vandalism.

Many urban farms are fully visible along inner-city streets that have significant amounts of car and foot traffic both day and night. Thus, vandalism, specifically theft, trampling or refuse dumping, can be a problem; but, as with contamination, it is a surmountable one. Urban agriculture practitioners generally consider vandalism less of a deterrent and more of an irritant, addressed by securing equipment in sheds, installing perimeter fencing and lockable gates (with keys issued only to those involved with the project), and immediately removing graffiti. The pragmatic nature of urban farmers ensures that they will not become complacent toward errant behavior that can threaten a significant investment in time and labor.

Cultivating relationships with neighborhood residents to gain and maintain their trust and support is important in combating vandalism. In a number of situations, residents have developed a sense of civic "ownership" over a project site, either through direct participation in its creation or management or by simply appreciating how the project improved the look of the area. This feeling of neighborhood ownership can lead to the well-known "eyes on the street" phenomenon, where the emotional attachment to a neighborhood amenity leads to heightened surveillance over it. The New Kensington open-space program in Philadelphia was deemed a success after neighborhood residents chased an individual caught in the act of stealing a newly planted tree from a vacant lot cleaned of garbage. The thief got away, but the tree was soon replaced.

3. Entrepreneurial urban agriculture projects are not economically viable as profit generators.

It is a common, almost defining characteristic of city farming operations that they are managed on very limited budgets by initiating organizations dependent on gifts and grants. The relative newness of urban agriculture as a community-building vehicle has meant little capitalization for what are essentially very modest projects when compared to conventional farming. Some money is needed, but typically little money is made. Yet, entrepreneurial urban agriculture need not be seen as throwing money down a hole. A reasonable goal for practitioners is to set a revenue target that matches, or slightly exceeds, the costs of doing business, in other words, self-sufficiency. Reaching this goal would allow projects to be less grant dependent, so that managers can spend less time writing grants and more time farming (or in teaching others to farm, as in the case of Growing Power, where 14 percent of its revenues comes from training and workshop fees).

In general, the key to overcoming this concern lies in considering the returns to an urban farming investment as some acceptable combination of earned revenue and less-quantifiable social outcomes. This is the conclusion of two reports on entrepreneurial urban agriculture:

> The economic development potential for these [entrepreneurial community] gardens *is modest, but important*. Successful projects create immediate employment opportunities in low-income areas. More important, they play a critical role in preparing low-income residents for better quality jobs over the long term. They do so by providing educational opportunities, developing leadership and life skills, instilling a sense of control, and in other ways, contributing to a higher quality of life. (Feenstra et al. 1999, 34; italics added)

> The Study's findings of viable urban agricultural businesses suggest that ventures
> serving niche markets warrant further exploration, *even if most are marginally
> profitable at best.* . . . Philadelphia does contain some key ingredients required for
> these ventures, namely the availability of vacant, unused land, the identification
> of viable urban agriculture business models, and the entrepreneurial spirit of a
> core group of organizations and individuals who support the growth of urban
> agriculture in Philadelphia. The development of select for-profit businesses could
> serve as one of many options in City government's plans for overall vacant land
> management.[4] A nearby market of restaurants and consumers seeking the fresh-
> est, highest-quality produce offers the potential for new business and employment
> opportunities in Philadelphia's neighborhoods. (Hope Wohl Associates 2000, 18;
> italics and footnote added)

Under this view, the social benefits of city farming (e.g., neighborhood beautification, improved access to fresh produce, job creation, community building,
youth development, even the positive value of seeing growth every day rather
than decay) would not be ignored in its advocacy. Because such projects are char-
acteristically run by community-based, nonprofit organizations, one should not
judge the worth of entrepreneurial urban agriculture on profitability alone.

A basic advocacy strategy would clarify the objectives and practices of
urban agriculture, and not its novelty as an unconventional activity—in other
words, "packaging" urban agriculture in a manner that convinces others of its
merits. Local and national media could play a significant role in promoting a
nontraditional urban activity that is both photogenic and filled with human
interest angles (projects with a focus on young people are especially appealing).
A significant vehicle for presenting city farming to the general public has been
the occasional feature story (with photographs) in national publications such as
the *New York Times* (Davey 2003) and *Preservation* (Wilson 2002) and in daily
newspapers such as the *Chicago Tribune* (Anderson 1997), the New Orleans
Times-Picayune (Usher 2003), the *Philadelphia Daily News* (Geringer 2001) and
the *Detroit Free Press* (Dixon 2001). Over three consecutive days in October 1997,
the *Philadelphia Inquirer* ran a series of articles on local urban agriculture projects
and project initiators (Goodman 1997).

Within a public policy framework, a clear and straightforward presentation of successful urban agriculture examples can only further its consideration
by decision makers, especially if data suggest that support for urban farming
represents an effective public investment. As an example, research conducted
at Rutgers University revealed that, under certain conditions, the increased
consumption of vegetables grown in Trenton's community gardens would save
approximately $500,000 per year in cancer treatment costs (Hamm et al. 1999).

The central importance given to urban agriculture and its economic potential by the Dudley Street Neighborhood Initiative in Boston is an example that
can be advertised to other nonprofit community developers. Former DSNI

---

4. Here the report implies the public/private facilitation of entrepreneurial urban agriculture
described earlier in this chapter.

director, Greg Watson, said in a May 1999 speech to the National Neighborhood Association:

> A key part of our economic development strategy is urban agriculture. We envision 10 acres of community farms, a 10,000-square-foot, commercially viable greenhouse used to create community wealth, and growing value-added foods that reflect the cultural diversity and excitement of being in Dudley.

At the national level, organizations such as the American Community Gardening Association and the Community Food Security Coalition have issued policy papers documenting the social and economic benefits of community gardens and urban agriculture, respectively.[5] These are largely directed at decision makers, both in and out of government, positioned to grant more substantial and longer-lasting support to urban agriculture. Here, the relevant indicators might include the amount of food produced (and the dollar amount of this food if bought in a supermarket), the number of jobs created, the health benefits of the food consumed and the results of neighborhood surveys showing satisfaction with having an urban farm in the area. One could begin by looking to relevant federally funded Community Food Projects as a data source for such advocacy.[6]

4. Entrepreneurial urban agriculture projects are run by people who, although energetic and committed, lack the necessary management and business skills to make such ventures successful.

Some managers of nonprofit entrepreneurial urban agriculture ventures come from farming backgrounds. Others are young people fresh out of college, whose previous growing experiences may have occurred on small, rural organic farms, a quite different setting from the inner city. Others have some experience in community development or sustainable, environmentally centered activities. The idealism and commitment of these individuals can sometimes overshadow their capacities as business managers. Thus, skepticism can develop over the ability of those running for-market urban farms to successfully manage them as businesses.

This concern can be addressed in several ways. The most ideal is to hire people experienced in market agriculture who can juggle multiple responsibilities, and, especially in minority communities, speak the language of the street. Will Allen of Growing Power possesses this mix of characteristics and functions well in his multiple roles as farmer, administrator and communicator. In addition to the difficulties in simply finding them, keeping individuals with such qualities from being lured away by other opportunities is a challenge. One direc-

---

5. See Payne and Fryman (2001) and Brown (2002).

6. Since 1996 the U.S. Department of Agriculture has been a significant urban agriculture supporter through this annual competitive grant program managed through the department's Cooperative State Research, Education and Extension Service. Under the Farm Security and Rural Investment Act of 2002, approximately $5 million in Community Food Project grants will be awarded through fiscal year 2007.

tor of an urban agriculture nonprofit retained a valued grower by rearranging the organization's budget to provide him with a higher salary. The grower not only had extensive horticultural knowledge, but related especially well to the homeless men hired to help grow and distribute food. Urban agriculture organizations now execute nationwide job searches over the Internet to increase the chances of finding competent managers.

None of these attributes, however, signifies an ability to successfully manage a business, in particular the direct marketing from which urban agriculture revenues are generated. This, then, becomes an area in which partnership or pro bono support is appropriate. The Centro Agricola in Holyoke used grants from USDA and the Massachusetts Cultural Facilities Program to pay a consultant to prepare a professional business plan outlining operations, a marketing plan, development costs and financial projections.

In short, an organization planning to initiate an entrepreneurial project would do well to recognize that market urban agriculture is no different from other businesses. In addition to hard work, it requires a well thought-out business plan showing direction, cost/revenue projections and short- and long-term objectives. It also requires an ability to anticipate what problems may lie ahead in order to establish appropriate contingencies.

5. Entrepreneurial urban agriculture practitioners do not work together sufficiently to promote the potential and overall value of city farming.

Media accounts of urban agriculture generally portray a collection of independent efforts fending for themselves, often with focused, charismatic individuals at the helm. This is not a totally inaccurate picture. The day-to-day management of urban agriculture can be very time-consuming, leaving little time to network and work cooperatively with like-minded individuals and groups. Experience, however, has taught growers in several cities the importance of establishing good lines of communication. When local or national information is shared on topics such as grant opportunities and best practices, the cause of urban agriculture is advanced through cooperative, rather than autonomous, action.

One emerging approach involves networked "seed groups" of urban growers who advocate for urban agriculture in their respective local settings. The Detroit Agriculture Network (DAN) started in 1995 as a group of organizations involved in various aspects of city farming. Meeting over occasional potluck suppers to pursue common interests, DAN members envisioned vacant lots transformed into community gardens, neighborhood farms and outdoor farmers' markets. In addition, community greenhouses would sell flowers and grower cooperatives would sell Detroit-grown produce and other local products at farmers' markets, restaurants and corner stores. In 1997 DAN secured a USDA Community Food Projects grant of $180,000 to develop entrepreneurial projects as a component of an alternative food-based economic sector. Today, DAN has more than 200 individual and organizational members supporting almost 40 project sites across Detroit and the older suburbs of Highland Park and Hamtramck.

A practical problem facing these local networks lies in the diverse nature of urban agriculture, making it difficult to merge the different interests of individual members into a single advocacy direction for the entire group. This issue confronted participants in Boston during discussions in the late 1990s about whether to favor market production activities over traditional nonmarket consumption by individual growers, the pattern typical of most community gardens.

A second type of local coalition, the food policy council, is more comprehensive in scope, involving groups of food security advocates who meet regularly to survey local conditions and lobby for improvements in the availability of affordable, healthy, accessible and culturally appropriate food for an entire metropolitan population, particularly for those of low income. Within these coalitions, examples of which exist in a growing number of communities, urban agriculture finds a ready niche amid efforts to improve the quality of school lunches, anti-hunger initiatives and attempts to lure supermarkets back to poor neighborhoods in central cities.

6. Entrepreneurial urban agriculture projects represent a temporary land use, lasting only until "real" revenue-producing development occurs.

It is vitally important to dispel the prevailing notion that community gardening/ urban agriculture is merely a temporary land use until "real" revenue-producing development can be arranged. Like the contamination issue, overcoming this concern involves either avoiding the issue completely (by concluding that a site is destined for development in the near future and thus looking elsewhere) or understanding the different avenues available to help nonprofits secure permanent land access.

Some examples of city farming occur on land owned by individuals, institutions or governments (acting in the public interest) that see the benefits these activities provide. In such instances, long- or short-term agreements for the use of their land have been established. But owning the land outright is clearly the best option for securing land tenure in most situations. Although the purchase of land for urban agriculture is possible, such action is infrequent, due to the costs involved for resource-strapped community organizations.

Public land trusts are an effective means of securing permanent sites for community gardens and entrepreneurial urban farms in the future. In Philadelphia the Neighborhood Gardens Association (NGA), a land trust founded by the Penn State Urban Gardening Program and Philadelphia Green in 1986, acquires existing gardens following solicitation by the gardeners and a careful review of site characteristics by NGA staff. The association has thus far acquired 23 garden sites in North, West and South Philadelphia. Similarly, the Boston Natural Areas Network is critical to the long-term stabilization of that city's community gardens, with almost 40 sites now under its ownership. And in Chicago the innovative NeighborSpace land trust, jointly funded by the city of Chicago, the Chicago Park District and the Cook County Forest Preserve District, is a model for land use partnership between local government and neighborhood organizations. After two years of operation, NeighborSpace had assumed title to more than 50 community parks, gardens and natural areas throughout Chicago. Of these, only seven were used for food production, a result of community preference and not NeighborSpace policy.

Establishing community gardens under city ownership and management is another possible solution. Doing this, of course, assumes that municipal governments become convinced of the value of urban agriculture (and its attendant administration) in serving specified community development objectives.

Conclusion

Addressing each of these six perceived obstacles presumes that advocates of entrepreneurial urban agriculture must play active and important roles. In some instances, they might focus on changing negative perceptions related to site contamination, vandalism and inadequate staff capacity. In other cases, their efforts would be directed at broadening the terms of the debate, such as judging for-market city farms on their ability to generate multiple benefits, rather than solely on the grounds of financial viability.

For starters, city farming advocates need political savvy, the ability to establish appropriate political and bureaucratic connections, and the patience to work with and through complicated bureaucracies. Identifying existing policy instruments as frameworks within which to insert entrepreneurial urban agriculture would be an example of appropriate proactive behavior. In Philadelphia a 1995 City Planning Commission policy report, written to further the local vacant land debate, implicitly suggested openings for urban agriculture within a concept of "neighborhood restructuring":

> The objective of this restructuring is to create more attractive and desirable urban neighborhoods by taking advantage of vacant land to reduce residential densities, provide more private living space for individual households, *and to make community open space "intentional"*—an asset and amenity for the neighborhood, rather than the unfortunate byproduct of public actions to remove dangerous buildings. (Philadelphia City Planning Commission 1995, 39; italics added)

Incorporating urban agriculture into municipal comprehensive plans as an *intentional* use of civic space would legitimize city farming, as would its recognition as an important component of a city's managed open-space strategy, with community stakeholders acting as stewards over individual sites. The manner in which Greensgrow began as a grassroots project within existing public- and private-sector vacant land initiatives in Philadelphia is an excellent example of planning actions facilitating creative community proposals.

Similarly, community-based nonprofits seeking grants for entrepreneurial urban agriculture should frame proposals more holistically, emphasizing the capacity of the project to address a variety of community benefits. This reflects an understanding that outside support would be more likely if proposals are set within a larger context—as part of an overall sustainable community approach, for example—rather than standing alone as independent efforts.

A direct promotional tactic could involve creating video presentations of successful urban agriculture elsewhere in the country. Interest could then be stimulated by showing the more appealing images of city farming—picking ripe tomatoes, making value-added products like salsa or jams from the products grown, and youngsters tending worm bins producing high-quality compost. Research by local universities could look at the social effects of growing food on urban sites. Such topics might include the possible savings in health care costs due to the consumption of city-grown organic produce, or the use of food-related businesses to aid local welfare-to-work programs by serving as a source of living wage jobs.

A proponent of urban agriculture in Philadelphia recently sketched her vision of an urban future as she looked at blocks of abandoned land in that city: "Try to imagine what it would feel like if there were food being grown all around here. How the energy would change if people could get entrepreneurial training, and eventually go out and start their own urban farm or business" (Goodman 1997). Those who would endorse such a vision hope to see entrepreneurial urban agriculture's now-small footprint increase in cities with abundant or modest supplies of vacant, abandoned land. There exists, at the same time, a more sobering reality for entrepreneurial urban agriculture: its enthusiasts are far outnumbered by its skeptics; its representative projects are underfunded, understaffed and confronted with difficult management and marketing issues; it is not seen as the highest and best use of vacant inner-city land by local policy makers; and it still suffers from the conventional view that food growing is something that takes place and belongs on rural land.

In the final analysis, many American cities are hard-pressed to maintain their residential viability. Municipal leaders want their middle-class residents to stay put rather than move to the suburbs. They wish for more market housing and small businesses on now-vacant land. They would like to see a strong back-to-the-city movement to fuel the revitalization of depressed neighborhoods. But, the reality is that the middle-class exodus continues in many of these cities, leaving behind vacant land as a long-term policy problem. It is true that some vacant parcels, because of their strategic locations near reviving downtowns, commercial thoroughfares or waterfronts will be attractive sites for future housing and business developments. Yet, considerable numbers of parcels in these same cities will likely remain vacant, unsightly and unproductive.

Every year, more civic actors begin to believe in the opportunities of using excess vacant land to grow food for the benefit of urban residents. Recent evidence suggests that the nascent movement of urban agriculture, particularly entrepreneurial urban agriculture, is worth a more concerted effort.

References

Anderson, Jon. 1997. Fish farming takes root in city. *Chicago Tribune*, December 24, B1.

Bailkey, Martin and Joe Nasr. 1999. From brownfields to greenfields: Producing food in North American cities. *Community Food Security News* (Fall 1999/Winter 2000): 6–8.

Bonham, J. Blaine, Jr., Gerri Spilka and Darl Rastorfer. 2002. *Old cities/new cities: Communities transform unmanaged land.* PAS report 506/507. Chicago: American Planning Association, Planning Advisory Service.

Boston Globe. 2002. Mission Hill masterpiece. *Boston Globe*, September 14, A12.

Brown, Katherine H. (principal author). 2002. Urban agriculture and community food security in the United States: Farming from the city center to the urban fringe. Policy paper. Venice, CA: Community Food Security Coalition. http://www.foodsecurity.org/urbanag.html.

Davey, Monica. 2003. A garden flourishes amid Chicago's projects. *New York Times*, August 25, A8.

Dixon, Jennifer. 2001. Detroit is friar's field of dreams. *Detroit Free Press*, April 16.

Feenstra, Gail, Sharyl McGrew and David Campbell. 1999. Entrepreneurial community gardens: Growing food, skills, jobs and communities. University of California Agriculture and Natural Resources Publication 21587.

Geringer, Dan. 2001. Growing lettuce in the city. *Philadelphia Daily News*, June 11.

Goodman, Howard. 1997. Sowing seeds of change: Down on the farm in Philadelphia. *Philadelphia Inquirer*, October 12–14.

Hamm, Michael, Matthew Griffin, Megan McGlinchy and Marty Johnson. 1999. Community gardening, vegetable intake, and the potential to reduce health care costs: A case study of Trenton, New Jersey. Paper presented at the joint meeting of the Agriculture, Food and Human Values Society and the Association for the Study of Food and Society, Toronto, Ontario, June 5.

Hope Wohl Associates. 2000. *The feasibility of urban agriculture with recommendations for Philadelphia*. Philadelphia: Pennsylvania Horticultural Society.

Jaffe, Mark. 1999. Growing a cleanser. *Philadelphia Inquirer*, June 14, C1.

Kaufman, Jerry and Martin Bailkey. 2000. Farming inside cities: Entrepreneurial urban agriculture in the United States. Working paper. Cambridge, MA: Lincoln Institute of Land Policy.

Kromer, John. 2000. *Neighborhood recovery: Reinvestment policy for the new hometown*. New Brunswick, NJ: Rutgers University Press.

Meyer, Brian. 1998. Bearing fruit: Brownfields "farm" produces first crop. *Buffalo News*, April 16, 1A.

Monroe-Santos, Suzanne. 1998. Recent national survey shows status of community gardens. *Community Greening Review 1998* (American Community Gardening Association) 8:12, 17.

Payne, Karen and Deborah Fryman. 2001. *Cultivating community: Principles and practices for community gardening as a community-building tool*. American Community Gardening Association.

Pennsylvania Horticultural Society. 1999. *From vacant land to open space: An evaluation of the New Kensington Neighborhood Open Space Management Program*. Philadelphia: Pennsylvania Horticultural Society.

Philadelphia City Planning Commission. 1995. *Vacant land in Philadelphia: A report on vacant land management and neighborhood restructuring*. Philadelphia: City Planning Commission.

Revkin, Andrew C. 1998. For urban wastelands, tomatoes and other life. *New York Times*, March 3, A1.

Rummler, Gary. 1997. Planting seeds of hope at Victory Park. *Milwaukee Journal Sentinel*, July 29, B3.

Usher, Nikki. 2003. A garden of hope: St. Thomas youths develop pepper sauce, job prospects. *(New Orleans) Times-Picayune,* July 21, B1.

Wilson, Charles. 2002. Asphalt eden. *Preservation* 54(3):58–65.

10 | Creative Brownfield Redevelopment

The Experience of the IBA Emscher Park Initiative in the Ruhr in Germany

Klaus R. Kunzmann

There is one feature traditional industrial regions have in common around the developed world: extensive blighted brownfields. Industrial cities in Europe, such as Birmingham, St. Etienne and Duisburg, and port cities, such as Genoa, Liverpool, Marseilles and Bilbao, have become symbols of the decline of traditional industrial economies in a globalized world. They all deal with the aesthetically unpleasant, environmentally hazardous and economically unprofitable brownfields, legacies of massive industrialization of the late nineteenth and twentieth centuries. Today, these cities have considerable difficulties in redeveloping such sites. The original landowners do not need the once heavily used land, and there is no property market that shows an interest in such sites, even if their property values are low. With little demand for such land, redevelopment is difficult, time consuming and costly. Hence, the sites remain idle for years or even decades, surrounded by wired fences and security guards. Brownfields are eyesores in the urban landscape of postindustrial society and physical barriers for future-oriented urban development.

There are, of course, exceptions. Brownfield sites at upscale inner-city locations in metropolises where property values are high are, as a rule, successfully revitalized. This is true also for sites at scenic locations, such as riverbanks, places of historic interest or within or adjacent to an attractive residential area. Most brownfields, however, are difficult to reuse, requiring more creative and visionary efforts to overcome the market failure. Planners, confronted with the challenge of finding new uses for brownfields, have three options:

1. They may demolish all structures on the site to make way for new public or private projects, malls, office development or infrastructure. Whether the enormous investment in demolishing the industrial structures and the subsequent environmental cleanup make economic sense depends on the location of the site within the city, the potential of the public sector, the market demand at the time of the factory's closing, and the interest of private investors to take risks.

2. Industrial conservationists may choose to maintain all or most of the structures on the brownfield site. This may require the transformation of such structures into flexible "containers" for artists or architects, theaters or nightclubs, for other cultural or creative uses, or for loft housing. Again, the location will determine the standards of such rehabilitation, which may range from minimum-cost, do-it-yourself adaptation to high-end modernization by renowned architects.

3. There may be good arguments for totally demolishing the industrial structures, covering the polluted ground with topsoil, and transforming the site into a public park or a "new" greenfield site, which at a later stage could be brought back into the market, once the location becomes attractive for new investment.

The Ruhr: A Difficult Terrain for Brownfield Redevelopment

An abundance of brownfields has been one of the problems in the long process of revitalizing the Ruhr in Germany. This region (Figure 10.1), once the industrial heart of Germany, where coal mining and steel production dominated the economy and the labor market, has been hit hard by structural change. The economic success of the past left a devastated industrial landscape, marred by roads, railways, waterways, gas or sewage pipes and countless brownfields. The urban industrial landscape, where soil and water are polluted and smoke stacks dominate the skyline, could no longer compete with other, thriving German cities such as Munich, Frankfurt and Düsseldorf.

The Ruhr, an area about 4,500 square kilometers, with 53 communities and a population of 5.2 million, has no one major city, but a few larger cities such as Essen, Duisburg, Dortmund and Bochum, which compete rather than cooperate with one another. Hence, none of these cities could be called the heart or the capital of the region. Neither influential feudal residences nor independent bourgeois towns (as in southern Germany) historically dominated the region along the Ruhr and Emscher rivers. The cities of Duisburg, Essen and Dortmund were only second-rank urban centers in this Prussian province before industrialization entered the region and rich coal resources transformed it into a dense network of industrial villages.

The vested interests of the coal mining and steel producing corporations dominated spatial development for decades. Coal mining companies built housing around the pits, and public infrastructure followed the mines and steel works. Similarly, rail transport served the industries first, before other demands of the community were met. Over the years, industrial villages grew into functional industrial towns, which developed their own local cultures and pride. But the usual features of declining industrial regions now characterize the Ruhr: high unemployment, environmental pollution, an unappealing urban fabric and deteriorating public infrastructure. All this is embedded in a socio-political climate where large corporations dominate, entrepreneurial spirit and

**Figure 10.1   The Metropolitan Region RheinRuhr, in North Rhine-
Westphalia**

Source: IRPUD

services are lacking, unions are strong and innovative actors are scarce (Kunzmann 2000). Understandably, such features are not attractive for potential
property developers and investors who are not familiar with the region and not
linked to their influential actors in a complex decision-making environment.
Intraregional jealousy and competition usually torpedo any rational division of
labor here (Benz et al. 2000). This traditional industrial region has been under
continuous pressure to modernize. However, the regional actors do not agree on
the means and goals of structural change, making urban and regional revitalization difficult and cumbersome.

The transformation problems of the Ruhr do not differ much from the problems most deindustrializing regions around the world face in times of globalization and technological change. Coal mining and the large industrial complex
are eroding. Modern services favor locations other than those between derelict
industries and industrial workers' colonies. Entrepreneurship is not a strength
of the region, where workers are accustomed to lifelong provision of services,
and industries, local governments and the labor force are dependent on generous

state subsidies. Unemployment is higher than elsewhere in western Germany, and for many reasons there is very little inward investment in the region.

The Ruhr also lacks provincial highlights and urban assets. Each major city in the multinodal region pursues its own local (and quite parochial) development aims. The smaller cities have neither the experience nor the means to form their own strategic alliances. Intercommunal competition dominates local decision making. Only since the 1960s has there been an open discourse on the future of the region as a whole.

Brownfield redevelopment has not been a major policy of the local and regional institutions in the Ruhr, at least not a successful one. The traditional landowners were not keen to sell property with environmental liabilities. Only occasionally were former pit sites cleared and turned into public industrial parks where local industries found new space for production and services. In other sites, transient users offered just short-term contracts for former office space and workshops to run their businesses or cultural activities. However, when some form of illegal squatting was reported, the public sector had to intervene.

As late as the early 1980s, when brownfields started to become a public issue, the state government of North Rhine-Westphalia established a rotating superfund for brownfields (US$250 million), to which local governments were offered access, and asked the state's *Landesentwicklungsgesellschaft* (development corporation) to manage the fund. However, the lack of financial resources was not the main constraint for successful brownfield redevelopment; rather, it was the lack of ideas about what to do with the sites. This is exactly what the ambitious IBA Emscher Park Initiative (Internationale Bauausstellung Emscher Park) aimed to overcome (Figure 10.2). It followed longstanding traditions of building exhibitions in Germany (e.g., Interbau 1957, IBA Berlin 1978–1984), which demonstrated state-of-the art approaches to urban development.

The IBA Emscher Park Initiative

The IBA Emscher Park Initiative was a 10-year (1989–1999) undertaking by the state government of North Rhine-Westphalia to revitalize a 20-by-50-mile industrial rustbelt in the heart of the still heavily industrialized region with more than 5,000 acres of brownfields. In the late 1980s the Ministry of Urban Planning and Transport of the State of North Rhine-Westphalia, inspired by its young and ambitious state minister Christoph Zöpel and his creative advisers Karl Ganser and Wolfgang Roters, launched the regional development initiative for a 15-mile corridor stretching 50 miles east from the Rhine River. In contrast to previous regional development programs, the initiative was aimed primarily at changing the physical appearance of the Ruhr and the negative image of the region. The ambitious state program was labeled "A Workshop for the Future of Industrial Regions" (IBA Emscher Park 1988).

Bypassing the region's existing institutional hierarchy, a small development agency was established to do the work. It was led by a manager who came from outside the regional political milieu and was appointed by the government of

Figure 10.2   Map of Emscher Park Region in the Ruhr

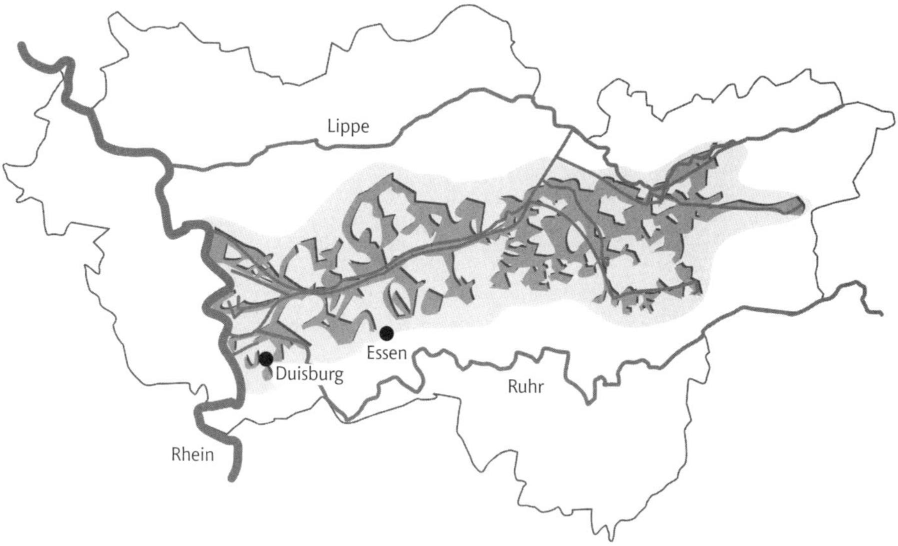

Source: IBA

North Rhine-Westphalia and given access to all state ministries and their budgets for regional and urban policy matters. The lean agency (with fewer than 30 staff members) was supported by four boards with members of the relevant state's ministries, as well as from regional institutions and local governments, representatives and experts.

This new, separate agency that was responsible for the day-to-day activities of the initiative was an affront to the regional establishment, local governments and the intercommunal regional authority, the Kommunalverband Ruhrkohlenbezirk (KVR). Traditionally, the local governments, via their political party networks, negotiated with the state government for support of development projects. The regional authority had hoped to be entrusted with the task of steering and managing the initiative. However, there were good reasons not to assign the 10-year project to this institution, which for more than two decades had failed to develop any future-oriented visions for the region as a whole. In bypassing the traditional regional policy networks, the project could be implemented outside corporate influence and party machinery (Kilper 2000). Given the political convention in the Ruhr and the post-war tradition of codetermination within the region's powerful coal and steel corporations, these policy networks were in the firm hands of the Social Democratic Party and the labor unions.

As part of a second strategic policy decision, the new agency did not have any control over an investment budget, except for its own operations and communication costs and some seed money for architectural and design competitions and for initiating innovative projects. This was done to avoid constitutional problems and also to prevent the local governments or private investors from shifting their money-seeking habits to the new agency.

The aims and action areas of the IBA initiative were defined in the original project memorandum as follows (IBA Emscher Park 1988):

- Ecological transformation and structural revitalization of derelict landscape;

- Renaturalization of the Emscher River;

- Conversion of derelict industrial land (brownfield redevelopment);

- Conservation of the industrial heritage;

- Construction of affordable model housing schemes;

- Promotion of architecturally outstanding new working environments, *Arbeiten im Park*; and

- Promotion of cultural industries and the arts to enhance the regional cultural environment and create new jobs.

These goals were pursued through strict application of several environmental, social and cultural principles, such as architectural merit, energy conservation, imaginative landscaping, accessibility to public transportation, conservation of sensitive micro-ecosystems, local commitment, partnerships, self-organization, procedural implementation and low maintenance costs. A long list of ambitious sustainability and quality criteria was developed and applied to judge each individual project and guide its implementation. Where the criteria were not accepted, no public money was offered.

Financial support came from the state government, and once the criteria were satisfactorily met and the IBA assessment boards had approved, projects were given the official go-ahead. In addition, substantial political support from the state's prime minister helped the IBA agency to overcome any bureaucratic and ideological constraints or local parochialism and nepotism. To guarantee that these principles were applied, the IBA Emscher Park Initiative undertook the following actions:

- International competitions among architects, urban designers and landscape architects were utilized to find the most creative solution for the brownfield site. The costs of the completions were borne by the IBA agency.

- With the help of conservationists and industrial historians in the public sector, outstanding industrial structures were listed as historical monuments the day they went out of use, making their likely demolition by the owners impossible.

- The brownfield sites were considered as spaces for incremental creative action, with no predetermined final stage. Hence, no blueprints were made and no feasibility studies were commissioned.

- Local civic groups were deliberately involved in the reutilization of the brownfields and their maintenance, thus giving them a sense of ownership and responsibility.

- To avoid infinite public subsidies, the transformation of industrial sites into industrial heritage museums was restricted to only a few sites with high architectural value. Preserving industrial structures was embedded in concepts of economic and cultural use, but transitional use of the site was not excluded, nor was its final demolition.

- Media-covered events, such as light shows, festivals, open-air concerts and art exhibitions, were used to make the sites accessible and regionally known. The provision of look-outs has contributed much to the popularity of the IBA flagship projects. In absence of cathedrals and bell towers, citizens had never had an opportunity to experience a bird's-eye view of the area. With the opening up of industrial structures, exciting new views of the urban landscape were made possible.

- To keep maintenance costs minimal, labor office–financed employment initiatives were used, and insurance issues and liability concerns were kept at a low profile. Although security concerns were taken seriously, only a few security guards control the industrial sites, relying on visitors to be responsible for their own safety.

- The rotating property fund made it feasible for the state's development corporation to buy up the industrial structures. A public-private foundation for the conservation of industrial heritage was established to take care of those structures, for which no new use has yet been identified.

The development of the projects was usually done by public-private partnerships, with the state's development agency as a key partner. Overall, the state government of North Rhine-Westphalia has invested about US$2 billion over 10 years in a broad range of activities to change the image of the Ruhr, to create jobs and to redevelop brownfields and public parks in the neglected industrial region (IBA 1999; Höber and Ganser 1999).

Two Examples of the IBA Approach to Brownfield Redevelopment

The reuse of derelict industrial structures on former coal or steel production sites has been a key concern of the IBA Emscher Park Initiative. Almost monthly, as a consequence of globalization and structural change, traditional industries are closed in this region, adding to the abundance of brownfield sites there. Due to the relatively unfavorable locations of the sites and because of the absence of pressing market demand, it is difficult to find new uses and users for the sites. The demand for industrial land is low, white-collar service industries prefer to invest near the city centers of Dortmund or Essen, and wholesale markets and shopping malls are reaching a saturation point in the region. Housing on former industrial sites is not well accepted by individual private investors or housing associations, for a variety of health reasons. In absence of true pressure from the real estate market, housing in nearby cities (e.g., Düsseldorf) or in suburban communities is more attractive and cheaper.

Because of such market factors, the public sector in the state of North Rhine-Westphalia has been forced to take the lead. Some sites have been cleared for innovative projects such as technology parks; a few have been transformed into museums of industrial history or new industrial parks; others have been turned into accessible public parks and linked to the larger regional park. For a few brownfield sites with historical industrial landmarks other uses had to be found, including four of particular interest: the Landschaftspark (landscape park) in the city of Duisburg-Meiderich; the Design Center of the State of North Rhine-Westphalia on the former pit site of the Zeche Zollverein in Essen; the garden festival and industrial park on Zeche Nordstern in Gelsenkirchen; and the Jahrhunderthalle in Bochum. Their transformation by the IBA initiative has contributed considerably to the changing image of the region. Two of the projects are described below.

The Landschaftspark in Duisburg

The Thyssen steelworks in Duisburg-Meiderich was one of the largest blast furnace plants in the Ruhr. It provided employment to more than 10,000 proud steel workers in this prototypical industrial city, with its coal mines, steel works and important inland port. When it closed in 1985 after 82 years of productive existence, there was little hope that the 5,000-acre site would bring new investment. The price of scrap metal was so low at the time that it was difficult to find a buyer. Even the Chinese government, always on the search in the Ruhr for reusable industrial production sites, showed no interest in dismantling the furnace, shipping it to China and rebuilding it in one of the country's industrial cities.

Faced with so little outside interest, the city government was desperate. They finally accepted an offer from the IBA Emscher Park Initiative to gradually develop the site into a large landscape park. In 1991 the state development corporation acquired the site for a symbolic fee of DM 1, and the owner, the Thyssen corporation, was convinced to offer US$2.5 million to start a fund for its development. The landscape architect Peter Latz and his team won the fierce international competition launched by the IBA agency. Latz proposed to transform the site into a new, ecologically sensitive landscape park around the huge steel furnaces and make the park accessible to the public at an early stage of the incremental development process. Over the following years, new uses were identified and realized for one structure after another. For example, a furnace was used as an open-air theater for operas, concerts and movie performances; a gas tank was transformed into a training ground for local divers; the coal storage bunkers were handed over to the local mountaineering club, who turned them into a paradise for climbers of all ages; and one of the large production halls was converted into a facility for world music performances. A small experimental theater was located in one of the former industrial structures, and a popular discotheque in another. The park has quickly become a favorite destination for weekend trips, for visitors from abroad and for the annual cultural festival of the city of Duisburg. It is managed by a small partnership funded by the state and the local government, with support from various local nongovernmental organizations.

The fact that the park was accessible to the public at no cost contributed much to its popularity. The light installations by Jonathan Park, the renowned British lighting engineer for the Rolling Stones, were also a draw. Park developed an impressive two-hour light show for the steel furnaces, which render the industrial structures into an imaginative, colorful mega-structure that can be seen from afar by passing motorists (Figure 10.3). The park, though initially not universally loved by the pragmatic local councilors, has now become widely accepted as a symbol of hope for the declining city in post-industrial times and has successfully replaced the images of derelict chimneys and steelworks.

The Zeche Zollverein in Essen

The Zeche Zollverein in Essen-Katernberg was opened as a coal pit in 1847 to exploit the high-quality coal found 180 to 800 meters below the surface. At that time it was the most northern coal pit in the Ruhr. Between 1928 and 1932 the architects Fritz Schupp and Martin Kremmer were commissioned to design a modern structure on the site. The result was an impressive industrial complex, which became a prototype of Bauhaus industrial architecture. When the pit was closed in 1986, around 15,000 workers lost their jobs or were transferred, and the local community lost its traditional economic center. The owners, the RAG, wanted to demolish the now obsolete structure, but public conservationists, on the order of the state minister, listed the building as a historic monument, thereby preventing its destruction.

Figure 10.3   Landschaftspark, Duisburg

Source: IBA

Following their philosophy of incremental transformation, the IBA agency proposed to turn the complex into a center of cultural industry (Figure 10.4). The British architect Norman Foster converted the power station into the Design Zentrum NRW (North Rhine-Westphalia Center of Design), a combination of a design museum and an office building. An upscale restaurant was built in a production hall; other buildings became conference facilities or workshops for designers, artists and other cultural employees. The well-known local modern dance company was given a former industrial edifice for training workshops and performance spaces. Over the years the whole precinct served as a magnet for creative types and entrepreneurs. A wonderful temporary exhibition on the use of energy was installed in the former coke plant, and a complex for start-ups in the creative industry was promoted by the city of Essen in another corner of the 13-kilometer area.

While the local neighborhoods and the traditional political milieu still struggle to accept this transformation, the Zeche Zollverein, just 20 minutes from the city center of Essen, the region's largest town, has become a hub of cultural activity. It is a site for international conferences, festivals and a must-see for tourists in the area, and there is still ample space for new ideas, cultural entrepreneurs and facilities. The local management team, a partnership of local organizations

Figure 10.4   Zeche Zollverein, Essen

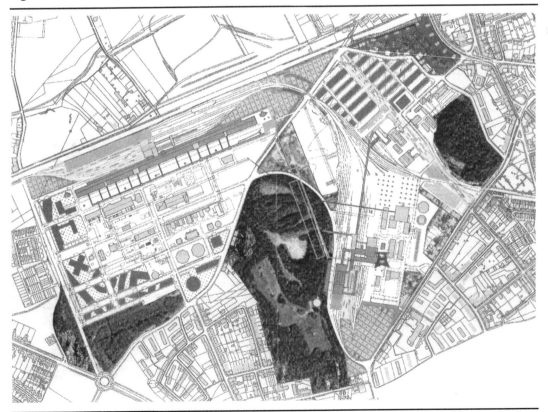

Source: IBA

and city and state governments, is now considering moving to Zeche Zollverein the local academy of fine and performing arts, the Folkwang Academy, one of the outstanding training institutions in the state, to create a cultural complex of international reputation. The Ruhr Triennial will use the site for ambitious theater productions as part of that cultural festival. In addition, a new International School of Design will soon be built on the site, based on the design of the Japanese architects Kazuyo Sejima and Ryve Nishizawa from the Tokyo-based studio SANAA, who won the international design competition.

Landschaftspark and Zeche Zollverein were among the best-known flagship projects of the IBA Emscher Park Initiative. They exemplify the potential to reuse industrial sites for the development of creative industries. These sites have contributed much to changing the face of the region and have become prototypes for the creative use of brownfield sites and industrial megastructures. No wonder they are the key stages for the new Ruhr Triennial, an ambitious effort by the state government to emulate the success of the Edinburgh and Salzburg cultural festivals (Figure 10.5). Gérard Mortier, the former director of the Salzburg Festival, has been selected as the Ruhr Triennial's artistic director. The inspiring industrial stages convinced him to accept the challenge of developing a cultural festival in a region that otherwise lacks attractions for international visitors.

Brownfield Sites and Cultural Industries

Cultural industries, the arts and entertainment were key components of the innovative public sector–led regional revitalization strategy in the Ruhr. The IBA Emscher Park Initiative has demonstrated that cultural applications in the broad sense are a perfect use (at least a perfect interim use) for brownfield sites in postindustrial times. Artists and developers searching for niches in the competitive real estate market are encouraged by the special features of such sites that offer productive spaces in a different environment (Bradke and Löwer 2000). There are at least three reasons why brownfield sites are attractive and particularly well suited for innovative urban development.

Visual innovation and creative settings. As a rule, brownfield sites, particularly if the structures are landmarks, industrial heritage sites or from the early ages of industrialization, offer new, photogenic centers for art, music or design activities in an environment where exciting visual experiences are sought. This is true for a whole range of cultural industries, from the up-market, where architects, designers, and music and multimedia producers can afford unique structures that are preferred over mass-produced office space, to the lower end, where artists, craftspeople, start-up companies and experimental theater groups seek affordable space for the production and presentation of their work. And visual reference to such sites in glossy brochures is of some importance to young entrepreneurs in cultural industries, as it conveys an avant-garde aspect that can be important for marketing efforts or just for the image of the artisans in such developments.

Figure 10.5   Site of the New Ruhr Festival: Ruhr Triennial

Source: Ruhrtriennale

High spatial flexibility and transitional use potential. While dependent on local regulations, such as fire or building codes, industrial structures on brownfield sites are usually more flexible in use than traditional buildings. The control is less rigid and the space is not as expensive. Hence, the combination of low-cost productive space and flexibility makes such projects appealing to those who, as a rule, do not wish to make longer-term commitment, take financial risks or pay for professional facility management. Such features make brownfields a perfect interim solution for start-ups in the financially risky cultural industries. The pioneers who have become passionate residents in such sites have ample space for creative renovation and incremental expansion, raising standards gradually according to their requirements and available means.

Noise resistance and event suitability. Generally activities on brownfield sites do not create major noise pollution, which could elicit neighborhood complaints. This appeals to nightclub managers, popular music groups and jazz clubs. The fact that such sites provide almost unlimited parking space also contributes to their popularity. For such reasons and because of their landmark character, they can easily accommodate big events, even if they occur only a few times a year. The event suitability may be another advantage in qualifying for public financial support, particularly when the site is a landmark of historical interest and is registered as such.

Additional arguments for the incremental reuse of derelict land in less-favored locations of city regions for creative industries may arise from the local political context. Recent interest in Europe in promoting creative industries (Cliche et al. 2002) will certainly encourage local governments to explore the use of obsolete brownfield developments for such innovative uses. Experience from the IBA Emscher Park Initiative demonstrates that three things are essential for developing brownfield sites for cultural industries: a visionary incremental approach, the involvement of creative expertise from outside the region, and trust in the enthusiasm of regional innovative networks.

Lessons Learned from the IBA Initiative

What are the lessons learned from the IBA initiative and its efforts to revitalize brownfields and transform the industrial landscape? Obviously, the flagship projects of the IBA initiative have become popular attractions in the Ruhr and serve as magnets for many activities in the region. They are symbols of transformation and of the region's potential to become a modern technopolitan center, where a new economic base is emerging from the fusion of traditional industrial knowledge and new communication and information technologies.

There is another, surprising effect of the IBA Emscher Park Initiative. In its early years, the private sector, particularly middle management of large energy and steel corporations, showed little enthusiasm or cooperative spirit. Entrenched in their local pragmatism, they could not imagine brownfields serving anything other than industrial production. Together with the local political stakeholders, they were primarily concerned with quickly getting rid of obsolete structures to clear the grounds for new development. Cultural industries and the arts were not the obvious, appropriate subsequent use to coal and steel production sites. However, once they witnessed the transformation and the positive regional and international media coverage of the flagship projects, they began to use the converted structures for their own image-building activities, including conferences and shareholder meetings. Moreover, single property arms of the corporations jumped on the bandwagon and began to develop private entertainment centers on their derelict properties. One such project is an artificial indoor ski slope on a former slagheap in Bottrop; comparable projects in other cities are in development. The IBA has demonstrated that urban entertainment is a moneymaking industry in a region where more than 15 million consumers live within a one-hour catchment area.

The IBA initiative was a holistic concept for regional revitalization, a continuous process of guided incrementalism that responded to efforts by visionary actors. No blueprint or comprehensive master plan has been designed for the region. Individual projects followed a vague long-term vision. In a design-by-progress manner, many projects, mainly on brownfield sites, were started even when the final product could not yet be defined. Only a few flagship projects were implemented on brownfield sites to illustrate the applied principles and to attract outside interest. The conservation of the rich industrial heritage and the promotion of cultural catalysts were seen as keys to regional modernization. The IBA initiative experimented with regional modernization that differed considerably from the usual developer-led regeneration approach that other regions and cities around the world, such as Pittsburgh, Pennsylvania, or the Docklands, in London, had adopted.

Although the 10-year initiative has many grassroots and bottom-up features, it was in fact a farsighted, rather subversive, top-down strategy. It was subversive because it applied grassroots ideas of sustainable and cultural development to the formulation, selection and implementation of projects and secured their political acceptance by financial support from the state. In many respects it acted against mainstream interests of local governments and the private sector, who were less courageous in embarking on brownfield redevelopment projects beyond their imagination. Hence, the IBA applied a rhizome approach to regional modernization, where individual projects are interlinked by an invisible web of principles and quality criteria and promoted by a network of individual agents of change. The initiative has illustrated that such an approach to regeneration can successfully guide a process of innovation and modernization in a region that the market bypasses or neglects. The factors distinguishing the IBA approach from traditional German and U.S. approaches to brownfield redevelopment are summarized in Table 10.1.

Conclusion

Can the experience of the Ruhr be transferred to other regions? The answer is yes and no. No, because the conditions for the successful launch of the strategy were very region specific. No, because other regions in need of more holistic and creative regional redevelopment approaches may not find the kind of financial support the Ruhr received from an enthusiastic state government over a 10-year period. However, the experience of the IBA initiative offers a wealth of ideas for regional revitalization (Sack 1999). Even if the starting point and the political-administrative context are different, the IBA may provide lessons in overcoming local and regional constraints to regenerating brownfields in regions where market forces do not encourage reusing formerly industrial land. The IBA has developed models for involving and networking with innovative actors, and how to use soft approaches and events for changing attitudes and public awareness. Combining top-down and bottom-up approaches to regional regeneration seems to inspire and foster creativity and imagination.

Table 10.1 IBA Versus Traditional German and U.S. Approaches to Brownfield Redevelopment

Features	IBA approach	Traditional German approach	Traditional U.S. approach
Spatial scope	Regional, local and site	Local and site, some site-focused only	Site only
Approach	Holistic. Occasionally in disagreement with local government and local stakeholders	Comprehensive	Project-centered
Leadership	Public-sector led. IBA Agency cooperating with local governments and regional and local public development agencies to initiate the project, then handed over to local development agency	Public-sector led. City government usually with a local or regional public developer	Private-sector led. Private developer in accordance with local government (but not always)
Citizen involvement	Considerable. Form varies, however, with project character: *high in housing, low in other projects*	Formalized. Following established planning regulation procedures	Depends on project
Budget	Drawn from a plethora of public-sector budget lines (EU, national, state, local); some private investment	Drawn mainly from public-sector budget (EU, national, state, local); some private investment	Private investment and banks
Project idea and content search	IBA Agency brainstorming or project idea submitted by local interest group to IBA, followed by international/national competition among architects and landscape planners	Local government with local planners and architects; occasionally competitions or concepts of private investors	Feasibility study by architectural and business consultants
Planning control	Local government	Local government	Public sector
Effectiveness of planning control	High-quality standards agreed upon by project stakeholders, then followed by routine control	Routine control following established regulations	Low
Implementation	Initial public investment of the state government, then highly incremental, responding to local interest and budget lines	Traditionally by local government with regional or local development agency and public pre-investment	Private investment, eventually with public support
Investment payback period	Long	Medium to long	Short to medium

It is clear that the IBA has not successfully regenerated the Ruhr or brought it back fully to its former status as the economic powerhouse of Germany. That was not its mission, and such a task would have exceeded the capability of any time-limited, regional development initiative. The Ruhr today is still suffering from structural economic change and unemployment; however, the IBA has demonstrated that creativity linked to strong aesthetic, social and ecological quality control, as well as intensive communication among open-minded stake-holders, can turn brownfields into pools of spatial inspiration and innovation. Tourists have discovered the Ruhr through the IBA flagships, which has rein-forced regional identity and given new hope for the people living there. The IBA brought about a turning point in the Ruhr's history.

When searching for new development strategies, other regions in North Rhine-Westphalia have used the IBA Emscher Park experience as a model for strengthening regional profiles and programming cultural development. Most sub-regions in the state pursue and apply modernization policies with respective lessons learned from the IBA , though with much less public financial support. In eastern Germany, where old industrial areas are struggling for survival in a competitive, post-reunification world, the IBA initiative has found much interest. Following the IBA model, the state of Saxony has initiated the IBA Fürst-Pückler Land 2000–2010 as a workshop for new landscapes (Kuhn 2000). This region, with famous eighteenth-century landscape parks of Count Fürst Pückler, and the former open cast lignite mining region, Oberlausitz, in eastern Germany, are using the soft endogenous development approach of the IBA to revitalize seriously damaged and impoverished industrial landscape and turn it into a tourist destination. And in Italy, planners informed by a special edition of the journal *Rassegna* and an exhibition of the IBA at the Architecture Biennial of Venice in 1996, which spurred numerous articles in Italian architecture and planning journals, were excited by the flexible and creative approach to regional revitalization (Rassegna 1990; Wachten 1996). In fact, hardly any other German planning achievement has attracted so much interest outside the country in recent years as the IBA Emscher Park Initiative. It is only paralleled by the Berlin project, the ambitious physical reconstruction of Germany's capital city.

Response in the U.S. has been less enthusiastic. Professional and political audiences, whether from Detroit, Pittsburgh or Buffalo, at first glance are impressed by IBA's flagship projects. However, upon further consideration they are skeptical as to whether the visionary incremental approach would meet U.S. regulation requirements, be accepted by U.S. insurance companies, and appeal to private developers who focus on short-term profits. However, the Americans usually concede that the many projects of the IBA initiative and their implementation processes offer a rich source of inspiration for creative brownfield redevelopment, at least at such sites where, in the absence of market pressure, brownfields in large urban agglomerations could benefit from unusual ideas and approaches.

References

Benz, Arthur, Dietrich Fürst, Heiderose Kilper, and Dieter Rehfeld. 2000. *Regionalisation: Theory, practice and prospects in Germany*. Stockholm: Swedish Institute for Regional Research.

Bradke, Markus, and Heinz-Jürgen Löwer. 2000. *Brachflächenreaktivierung durch kulturelle Nutzungen*. Ph.D. dissertation, School of Planning, University of Dortmund.

Cliche, Danielle, Ritva Mitchell, and Andreas Wiesand. 2002. *Creative Europe: On governance and management of artistic creativity in Europe*. Bonn: ERICarts.

Höber, Andrea, and Karl Ganser, eds. 1999. *Industriekultur. Mythos und Moderne im Ruhrgebiet*. Essen: Klartext.

IBA Emscher Park. 1988. *Werkstatt für die Zukunft von Industrieregionen. Memorandum der internationalen Bauausstellung Emscher Park*. Gelsenkirchen: Internationale Bauausstellung Emscherpark GmbH.

———. 1999. *Memorandum III. Erfahrungen der IBA Emscher Park. Programmbausteine für die Zukunft*. Gelsenkirchen: Internationale Bauausstellung Emscherpark GmbH.

Kuhn, Rolf. 2000. Internationale Bauausstellung Fürst-Pückler-Land-Eine Werkstatt für neue Landschaften. In *Jahrbuch Stadterneuerung 2000*, ARGE Stadterneuerung, ed., 285–296. Berlin: Institut für Stadt- und Regionalplanung TU Berlin.

Kunzmann, Klaus R. 2000. The Ruhr in Germany: A laboratory for regional governance. In *The changing institutional landscape in Europe*, Louis Albrechts, Jeremy Alden, and Rosa da Pires, eds., 133–158. London: Aldershot.

Rassegna. 1990. Trimestrale, Anno XII, 42(2).

Sack, Manfred. 1999. *Siebzig Kilometer Hoffnung. Die IBA Emscher Park. Erneuerung eines Industriegebiets*. Stuttgart: DVA.

Wachten, Kunibert, ed. 1996. *Chance without growth? Sustainable urban development for the 21st century*. Architecture Biennial of Venice. Bonn and Berlin: Federal Minister for Regional Planning, Building and Urban Development.

11 Once Upon a Brownfield

Toward a Vision of Sustainable Development in Boston's South Bay

William Shutkin

From 1959 until it closed by court order in 1974, Boston's South Bay Incin-erator (the Incinerator) burned hundreds of tons of municipal trash and spewed a toxic plume of lead, mercury, dioxin and other poisons above a thickly settled area. Pollution from the stacks, from fuel storage tanks on the site and from asbestos insulation and lead plumbing in the structure settled into the soil and groundwater. For two decades after the Incinerator shut down, the site was used for storage by the city's Department of Public Works. Today, the Incinerator site is a quintessential brownfield (Figure 11.1).

In the early 1990s a proposal to build an asphalt plant on a nearby prop-erty sparked an outcry from the surrounding communities. Their protest succeeded in preventing yet another polluting facility from moving into the neighborhood, and initiated a comprehensive visioning process undertaken by community groups, environmental organizations and government agencies with greener, cleaner development in the South Bay as the goal. The need of the surrounding racially, ethnically and economically diverse communities for development that would provide economic benefits without producing envi-ronmental harm meshed with the vision of sustainable development advocated by a number of environmental organizations, which took an interest in the Incinerator site.

Historically, development of land and natural resources has come at the expense of environmental quality in the inner city and beyond. Suburbaniza-tion has separated the places people live from the places they work, shop and play, resulting in air pollution from an ever-increasing number of vehicle miles traveled and destruction of woodlands, wetlands and other habitats for devel-opment. In addition, after World War II, white, middle-class families from America's inner cities fled to the suburbs; such wholesale economic disinvest-ment left behind brownfields in the midst of struggling neighborhoods popu-lated largely by minorities and immigrants (Katz and Bradley 1999). Restoration

Figure 11.1   Aerial Views of the Incinerator Site

Before Demolition, 1995

After Demolition, 2001

Source: MassGIS, courtesy Boston Redevelopment Authority

of these diverse urban communities is a matter of economic development and environmental justice. The greatest challenge is to promote development that advances both.[1]

Envisioning Sustainable Communities

Most environmental harms—brownfields, water pollution, climate disruption, habitat destruction—are a function of land use decisions: how land and natural resources are developed or preserved for the purposes of production, consumption or conservation. Environmental law and policy, designed to control and mitigate pollution and the loss of natural areas, can, therefore, be understood as a response, if only indirect, to land use decisions (Landy et al. 1990, 22–49). However, these laws and policies have focused on controlling individual pollutants in the air, water or soil, rather than on the underlying land use and development patterns determined by local zoning and planning boards.

More recent environmental policy initiatives have sought to bridge this gap and to move toward an ideal of sustainable communities rather than relying on a fragmented, pollutant-by-pollutant approach to regulation. Such initiatives include brownfields revitalization programs, smart growth and industrial ecology, among others. Each concept has a different emphasis; however, each embraces the notion of vibrant economic activity informed and enlivened by ecological principles such as carrying capacity and waste recycling. Each is concerned with land use and involves community planning. Each promotes a preventive, proactive approach to environmental problem solving rather than the conventional focus on one pollutant at a time. Putting these concepts into practice can restore and protect the environment and reinforce a sense of place, while promoting economic development and community revitalization (Mazmanian and Kraft 1999, 3–43).

Brownfields mitigation and reuse direct environmental cleanup and new investment to abandoned, contaminated sites typically found in urban centers and older, first-ring suburbs, bringing economic growth to these neighborhoods while protecting the natural systems and the overall character of rural and suburban areas. Smart growth initiatives plan for and target economic development according to the carrying capacity, natural resources and existing physical infrastructure of communities, at both local and regional levels (Calthorpe and Fulton 2001, 1–12). Industrial ecology (IE) provides tools for analyzing the energy and material flows involved in production processes, from extraction of raw materials through consumption and disposal. It encourages design standards and production methods that reduce waste, eliminate toxic products,

---

1. For 12 years the author has worked as an environmental lawyer and social entrepreneur in neighborhoods in and around Boston with more than their share of toxic sites, among numerous other environmental threats. The focus of his work has been on assisting and empowering those who have traditionally not been part of any environmental constituency, but are among the most powerful proponents of environmental protection.

by-products and emissions, and mimic the recycling and replenishing functions of natural systems (Ehrenfeld 1998; and Powers and Chertow 1995, 24–25). Taken together, industrial ecology, smart growth and brownfields remediation suggest a new paradigm of environmental policy that links economic vitality, ecological integrity, civic activism and social well-being within the conceptual framework of sustainable development (Hempel 1999, 45–51). Environmentalism becomes a unifying thread weaving together industry and ecology, city and nature, individual and community, and transforming areas of blight and sprawl into sustainable communities.

As efforts to redevelop the South Bay Incinerator site evolved, the vision of environmental organizations converged with that of nearby communities for economically beneficial development without environmental contamination. Despite the concerted efforts of environmental and community-based groups, redevelopment of the site has been enmeshed in a long and complex process, which involves mending Boston's neighborhood Balkanization, negotiating a maze of federal, state and city agencies (each of which claims some piece of the decision-making process about the disposition and use of the property), and choosing among competing proposals for use of the site.

Two other recent attempts to undertake sustainable development of industrial sites have seized upon similar opportunities, faced similar difficulties and provide similar lessons. In the Banana Kelly section of the South Bronx, in New York City, the Natural Resources Defense Council, a nationally prominent environmental group, teamed up with a local community development corporation (CDC) to develop a state-of-the-art recycled paper mill on an abandoned, polluted rail yard. With environmental cleanup and plenty of jobs to offer, the project was heralded as a "green" milestone in the history of New York City development (Harris 1995). However, investors walked away and the paper mill project eventually folded after years of litigation brought by community groups opposed to the project who claimed the new facility would only further contribute to local air quality problems. This, in combination with internecine conflict among competing community organizations and a host of financial difficulties, doomed the project. The South Bronx case proved just how contentious and costly a good idea can be when it comes to actually implementing sustainable development on the ground.

In 1997 the Stonyfield Farm Yogurt Company in Manchester, New Hampshire, spearheaded an effort to build an "eco-industrial" park (EIP). An EIP consists of firms clustering together to facilitate the practice of industrial ecology. Energy can be shared; one firm's effluent or by-product may become another firm's input; and, as a whole, an EIP can accomplish a closed-loop production system with little or no waste and more efficient use of resources. Stonyfield's proposed EIP was on 100 acres of woodland, zoned for industrial use, abutting its factory. Known as an environmentally responsible business, Stonyfield wanted to take its philosophy to the next level to show that IE was not just a great environmental idea, but a great business practice (Wasserman 2001). While Stonyfield Farm significantly reduced its role in the project, bringing private developers in to manage the effort, the eco-industrial park remains an ongoing enterprise. To date, progress has been slow. Only one industrial user, a natural gas power plant, has chosen to locate in the park. As with the South Bronx example, sustainable development, despite its many theoretical virtues, can be a tough sell.

The South Bay and the Incinerator Site

The South Bay section of Boston is an industrial and commercial district abutting an interchange for Interstate 93 (known locally as the Southeast Expressway) and surrounded by five culturally and economically diverse neighborhoods: Chinatown and the gentrified South End to the north; Roxbury, predominantly African American and Boston's poorest neighborhood, to the west; Dorchester, with large African American, Latino, Cape Verdean and Southeast Asian immigrant populations, to the south; and traditionally blue-collar Irish, but gentrifying South Boston to the east. The South Bay includes a recently developed shopping center and the Newmarket Industrial District, one of Boston's oldest and most concentrated industrial zones (BRA 1998, 11). Newmarket retained its industrial base throughout the latter half of the twentieth century, despite the hemorrhaging of manufacturing jobs in Boston after World War II. Between 1970 and the late 1990s alone, Boston experienced a 43.5 percent decline in industrial employment, a loss of more than 22,000 jobs (BRA 1998, 6).

What kept Newmarket relatively stable throughout this period, despite a considerable build-up of underutilized and vacant land and deteriorating physical infrastructure, was its base of meat and food processing and distribution firms and its access to major transportation infrastructure. The Newmarket Business Association (NBA), an organization founded in 1977 to promote area revitalization, brought visibility and a political voice to Newmarket, leveraging the power of its roughly 150 member firms and their 1,800 workers (BRA 1998, 11–12).

Efforts to redevelop the Incinerator site brought neighborhood groups, environmental organizations, elected officials, city and state agencies, and businesses into an evolving and ambitious attempt to reconcile two seemingly contrary goals: the reindustrialization of the Incinerator site and the South Bay in general, and the implementation of environmentally responsible development. The vision of sustainable development—brownfields cleanup and reuse, containment of sprawl, and industrial ecology—dovetails with the expressed need of neighboring communities for environmentally sound economic development.

On Becoming Brownfield, from Tidal Marsh to Industrial Zone: 1900–1970

For centuries the South Bay was an intertidal marshland along the narrow tract of land called Boston Neck that connected the seventeenth-century town of Boston to the mainland. As the population grew and industrialization increased, the city annexed nearby settlements, including the towns of Roxbury and

Dorchester south of Boston Neck, and embarked on major projects to fill in and develop the marshes and tidal flats at the edges of the original city. Once a major shipping port, the South Bay was annexed and gradually filled by the city to expand its land area and accommodate rapid industrial development. The area was an environmental problem even before the Incinerator began operations in the late 1950s. The urban fill used to cover the South Bay tidal flats beginning in the late nineteenth century generally consisted of coal ash and other waste debris, much of which would be regulated today as hazardous material in Massachusetts (Massachusetts Division of Capital Asset Management 1999, 3).

By 1900 maritime activities in the South Bay mostly had come to a halt. The Incinerator site itself was filled around this time to accommodate development of a rail yard. In the 1950s the last of the South Bay's marshes were filled to make way for the Southeast Expressway (CDM 2000, 1). In 1957 the city of Boston, in need of greater capacity to handle a mounting solid waste stream, selected a pie-shaped piece of land, just shy of three acres, in the South Bay to build a new municipal trash incinerator. The Incinerator began operation in 1959, predating by several years the federal Clean Air Act of 1970, which sets emissions limits for key air pollutants, and the Resource Conservation and Recovery Act of 1976, which regulates the transport and disposal of hazardous and solid wastes. The Incinerator was subject only to a weak, patchwork system of state and local air quality and public health rules, some of which dated to the late nineteenth century and were, in general, loosely enforced.[2] As a result, the Incinerator was equipped with virtually no pollution controls, save for the stacks themselves, exposing workers and residents in nearby heavily developed sections of the city to significant contamination, at the mercy of Boston's frequently shifting winds.

Among the Incinerator's emissions were some of the most dangerous toxins—lead, mercury and dioxins. In addition, a host of other contamination sources was associated with the operation of the Incinerator. Underground and aboveground storage tanks for fuel oil and kerosene, boilers, piles of municipal garbage and construction debris, and incinerator ash all contributed to the contamination of the site itself (CDM 2000, 2). Arsenic, beryllium, cadmium, chromium, copper, lead, mercury, zinc, polychlorinated biphenyls (PCBs), dioxin, cyanide and polycyclic aromatic hydrocarbons (PAHs), among other pollutants, were released into the surface and subsurface soils, resulting in several contamination "hot spots" around the Incinerator site. Volatile organic compounds (VOCs), PAHs, lead, arsenic, mercury and dioxin leached into the groundwater (CDM 2000, 2–3). The facility itself was lined with hazardous building materials including asbestos insulation and lead plumbing. Its concrete slab, flooring and walls were coated with toxic ash, oils and solvents. Over time, these and other pollutants rendered the Incinerator, in addition to the plume emitted continuously from its stacks, dangerous and forbidding.

---

2. For example, the statute empowering local public health boards in Massachusetts to prevent noxious or injurious industrial activities was enacted in the mid-1800s and serves as the basis for Massachusetts's air pollution control regulations, which were adopted more than a century later.

The Incinerator Shutdown: 1970s–1980s

During the 1970s a growing awareness of the dangers of industrial pollution sparked a public outcry against sources of pollution, including the Incinerator. In 1974 a state court judge ordered the city to shut down the Incinerator. For more than two decades following the ruling, the site was used as a storage yard for the Department of Public Works, but little attention was paid to the site's potential or problems.

A 1988 master plan for the Newmarket Industrial Area, including the Incinerator site, was prepared by the Boston Redevelopment Authority (BRA) and its Economic Development and Industrial Corporation (EDIC), whose mission is to promote neighborhood revitalization. The study chronicled an area in decay and study found:

> Scattered vacant and underutilized parcels throughout the area are frequently targets for illegal dumping. . . . Major obstacles to full development of the area include: an inadequate road system, outdated utility infrastructure, illegal dumping and incompatible uses, in particular the transfer stations. The lack of a positive district-wide identity is a major problem. The proliferation of loading docks and illegally parked cars which clog the . . . streets, the unregulated signage and divergent architectural treatments all contribute to a functional and aesthetic chaos. (Boston EDIC 1988, 1)

The South Bay's blighted conditions were part of a degenerative land use cycle common to most inner-city areas. Vacant, trash-strewn lots invite unwanted uses and illicit activities, from dumping to drug dealing (Shutkin and Mares 2000, 60–62; Urban Habitat Program 1999, 1–12; Goldstein, Jensen and Reiskin 2001). Such sites tend to attract development, such as trash transfer stations, incinerators, landfills, polluting industries and parking lots, that most communities deem undesirable because of their adverse environmental impacts and negative effect on local property values. These locally unwanted land uses (LULUs) are the stuff of not in my back yard (NIMBY) campaigns. The Incinerator site and other nearby brownfields have attracted more than their share of proposed LULUs. However, the resulting NIMBY protests transcended the effort to thwart unwelcome development and evolved into a process for envisioning and engaging in sustainable development.

A NIMBY battle in the early 1990s involving a site directly across the street spilled over to the Incinerator site, bringing it long-overdue attention. In 1992 Todesca Equipment Corporation, a Boston construction company, proposed to build an asphalt plant on Cummings Street, a stone's throw away from the Incinerator. Carrying the banner of environmental justice for Boston's inner city, a small group of activists representing dozens of community organizations from the five neighborhoods that abut the South Bay formed the Coalition Against the Asphalt Plant (CAAP) in 1993. Environmental justice—a movement that asserts that people of color and low-income communities, which have traditionally borne the brunt of environmental harms, deserve the same environmental protection as white and economically advantaged communities—came of age in the early 1990s as an organizing issue and social critique (Gottlieb 1993). A new, Roxbury-based environmental justice law center, Alternatives for Community and Environment (ACE), joined with CAAP to oppose the asphalt plant project (Friday 1996, 29).[3]

The effort to oppose the plant was a milestone in the history of Boston community activism. Never before, according to CAAP, had such a diverse group of residents come together in Boston, where political battles between neighborhoods and interest groups often left citizens worse off and benefited few. Blue-collar Irish Americans from South Boston, African American mothers from Roxbury, Asian Americans from Chinatown, and gay men from the South End found a common goal in thwarting the asphalt plant, which, CAAP alleged, would add to the inner city's already poor air quality and exacerbate public health problems, while bringing very few jobs or tax revenues. Boston University public health experts called the area a Zone of Death because of the high incidence of cancer and upper respiratory disease among local residents, which some attributed to environmental factors like air pollution (Lopez 1996).

Responding to CAAP's formidable legal and political pressure, state environmental officials required four rounds of environmental impact reporting. The reports found that the fully automated asphalt manufacturing plant would offer only a handful of low-paying jobs, which from CAAP's point of view did not begin to offset the considerable truck traffic, noise and air pollution the facility would generate. The campaign brought into sharp relief the frustration and despair many in the five neighborhoods felt regarding environmental conditions and land uses in the inner city. The plant, they believed, was yet another blow, an insult that would further undermine the South Bay's ability to shed its blighted past and become the vibrant gateway district so many residents, and the city's own planning agencies, wanted to create.

The battle against the plant raged for years, in front of the Boston zoning board of appeal, in state courts and administrative agencies, in the media, on the street and, finally, before the city's board of health, which voted in 1996 to ban the siting of the plant, using its broad power to regulate "noxious" and "injurious" facilities (Chacon 1996, 30). After several appeals by Todesca, the plant proposal finally expired of its own weight in 1999.

The intensity, discipline and organization of the CAAP campaign not only defeated Todesca's proposal, but helped shine the spotlight on the South Bay's environmental degradation and overall physical decay. In fall 1994, looking beyond the four corners of the asphalt plant site on Cummings Street, some of the CAAP member organizations, led by ACE, the Roxbury-based Dudley Street Neighborhood Initiative (DSNI) and the Environmental Diversity Forum (EDF), formed the Incinerator Collaborative to focus attention on the hulking mass of the nearby incinerator. Dotted with debris piles up to 15 feet high, the site had become a shelter for scores of homeless people who took up residence

---

3. At the time, the author was codirector and senior attorney at ACE and represented CAAP in the asphalt plant campaign.

in the massive structure, unaware of its many hazards. The Incinerator site, like its dispossessed denizens, called out for relief.

Building on CAAP's experience, the Incinerator Collaborative first looked for a responsible party, a bad actor like Todesca, to shame into remedying the eyesore that stood abandoned and dilapidated for 20 years. However, unlike the asphalt plant, the Incinerator was a lingering liability for the community, who had no clear legal strategy for redress. Although it loomed over the area as a symbol of neglect and blight, its environmental effects had not been quantified in tons per day or vehicle trips per hour for easy attack by environmental activists, nor spelled out in neatly bound reports for public scrutiny. Relatively little was known about the Incinerator in 1994 beyond the urban folklore that the facility had been shut down because it was spewing poison into the surrounding neighborhoods, a scourge on Boston's poor and disenfranchised communities. Mysteriously, the city-owned property was transferred in 1991 to the Massachusetts Division of Capital Asset Management (DCAM, then called the Division of Capital Planning and Operations), the state's real estate arm. William Bulger, at the time the powerful state senate president and a South Boston politician whose district included the Incinerator, may have brokered the deal in the interest of his constituents, so as to utilize state resources to clean up and reuse the site.[4]

Ownership and control of the site, while a significant issue, never presented a barrier to the Incinerator Collaborative. Having worked diligently on the asphalt plant campaign and many other land use–related problems over the years, members of the collaborative felt a sense of entitlement regarding the site's fate, what one noted community development leader has called "moral site control."[5] Regardless of who owned the site, the Incinerator Collaborative was committed to exercising control over its cleanup and reuse as active partners.

EPA and Cleanup Efforts: 1994–1995

Beginning in late 1994 opportunities at both federal and state levels conspired to raise the profile of the Incinerator site among key decision makers and the public at large, and to build the Incinerator Collaborative's case for action. In the fall the EPA announced a new round of funding under its recently launched Brownfields Economic Redevelopment Initiative Pilot Assessment Program for municipalities interested in investigating and redeveloping brownfield sites. Working with the city's Environment Department, the lead applicant for the Brownfield Pilot Program proposal, the Incinerator Collaborative successfully applied for the award in March 1995, helping to galvanize local, state and federal interest in the Incinerator site.

---

4. Interview with Byron Rushing, Democratic Representative, Massachusetts House of Representatives.

5. This term was coined by Bill Traynor, executive director of Lawrence Community Works, a CDC in Lawrence, Massachusetts, where vacant brownfields are persistent and ubiquitous.

The Incinerator Collaborative also took advantage of Massachusetts Governor William Weld's Clean State Initiative (CSI), established in 1993 through Executive Order 350. The CSI mandated that state agencies comply with all state environmental regulations by June 30, 2000, and committed the state to being a leader in "community enhancement."[6] With the CSI in hand, the Incinerator Collaborative approached DCAM in late 1994 to compel the agency to comply with the executive order and clean up the Incinerator site. Both DCAM's deputy general counsel and the agency's commissioner were responsive to the plea.

Thanks to the collaborative's involvement in the Brownfield Pilot Program, EPA officials from the New England regional office became champions of their efforts. Several senior EPA staff took a personal as well as professional interest in seeing the Incinerator demolished and the land cleaned up. Starting in January 1995 and led by an attorney from the Resource Conservation and Recovery Act section, EPA, helped to convene key officials from the city and state, as well as members of the Incinerator Collaborative, in an informal negotiation process. These stakeholders soon came to call themselves the South Bay Incinerator Community Collaborative (ICC).[7]

As part of the larger ICC, the Incinerator Collaborative proposed an extensive, three-tiered list of steps to be undertaken by DCAM, the site owner, and the city, which, as the former owner and operator, was still a responsible party under Massachusetts and federal environmental laws. On a short-term basis, the Incinerator Collaborative wanted a barrier erected around the site; storage of road salt halted for fear that it was blowing around toxic particulates; and the Brownfield Pilot Program application prepared by the March 1, 1995, deadline.

Long-term requests focused on cleanup and development issues. With respect to cleanup, the collaborative proposed that the Incinerator be demolished; that the site be remediated to a level commensurate with future development plans; that a public participation process be established so citizens could have access to information about cleanup activities and be involved in site-related decision making; that DCAM secure adequate funding to cover the full cleanup costs; and that the ICC adopt a nonbinding memorandum of understanding (MOU) that would govern the cleanup process.[8]

Concerning development, the Incinerator Collaborative urged the DCAM to transfer ownership of the site to a local CDC for redevelopment; that it be redeveloped in an environmentally sound manner with an end use such as a recycling facility; that the reuse maximize job opportunities for low-income, low-skilled workers in Boston; that the city and state provide both debt and equity funds for redevelopment; and that the city and state apply for a Brownfields Pilot

6. http://www.state.ma.us/envir/cleanstate.htm.

7. South Bay Incinerator Community Collaborative, Draft Agreement, April 24, 1995 (on file with the author). The collaborative included representatives from DCAM, the city of Boston, EPA, the Massachusetts Attorney General's Office, the Massachusetts Department of Environmental Protection, DSNI, ACE, EDF and three other community-based organizations, Nuestra Communidad, a CDC, the South End Neighborhood Action Project, and South Boston Community Housing.

8. South Bay Incinerator Community Collaborative Meeting Agenda, February 3, 1995 (on file with the author).

Program grant in partnership with the Incinerator Collaborative.[9] On a more systemic level, the Incinerator Collaborative proposed that the cleanup become a model to be studied and replicated; that the city should institute a CSI-type program to deal with its own brownfield sites; and that the Incinerator should serve as a springboard to other collaborative, timely brownfield redevelopment projects in and around Boston.[10]

Signing of the MOU in May 1995 formally launched the campaign to redevelop the Incinerator site. The ICC had become a closely knit group committed to following through on the MOU's directives. Later in the year, several of the ICC members, from both the community organizations and the government agencies, participated in the Boston Brownfield Pilot Program as it got under way. Between the two parallel efforts, redevelopment plans for the Incinerator site were well considered.

Controversial Development Proposals: 1996–1998

While community groups and public agencies considered the remediation issues involved in reuse of the Incinerator site, a string of controversial development proposals was put forward encompassing this site and others nearby. As early as 1993, the South Bay, thought to be a no-man's land by many Bostonians, was under consideration for a possible "megaplex" project, combining a sports stadium, convention center and hotel that would cover most of the South Bay and Newmarket areas and encroach upon portions of Roxbury and the South End, much to the ire of area residents. For its part, the city had been looking to build a large convention center for years.

The megaplex idea never got off the ground, but the stadium proposal was reinforced by threats from the owner of the New England Patriots football team to leave the state if the team could not replace its outdated Foxborough, Massachusetts, facility. In 1996 both Governor Weld and Boston Mayor Thomas Menino were openly courting the Patriots, and the South Bay was a prime target (Cassidy and Vaillancourt 1996). CAAP, the Incinerator Collaborative, and other community activists watched warily for four years as one day the stadium project had the green light, the next it was dead in the water (Flint 1999). Finally, in late 1999, the Patriots decided to build a new stadium at the existing Foxborough location. The South Bay also came into play as a potential site for the new home of the Boston Red Sox. After much publicly reported speculation about a possible move from the baseball team's venerable Fenway Park, it now seems unlikely that the Red Sox ownership will relocate to the South Bay.

The megaplex and stadium proposals were just the beginning. Equally ominous in the minds of the Incinerator Collaborative were several smaller, less glamorous, but no less undesirable, potential development projects, among them a new central lock-up facility for the Suffolk County House of Corrections,

---

9. Ibid.

10. Ibid.

located just north of the Incinerator site.[11] GeoTek, a North Carolina company, considered the site for a tire recycling plant using technology called tire pyrolysis, which heats tire feedstock without oxygen, resulting in solid carbon, a liquid fuel similar to oil, and a gas fuel. Though seemingly a "green" technology, tire pyrolysis generates significant air pollution—in this case, up to 65 tons per year of sulfur dioxide—while providing very few jobs.[12] To the Incinerator Collaborative, the GeoTek proposal was a nonstarter.

Yet another proposal came from the Medical Academic and Scientific Community Organization (MASCO), a private corporation responsible for managing the transportation and other infrastructure needs of Boston's expansive Longwood Medical area, home to many of the city's teaching hospitals and colleges. In summer 1997 MASCO proposed to build a 600-plus-space parking lot on the Incinerator site (MASCO 1997). With just a couple of jobs and hundreds of vehicle trips per day at issue, the MASCO proposal met with considerable resistance right off the bat and soon fell through.

After engaging in opposition to so many South Bay development proposals, in 1997 the Incinerator Collaborative adopted a new name, Neighborhoods United for the South Bay (NUSB), and sought to emphasize a proactive approach to development rather than a NIMBY posture. By this time, NUSB had established enough of a presence in the South Bay that developers were approaching NUSB at very early, predevelopment stages to test the waters, before lobbying city and state officials or other businesses.

Green Village, New Ecology, and A Vision of Sustainable Development: 1998

In 1998 a unique and powerful development proposal offered NUSB a concrete opportunity to implement its ideas for sustainable green development and balancing economic and environmental goals. For two years a small manufactured housing company called Green Village, based in nearby Cambridge, had been looking for a Boston site to build a factory for its housing product. A consortium of environmentally conscious engineering, architecture and real estate development firms, Green Village specializes in multifamily and cluster housing, using custom-designed modular EcoDynamic Houses. These homes cost less to manufacture and buy (15 percent or more project cost savings) than traditional houses, are easily adapted to urban environments, use recycled and nontoxic materials (20 percent less use of nonrenewable resources, 10 percent less water use and 40 percent improvement in indoor air quality), and provide dramatic energy savings (65 percent less energy use).[13] The business advantage of modular

---

11. R. Rouse, Suffolk County (MA) Sheriff, letter to author, February 24, 1998 (on file with the author).

12. R. Nadkarni, Environmental Engineer, letter to author, December 23, 1996 (on file with the author).

13. Green Village Company, marketing materials, June 1996 (on file with the author).

housing is that it comes out of the factory fully equipped with electrical, plumbing and finish work, saving time and money. The product is then shipped by truck to the job site where the individual modules are fitted together and the final structure is "zipped up." From the first nail in the factory to move-in can take as little as a few weeks.

With two projects completed, including a much-celebrated cohousing development in North Cambridge, whose expensive units (over $500,000) and tasteful design belied the notion that modular housing was a cheap alternative to conventional, more resource-intensive construction, Green Village was interested in building a factory in the heart of Boston. It wanted to take advantage of the growing need for lower-cost and affordable housing, in the city and beyond, and to produce the homes close to its market, employing a local workforce of approximately 100. Green Village's manufacturing operations were based in Peabody, New Hampshire, just outside Concord, where another modular housing company, Epoch Corporation, produced the units for Green Village. As the 1990s economy heated up, Epoch's production demand increased while New Hampshire's available workforce all but disappeared. If it were to grow and compete, Green Village realized it could not rely on Epoch's production capacity.[14]

Green Village's management team scanned the city looking for six to eight acres to accommodate a 30,000-square-foot building and a large loading/unloading area for trucks. They had been in touch with the Boston Brownfield Pilot Program, recognizing that any suitable site would most likely be polluted. The management team contacted DSNI and several other CDCs from the Roxbury and Dorchester neighborhoods, as well, to inquire about possible sites. In summer 1997 DSNI and ACE invited Green Village to make a presentation about their company to a group of Roxbury residents from the economically hard-hit Grove Hall section. Residents there had for years been complaining to the city about a lack of high-quality, affordable housing and about numerous vacant, blighted parcels that blanketed the area. Green Village offered a solution to both these problems. Unfortunately, the meeting dissolved into a debate between Green Village's white management team and several African American residents about economic justice and the appropriateness of a white-owned business looking to, in the words of the residents, "capitalize on the neighborhood's distress." Neither the residents nor the Green Village representatives were prepared for such an encounter.

Green Village continued its search for a manufacturing location in Boston. In 1998 they were introduced to the Incinerator site by New Ecology, Inc. (NEI), a nonprofit launched in 1998 whose mission is to promote environmentally responsible development in distressed urban areas.[15] NEI's mission is grounded in the belief that land use and development are the principal drivers of environmental change, whether good or ill.

---

14. Steve Stuntz, CEO, Green Village, interview with author, Cambridge, MA.

15. NEI was started because of development opportunities like Green Village and the Incinerator site, which ACE, a law and education organization, was neither designed nor equipped to pursue.

With the emergence of NUSB, the effort to redevelop the Incinerator site had evolved from a narrowly focused NIMBY battle over one small piece of property into an integrated planning process for a significant segment of Boston's landscape. Taking a further step along that trajectory, a number of interested parties, including NUSB members, State Representative Byron Rushing, NEI, and NBA, which took on a leadership role, formed an expanded but looser coalition known simply as the Working Group. The Working Group began to develop a strategy for approaching the legislature and for working effectively with DCAM to expedite disposition of the Incinerator site without violating the complex rules set in place in the 1970s to control corruption and mismanagement of land under the state's jurisdiction.

The tax-exempt nongovernmental organizations (NGOs), like NEI and DSNI, which are legally prevented from lobbying, played an advisory role, investigating and educating other Working Group members about "best practice" policies for enabling environmentally sound development. In 2000 Rushing introduced House Bill 3630, which, after careful shepherding, was passed by the House and Senate and signed into law in 2002. The bill balances environmental and economic concerns in regard to redevelopment of the Incinerator site, instructing DCAM to encourage light industrial/manufacturing uses, and the provision of one new job paying at least twice the Massachusetts minimum wage for every 500 square feet of built space. DCAM must also encourage developers to hire 80 percent of employees at the site from Boston residents, maximize the use of public transportation and minimize the need for off-site or on-street parking. In August 2003 the BRA moved redevelopment one step further with a decision to commission a planning study for the South Bay.

Meanwhile, Green Village decided to locate its factory in Worcester, Massachusetts, an aging industrial city 45 miles west of Boston, where land was cheaper and the city government was eager to attract industrial development. While this is a setback for the prospect for sustainable development of the Incinerator site, it is a success in its own terms—providing a valuable and environmentally sound economic resource to a city badly in need of rehabilitation.

Conclusion

That the redevelopment of the Incinerator site is still a work in progress is perhaps the most meaningful lesson to be gleaned from this story. Places like the South Bay, with its checkered land use history and persistent identity and infrastructure problems, present formidable redevelopment challenges, whether or not they are brownfield sites. In the absence of robust, comprehensive planning and policy interventions such as master planning, economic incentives, political leadership of key local and state officials, and local capacity to undertake difficult redevelopment projects, hard-hit areas like the South Bay are prone to languish or attract "business-as-usual" redevelopment efforts, which may reintroduce undesirable land uses. This is a truism of inner-city economies.

Even when good planning, political leadership and local capacity exist, there is very little certainty and a long lead time associated with these projects. In the case of the Incinerator site the usual obstacles become even more problematic with the very aspirations that have made the effort itself so important. Instead of settling for development-as-usual or LULUs, the Working Group has insisted on a better, but more challenging, approach to brownfields redevelopment, grounded in a vision of best practice linked to the concept of sustainability. These efforts, it seems, must be measured not in years but in decades, with major milestones recorded and celebrated as they occur. From this overarching lesson flow a number of more discrete lessons about redevelopment embedded in the Incinerator history.

Perseverance. As the Incinerator story suggests, inner-city brownfields require intensive effort on the part of a variety of stakeholders through many years and under constantly changing circumstances. Over time, personnel within agencies, legislatures, firms and community-based organizations turns over, undermining the institutional memory and continuity of political support that can go a long way in advancing a project. The constantly shifting political and economic landscapes make particular redevelopment schemes more or less viable at any given moment. The consistent presence of certain institutions and individuals in the Incinerator effort has at least kept the project alive in the face of rapidly changing external circumstances.

Multi-sectoral alliances. Innovations in the economic development arena, such as the eco-industrial and sustainable development models envisioned for the Incinerator site, demand the commitment of resources and talent from a diverse group of stakeholders that cuts across public, private and community sectors. While such alliances necessarily entail delicate negotiations and pivotal compromises, the social capital gains and creative tension that result can offset these downsides and keep the project viable in the face of resistance or inertia. In the Incinerator case, the NBA has proved to be the most important party, even though the community organizations were responsible for initiating the effort. The NBA's involvement allowed the Working Group to leverage its political clout and access, resulting in the creation and passage of Rushing's bill. At the same time, because of the NBA's role, some of the more ambitious environmental goals for the Incinerator site advocated by groups like NEI and DSNI had to be abandoned in the interest of compromise. While sympathetic to these goals, the NBA does not pretend to be an environmental group.

Political leadership. While far from being a power broker within the legislature, Byron Rushing used his position and influence to build support for the bill and, more generally, for the idea of sustainable development in the South Bay. In conjunction with the other Working Group members, Rushing helped to move the redevelopment of the neighborhood beyond the numerous planning studies that for years sat gathering dust on the BRA's bookshelves to a programmatic series of action steps aimed at redevelopment. As has the NBA, Rushing has played an essential role in keeping the Incinerator site on the agenda of key decision makers.

Sustainable development. Looking beyond the Incinerator itself, there is no more important lesson to be learned from the brownfields problem in general than the imperative of environmentally responsible development. Sustainable development must be the framework within which policy makers and practitioners alike approach brownfields redevelopment. Adherence to the principles of sustainable development forces a reckoning with the corrosive externalities of conventional real estate development and economic production practices. As with any systems-change strategy, success is measured in both demonstrated performance (the physical proof, embodied in a development project or policy, of the benefits and virtues of the sustainable development model) and behavioral change (in consciousness and practices). Behavioral change is both a necessary precursor to and a consequence of performance. They are mutually reinforcing outcomes that point the way to further steps along the path to sustainable development.

Small steps toward a grand vision. Especially with brownfields projects, where the environmental imperative is strongest, sustainability is and must become best practice. To achieve this will require several practical steps, from designing RFPs to encourage green building practices (as in the Incinerator story), to creating tax and other financial incentives to support green space, renewable energy and eco-industrial development, to cataloguing sustainable development case studies and techniques within agencies like the BRA. While the economies of scale of sustainable development remain formidable barriers, states such as Massachusetts have developed a substantial capacity (even more than is reflected in the Incinerator site example), embodied in a suite of programs, policies and institutions straddling the public, private and nonprofit sectors, to implement sustainable development plans and projects.[16] Other states, such as Minnesota, New Jersey and Oregon, have even more robust capacity to achieve sustainable development, and others are following their lead (Resource Renewal Institute 2001).

Sustainable brownfields redevelopment ultimately requires a more rigorous standard for assessing project success, going beyond conventional measures that, like the GDP, fail to account for the negative environmental externalities associated with redevelopment. Sustainable brownfields redevelopment applies

---

16. For example, Massachusetts has the following sustainable development capacity in place (partial list): (1) *Public sector*: Massachusetts Renewable Energy Trust, Clean State Initiatives, Community Preservation Act, Massachusetts Office of Brownfields Revitalization; (2) *Private sector:* Developers (Lyme Properties, Hickory Consortium, Gravestar) and architects (Arrowstreet) with green building/planning experience; (3) *Nonprofit*: New Ecology, Inc., Chelsea Center for Recycling and Ecomomic Development, Lowell Center for Sustainable Production, CLF Ventures, MIT Environmental Programs Office, Center for Environmental Technology, Sustainable Step New England, Massachusetts Energy Consumers Alliance, and Tellus Institute.

both to sites left behind by conventional market forces and public policy and to sites that have been redeveloped, and asks the questions: What will this site and this community be like a generation from now? What will the buildings, roads and sidewalks look like? Who will live here? What kind of businesses will be located here? What will the quality of the environment and the quality of life be?

References

Boston Economic Development and Industrial Corporation (EDIC). 1988. *Newmarket Industrial District plan: Recommended master plan*.

Boston Redevelopment Authority (BRA). 1998. Economic development plan for Newmarket Industrial District, draft (July 11).

Calthorpe, P. and W. Fulton. 2001. *The regional city*. Washington, DC: Island Press.

Camp, Dresser and McKee (CDM). 2000. *Phase II and Phase III report, former South Bay municipal incinerator site* (March).

Cassidy, T. and M. Vaillancourt. 1996. Weld would give state site to Patriots. *Boston Globe*, December 20.

Chacon, R. 1996. City board rejects South Bay asphalt plant. *Boston Globe*, May 2, 30.

Ehrenfeld, J. 1998. Cultural structure and the challenge of sustainability. In *Better environmental decisions: Strategies for governments, businesses and communities*, K. Sexton, Alfred A. Marcus, K. William Easter and Timothy D. Burkhardt, eds. Washington, DC: Island Press.

Flint, A. 1999. Focus back on incinerator site. *Boston Globe*, April 18.

Friday, A. Walker. 1996. Neighborhood residents file suit to halt Newmarket Asphalt Plant. *Boston Globe*, January 26, 29.

Goldstein, J., M. Jensen and E. Reiskin. 2001. Urban vacant land redevelopment challenges and progress. Working paper. Cambridge, MA: Lincoln Institute of Land Policy.

Gottlieb, R. 1993. *Forcing the spring: The transformation of the American environmental movement*. Washington, DC: Island Press.

Harris, L. 1995. Banana Kelly's toughest fight. *New Yorker*, July 24.

Hempel, L. Conceptual and analytical challenges in building sustainable communities. 1999. In *Toward sustainable communities: Transition and transformations in environmental policy*, D. Mazmanian and M. Kraft, eds., 45–51. Cambridge, MA: MIT Press.

Katz, B. and J. Bradley. 1999. Divided we sprawl. *Atlantic Monthly* (December).

Landy, M., M. Roberts and S. Thomas. 1990. *The Environmental Protection Agency: Asking the wrong questions*. New York: Oxford University Press.

Lopez, R., executive director, Environmental Diversity Forum. 1996. Letter to the editor. *Boston Globe*, December 20.

Massachusetts Division of Capital Asset Management (DCAM). 1999. *Phase II comprehensive site assessment scope of work, South Bay Incinerator* (January).

Mazmanian, D. and M. Kraft. 1999. The three epochs of the environmental movement. In *Toward sustainable communities: Transition and transformations in environmental policy*, 3–43. Cambridge, MA: MIT Press.

Medical Academic and Scientific Community Organization, Inc. (MASCO). 1997. *Analysis of system wide Parker origins, South Bay lot planning* (August 11).

Powers, C. and M. Chertow. 1997. Industrial ecology: Overcoming policy fragmentation. In *Thinking ecologically*, Marian Chertow and Daniel C. Esty, eds., 24–25. New Haven: Yale University Press.

Resource Renewal Institute. 2001. *The state of the states: Assessing the capacity of states to achieve sustainable development through green planning* (August).

Shutkin, W. *The land that could be: Environmentalism and democracy in the twenty-first century.* 2000. Cambridge, MA: MIT Press.

Shutkin, W. and R. Mares. 2000. Brownfields and the redevelopment of communities: Linking health, economy, and justice. In *Reclaiming the environmental debate: The politics of health in a toxic culture*, R. Hofrichter, ed., 60–62. Cambridge, MA: MIT Press.

Urban Habitat Program.1999. *Building upon our strengths: A community guide to brownfields redevelopment in the San Francisco Bay area.*

Wasserman, S. 2001. Sustainable development: The case of implementing industrial ecology. Master's thesis, Department of Urban Studies and Planning, MIT, Cambridge, MA.

Glossary

Bioshelter

An enclosed structure—typically allowing solar energy to enter—that houses activities designed to replicate ecological processes in which the subsystems interact with one another to collectively create a self-regulating whole.

Brownfield

Any former commercial or industrial land that is abandoned, idle or underused because redevelopment and/or expansion is complicated by either real or perceived environmental contamination.

Business Improvement District (BID)

A physical area, a class of government or a nongovernmental organization. As a nongovernmental organization, it is made up of property owners and/or leaseholders in a designated area, the majority of whom have agreed to be governed by the BID. As a class of government, the state grants certain powers, including collecting taxes or fees to those within the district. As an organization, the members of the BID decide what services to provide, such as street and sidewalk cleaning and repair, auxiliary police, parking, beautification, lighting and various development projects to improve the district.

CERCLA

Comprehensive Environmental Response, Compensation, and Liability Act of 1980. *See* Superfund.

Clouds (on title)

Liens, taxes or mortgages still owed on a property that preclude a transfer of the title.

Community-based organization (CBO)

A private nonprofit organization or group that works to improve some aspect of a community. CBOs deal with interventions at the community level.

Community development corporation (CDC)	A corporation, usually nonprofit, that provides economic and social support to a community through programs that promote job creation, economic development, improved housing stock, community organization, policy advocacy and fulfill a variety of other needs. Historically, CDCs have focused on building and managing housing; many have expanded beyond these activities.
Community Food Project	A designation by the U.S. Department of Agriculture of activities receiving USDA grants to, among other objectives, increase the access to fresh, nutritious food by low-income individuals.
Community supported agriculture (CSA)	A farming model in which subscribers pay a local farmer at the start of the growing season for food that will be delivered, as harvested, on a regular basis throughout the season.
Compact city (policy)	An effort to concentrate dense development activity in and around existing towns.
Comprehensive Development Area (*Zone d'aménagement concrete* [ZAC])	A tool for redeveloping French vacant land. The designation provides for agreements between public and private developers for land assembly, infrastructure investment and development according to a comprehensive plan.
COSTAR Group	A leading provider of electronic commercial real estate information.
Deferred Development Zone (*Zone d'aménagement différé* [ZAD])	A designation of an area in France that is not being developed nor under consideration for development. The ZAD designation gives a public authority the right of first refusal on any property that is to be sold.
Deindustrialization	The process through which the physical and socioeconomic attributes of the economy change by a shift from traditional heavy industry toward other forms of production; the contraction and decline of production and/or employment in the manufacturing sector.
Derelict land	Land that has been so damaged by industrial or other development that it is incapable of beneficial use without treatment.

Economies in transition	States or governments moving from a planned economy to a market economy. Often applied to former Soviet states and some Eastern European countries.
Eminent domain	The police power whereby the government takes private property for public use through condemnation proceedings in exchange for "just compensation" to the owner.
Empowerment Zone (EZ)	A designation in the U.S. of an urban district that suffers from a long-term lack of investment, intended to harness public, private and community resources to attract the investment necessary for sustainable economic and community development. It allows tax advantages for businesses locating within the zone.
Empowerment Zone/ Enterprise Community (EZ/EC) program	Established in fall 1993 under the U.S. federal community revitalization strategy, the program is designed to empower people and communities to develop strategic plans to create jobs and opportunities in impoverished rural areas.
Enterprise zone	An area of distress, decay and blight in which redevelopment efforts are concentrated, typically through such financial mechanisms as job credits, sales tax exemption and property tax reductions or abatements.
Entrepreneurial urban agriculture	The cultivation of food and other agricultural products in urban areas for market sale.
Environmental assessment (EA)	An investigation of a property to determine the extent and location of potential contamination. Federal legislation requires EAs of a brownfield property before a potential buyer can consider purchasing it.
Environmental justice	The fair treatment of people of all races, cultures, incomes and educational backgrounds with respect to the development and enforcement of environmental laws, regulations and policies. Fair treatment implies that no population should be forced to shoulder a disproportionate share of exposure to the negative effects of pollution due to lack of political or economic strength.

EPA	U.S. Environmental Protection Agency. The lead executive agency in carrying out Superfund site designation and remediation.
EPA Sustainable Development Challenge Grants	A program of EPA's Region 3 that, between 1996 and 1999, provided seed money to 13 demonstration projects for possible replication in other locations.
Friche	The French term for vacant land, abandoned sites and structures, or brownfields.
Greenbelt	A belt of parks or rural land surrounding a town or city.
Greenfield	Undeveloped land whose protection has become a major policy concern, especially when located on the urban fringe.
Green space	Undeveloped urban spaces, often designated as open space, intended to provide city residents with recreational and environmental benefits in their neighborhoods or to protect natural resources.
Hydroponics	A technology for growing plants in solutions of water and fertilizers, with the optional use of nonsoil materials such as sand, gravel or rockwool. Used in urban agriculture.
Industrial ecology (IE)	The shifting of industrial process from open-loop systems, in which resource and capital investments move through the system to become waste, to a closed-loop system, where wastes become inputs for new processes.
Industrial heritage	Monuments such as water towers, gas tanks, pit heads, steel furnaces and coke plants that reflect the history of industrial production in a region and are, as a rule, protected by conservation laws.
Infill	Development of vacant urban land that sits among developed parcels; the smart growth principle of directing development and revitalization efforts toward underutilized land in existing urban communities.

Land banking	The process by which vacant and abandoned city properties are acquired by municipal government and held as strategic assets for future use.
Land trust	Typically a private nonprofit organization that acquires land titles for specific uses and/or the benefit of specific constituencies or the general public.
Land use plan (POS)	The guide for new development in France.
Limited liability corporation (LLC)	A state statutory construct that is a hybrid of a legal corporation and a partnership. It is used for property ownership and investment, with the tax advantages of a partnership and the liability protection of a corporation.
LULUs	Locally undesirable land uses. The term is most often used by planners to identify those land uses that are unwanted by the community.
LUST	Leaking underground storage tank. Prior to the Small Business Liability Relief and Brownfields Revitalization Act of 2002, federal funding excluded the remediation of LUSTs; thus, they were previously a significant barrier to brownfield redevelopment.
Mothballing	Keeping property, usually owned by large corporations, underutilized, undeveloped or vacant to avoid liability and remediation costs.
National Priorities List (NPL)	Intended primarily to guide the EPA in determining which contaminated sites warrant further investigation. Sites on the NPL have known or threatened releases of hazardous substances, pollutants or contaminants. *See also* Superfund site.
NIMBY	Not in my back yard. Describes opposition on the part of neighboring residents or business people to an unwanted land use.
No-Further Requirements letter/ document (NFRD)	Issued by the state declaring that the owner has cleaned the property to an acceptable standard. The NFRD may be conditioned on future land use restrictions and contain certain physical maintenance requirements.

Orphan property	An abandoned property, often with clouds on the title, that is no longer claimed by the previous owner or whose previous owner cannot be determined.
Phytoremediation	The use of plants to remove, degrade or contain site contaminants through the uptake and transpiration of water from the ground. Used in urban agriculture.
Progetto urbano	A designation in Italian land use planning and development for an urban project; an intermediate level of planning in Italy, which is smaller than citywide master planning, but larger than an individual site.
Sanborn maps	A collection dating from 1866 of more than 1.2 million maps chronicling approximately 12,000 U.S. cities and towns. The firm EDR has acquired and digitized the Sanborn Map Company collection.
Smart growth	Development principles, policies and practices that advocates claim discourage sprawl by promoting affordable and varied housing, mixed land uses, open space preservation, a sense of community, transportation choices and infill/redevelopment.
Split-rate (two-rate) tax	A tax that applies two different rates on land and buildings (unlike the local property tax).
Superfund	Common name for CERCLA, the law that established the federal program to clean up uncontrolled hazardous waste sites. The EPA works with communities, potentially responsible parties, scientists, researchers, contractors and government authorities to identify sites, test conditions, formulate cleanup plans and undertake remediation.
Superfund site	Any land in the U.S. contaminated by hazardous waste and identified by the EPA as a priority candidate for cleanup as a risk to the environment and/or public health.
Sustainable development	Development that meets present needs without compromising those of future generations; a multifaceted approach to managing environmental, economic and social resources over the long term.

Tangentopoli	A scandal in Italy in the early 1990s that revealed the longstanding corrupt practice of paying conspicuous amounts of money to the party or person who facilitated a planning license.
Tax increment financing (TIF)	Creating funds for redevelopment of a district in need by allowing a portion of the tax revenues generated by new development to be directly reinvested in the special district created or leveraged with bonds. TIF designation typically lasts approximately 20 years, but varies from city to city.
Tax-lien foreclosure	The process by which a state or local government takes title to or forces the sale of real estate for nonpayment of taxes; the enforcement of property tax collection to return tax-delinquent vacant land and abandoned structures to productive use.
TOADs	Temporarily obsolete, abandoned and derelict land.
Underutilized land	Properties not being used to their full economic or social potential.
Urban development corporation (UDC)	A group in British planning and development legislation that provides incentives for the reuse of abandoned and underutilized urban sites to attract private investors and occupiers.
Urban growth boundary (UGB)	A containment line drawn around an urban area to confine development.
USDA	U.S. Department of Agriculture.
Vermiculture	The cultivation of earthworms in controlled conditions to produce organic fertilizer (known as *vermicompost*) by feeding on decomposing materials such as vegetable scraps. Used in urban agriculture.
Voluntary cleanup program (VCP)	Program initiated at the state level in which land owners enter into voluntary agreements for brownfield remediation. Elements include cleanup standards, engineering and institutional controls, and liability relief from third-party and public actions.

Web Sites of Referenced Organizations and Programs

Local and regional organizations

Boston Natural Areas Network	www.bostonnatural.org
Dudley Street Neighborhood Initiative, Boston	www.dsni.org
Green Environmental Coalition, Ohio	www.greenlink.org
Greensgrow, Philadelphia	www.greensgrow.org
Growing Power, Milwaukee	www.growingpower.org
Neighborhood Gardens Association, Philadelphia	www.ngalandtrust.org
NeighborSpace Program, Chicago	www.neighborspace.org
New Jersey Regional Coalition	www.regionequity.org
Nuestras Raices, Holyoke	www.nuestras-raices.org
Philadelphia Green/Pennsylvania Horticultural Society	www.pennsylvaniahorticulturalsociety.org
Village Farms, Buffalo	www.villagefarms.com

National organizations

American Community Gardening Association	www.communitygarden.org
American Planning Association	www.planning.org
Community Food Security Coalition	www.foodsecurity.org
Smart Growth Network	www.smartgrowth.org

State and federal government agencies and initiatives

Maryland Department of the Environment	www.mde.state.md.us
Massachusetts Department of Housing and Community Development	www.state.ma.us/dhcd

Oregon Department of Land Conservation and Development	www.lcd.state.or.us
Pennsylvania Land Recycling Program	www.dep.state.pa.us/dep/deputate/ airwaste/wm/landrecy/default.htm
U.S. Department of Housing and Urban Development	www.hud.gov
USDA Community Food Projects Grant Program	www.csrees.usda.gov

Contributors

Martin Bailkey is a lecturer in the Department of Urban and Regional Planning at the University of Wisconsin-Madison. As a 1999–2000 Lincoln Institute Dissertation Fellow, he studied the social and political relationship between municipal vacant land policies and community-initiated open spaces in particular U.S. cities. He has written and spoken on various aspects of urban agriculture and their ties to the broader issues of community food security, public planning and urban land use. For more than 15 years, he has taught urban planning, landscape architecture and architecture at University of Wisconsin-Madison, University of Oregon, Eugene, and Drury University, Springfield, Missouri.

Ann O'M. Bowman is the James F. and Maude B. Byrnes Professor of Government at the University of South Carolina, Columbia. Her areas of interest include state and local government and politics, federalism and intergovernmental relations, and public policy. She and Michael Pagano are coauthors of *Terra Incognita: Vacant Land and Urban Strategies* (Georgetown University Press 2004). Her article "Horizontal Federalism: Exploring Interstate Interactions" appears in the October 2004 issue of the *Journal of Public Administration Research and Theory.*

Lavea Brachman is director of the Ohio office of the Delta Institute, a nonprofit organization that works on brownfields and sustainable development projects in the Great Lakes region. She was previously a practicing environmental attorney, a partner at a brownfields consulting firm, and an appointee to the Clean Ohio Council, which developed statewide brownfield funding policies and project selection. As a 2004–2005 Visiting Fellow at the Lincoln Institute of Land Policy, she is writing a guidebook on brownfield redevelopment for community-based organizations and designing a set of program activities for redeveloping vacant, abandoned, underutilized and brownfield land in urban areas.

Sabina Deitrick is associate professor at the Graduate School of Public and International Affairs at the University of Pittsburgh, where she is also codirector of the urban and regional research program at the University Center for Social and Urban Research. She teaches courses in economic development, community and neighborhood planning, and urban and regional policy. Her research focuses on economic restructuring in communities and regions in

U.S. and international contexts, with emphases on regional revitalization and brownfield redevelopment.

Margaret Dewar is Emil Lorch Professor of Architecture and Urban Planning in the Urban and Regional Planning Program at the University of Michigan, Ann Arbor. She teaches and researches urban redevelopment, economic development and land use. Her most recent work concerns the effects of the Detroit Empowerment Zone on economic opportunity and the state of institutions for handling tax-reverted property in Detroit. She directs the Detroit Community Partnership Center, which matches faculty/student teams with projects addressing community-identified needs related to planning and design in Detroit community-based organizations and city agencies.

Alan W. Evans is professor of economics at The University of Reading, in England, where for 15 years he was responsible for the school's residential accommodation for some 5,000 students. He has also served as pro-vice-chancellor and deputy vice-chancellor of the university. Evans has researched the economics of towns and regions, specializing recently in the economics of the land and property market and the economics of land use planning. He has published several books and articles, including *Economics, Real Estate and the Supply of Land and Economics* and *Land Use Planning* (Blackwell 2004).

Sarah S. Gardner teaches environmental planning at Williams College, in Williamstown, and serves on local and regional planning commissions in Berkshire County, Massachusetts. She conducted her doctoral research on brownfield sites in New Jersey and previously worked in the New Jersey Office of State Planning and the New York City Recycling Program. Her recent work focuses on the environmental effects of sprawl and land use politics on agriculture in New England.

Rosalind Greenstein is senior fellow and cochair of the Department of Planning and Development at the Lincoln Institute of Land Policy. Prior to joining the Lincoln Institute, she was a senior regional economist at the economic consulting firm formerly known as DRI/McGraw-Hill, and research director for the Commonwealth of Massachusetts' Industrial Services Program. She taught public policy at Clark University, in Worcester, and urban and regional planning at the University of Wisconsin-Madison. Her writing on regional political economies focuses on the social dimensions of economic development.

Marie Howland teaches economic development and urban economics in the Urban Studies and Planning graduate program at the University of Maryland, College Park, where she is also affiliated with the National Center for Smart Growth. Howland is the author of *Plant Closings and Worker Displacement: The Regional Issues* (Upjohn Institute 1988) and coauthor of *From Combines to Computers* (SUNY Press 1995), and has also published several studies on the impact of contamination on central city industrial land markets.

Jerome Kaufman is professor emeritus in the Department of Urban and Regional Planning, University of Wisconsin-Madison. Retired in 2001, he recently served as guest editor of the *Journal of Planning Education and Research* issue on Planning for the Food System (Summer 2004) and is co-coordinator of sessions for the 2005 conference of the American Planning Association on the same subject. He coauthored the Lincoln Institute working paper "Farming Inside Cities: Entrepreneurial Urban Agriculture in the United States" (2000), which serves as the basis for his chapter in this volume. Kaufman is currently chair of the board of the nonprofit urban agriculture organization Growing Power, in Milwaukee.

Klaus R. Kunzmann holds a Jean Monnet professorship for European Spatial Planning at the School of Planning of the University of Dortmund, Germany, since 1993. He studied architecture and urban planning at the Technical University of Munich and the Technical University of Vienna, Austria. His present research interests are in urban policy and European spatial planning, regional restructuring, and the role of creativity and the arts in spatial and endogenous economic development. In his home region in Germany, in the Ruhr, he is actively involved as an adviser on regional policy matters.

Nancey Green Leigh is a professor in the City and Regional Planning Program at the Georgia Institute of Technology, Atlanta, specializing in economic development planning. Leigh teaches, conducts research and publishes in the areas of local economic development planning, urban and regional development, industrial restructuring and brownfield redevelopment. She is the author or coauthor of several books and articles, including *Economic Revitalization: Cases and Strategies for City and Suburb* (Sage 2002).

Michael A. Pagano is professor of public administration and director of the Graduate Program in Public Administration at the University of Illinois at Chicago (UIC). He is coeditor of *Urban Affairs Review*, faculty fellow of UIC's Great Cities Institute, and a member of the Committee for the Study of the Long-term Viability of Fuel Taxes for Transportation Finance, of the Transportation Research Board, a unit of the National Academy of Sciences. He is coauthor with Ann O'M. Bowman of *Terra Incognita: Vacant Land and Urban Strategies* (Georgetown University Press 2004) as well as *Cityscapes and Capital* (Johns Hopkins University Press 1995).

William Shutkin is president and chief executive officer of The Orton Family Foundation, the Vermont- and Colorado-based operating foundation that seeks to promote sustainable development by engaging and empowering citizens in land use planning to make informed decisions affecting their environment and quality of life. He is founder and former president of New Ecology, Inc., a nonprofit environmental organization based in Cambridge, Massachusetts, that promotes sustainable urban development. He also cofounded the Boston-based Alternatives for Community & Environment, an environmental justice law and education center. Shutkin is a research affiliate and has taught environmental law and policy in the Department of Urban Studies and Planning at Massachusetts Institute of Technology, Cambridge.

Yesim Sungu-Eryilmaz is a research associate at the Lincoln Institute of Land Policy. She is currently a PhD candidate at the Graduate School of Public and International Affairs, University of Pittsburgh. She specializes in urban and regional economic development and international development, and has served as a research assistant in various projects including brownfields redevelopment, affordable housing, and interactive intelligent spatial information systems for disaster management.

Barry Wood is assistant dean of undergraduate studies at the University of Newcastle upon Tyne, England, and is currently visiting professor at the School of Architecture at the University of Bratislava, Slovakia. Wood's key areas of research and teaching have been economics and property development, combined with spatial planning, particularly in Europe. He is author or editor of several books and papers on spatial planning.

Index

About the Lincoln Institute

The Lincoln Institute of Land Policy is a nonprofit and tax-exempt educational institution established in 1974 to study and teach land policy, including land economics and land taxation. The Institute is supported primarily by the Lincoln Foundation, which was established in 1947 by Cleveland industrialist John C. Lincoln. He drew inspiration from the ideas of Henry George, the nineteenth-century American political economist, social philosopher and author of the book *Progress and Poverty*.

The Institute's goals are to integrate theory and practice to better shape land policy decisions and to share understanding about the multidisciplinary forces that influence public policy in the United States and internationally. The Institute organizes its work in three departments: valuation and taxation, planning and development, and international studies, with special programs in Latin America and China.

The Lincoln Institute seeks to improve the quality of debate and disseminate knowledge of critical issues in land policy by bringing together scholars, policy makers, practitioners and citizens with diverse backgrounds and experience. We study, exchange insights and work toward a broader understanding of complex land and tax policies. The Institute does not take a particular point of view, but rather serves as a catalyst to facilitate analysis and discussion of these issues— to make a difference today and to help policy makers plan for tomorrow.

Lincoln Institute of Land Policy
113 Brattle Street
Cambridge, MA, 02138-3400 USA

Phone: 617-661-3016 x127 or 800-LAND-USE (800-526-3873)
Fax: 617-661-7235 or 800-LAND-944 (800-526-3944)
E-mail: help@lincolninst.edu
Web: www.lincolninst.edu